Human Rights, Regionalism and the Dilemmas of Democracy in Africa

Edited by
Lennart Wohlgemuth
& Ebrima Sall

CODESRIA

**Council for the Development of Social
Science Research in Africa**

Nordiska Afrikainstitutet
The Nordic Africa Institute

©Council for the Development of Social Science Research in Africa 2006
Avenue Cheikh Anta Diop Angle Canal IV, BP 3304 Dakar, 18524 Senegal.
http:\\www.codesria.org

In association with the Nordic Africa Institute,
P O Box 1703 SE-751 47 Uppsala, Sweden
http:\\www.nai.uu.se

ISBN-13: 978-2-86978-192-4
ISBN: 2-86978-192-X

Typesetting by Hadijatou Sy

Cover design by Ibrahima Fofana

Distributed in Africa by CODESRIA

Distributed elsewhere by the African Books Collective
www.africanbookscollective.com

The Council for the Development of Social Science Research in Africa (CODESRIA) is
an independent organisation whose principal objectives are facilitating research,
promoting research-based publishing and creating multiple forums geared towards the
exchange of views and information among African researchers. It challenges the
fragmentation of research through the creation of thematic research networks that cut
across linguistic and regional boundaries.

CODESRIA would like to express its gratitude to African Governments, the Swedish
Development Co-operation Agency (SIDA/SAREC), the International Development
Research Centre (IDRC), OXFAM GB/I, the Mac Arthur Foundation, the Carnegie
Corporation, the Norwegian Ministry of Foreign Affairs, the Danish Agency for
International Development (DANIDA), the French Ministry of Cooperation, the Ford
Foundation, the United Nations Development Programme (UNDP), the Rockefeller
Foundation, the Prince Claus Fund and the Government of Senegal for support of its
research, publication and training activities.

Contents

Contributors

Lennart Wohlgemuth is a senior lecturer at the Göteborg University, Sweden.

Ebrima Sall is Head of the Department of Research, CODESRIA, Senegal.

Julia Dolly Joiner is Commissioner for Political Affairs, Commission for the African Union, based in Addis Ababa, Ethiopia..

Germain Baricako is a Lawyer and has been the Secretary of the African Commission on Human and Peoples' Rights (ACHPR) since April 1994.

Hassan Bubacar Jallow is Under-Secretary General of the United Nations and Prosecutor of the International Criminal Tribunal for Rwanda.

Paul Tiyambe Zeleza, Professor of African Studies and History, Pennsylvania State University, USA

Jibrin Ibrahim is formerly in the Department of Political Science at Ahmadu Bello University in Zaria, is now the director of Global Rights in Nigeria.

Frans Viljoen, Professor at the Centre for Human Rights, Faculty of Law, University of Pretoria, Pretoria, South Africa.

Ibrahima Kane, Legal Officer for Africa, Interights, London, UK.

Hannah Forster, Executive Director, African Centre for Democracy and Human Rights Studies (ACDHRS), Banjul, The Gambia.

Chapter 1

Introduction: Human Rights, Regionalism and the Dilemmas of Democracy in Africa

Lennart Wohlgemuth & Ebrima Sall

Background

Human history, worldwide, has always seen a struggle between individualism (individual power and wealth creation) and communalism (humanitarian considerations). Most societies have succeeded in bringing out a balance between the two, but whenever the balance has tilted too much, popular movements have usually been established to change the situation. The English Magna Carta, 1215, the Petition of Rights, 1628, the Bill of Rights, 1689, the American Declaration of Independence 1789 and the French Declaration of the Rights of Man and Citizen, 1789, are major historical landmarks in this respect.

According to Kofi Annan, 'The vision of "a government of laws and not of men" is almost as old as civilization itself'. He tells of a replica of the code of laws promulgated by Hammurabi more than three thousand years ago, in what is now Iraq, and on which are written '... principles of justice that have been recognized, if seldom fully implemented, by almost every human society since his time: legal protection for the poor; restraints on the strong, so that they cannot oppress the weak; laws publicly enacted, and known to all. That code was a landmark in mankind's struggle to build an order where, instead of might making right, right would make might'.

It has often been argued that the concept of Human Rights is an artifact of modern Western Civilisation and what is described as Human Rights in traditional societies of the South would just be privileges granted to members of a group if certain duties were performed. Such descriptions are hardly either accurate or constructive.[1] As Zeleza writes in his paper (also citing Heiner Bielefeldt):

> Indeed, it is ultimately counterproductive to turn the idea of Human Rights into 'Western', 'Asian', 'African' or 'Islamic', for that would turn the language of Human Rights 'into a rhetorical weapon for intercultural competition.... What is needed...is a critical defence of universal Human Rights in a way that gives room for different cultural and religious interpretations and, at the same time, avoids the pitfalls of cultural essentialism'.

With the industrial revolution, colonisation and the technical improvements of weapons, the situation became more complicated. The atrocities of the Second World War shocked the world. Human Rights were no longer only an internal issue of each country, but a universal concern.

Human Rights issues have come even more into focus after the end of the Cold War, which took the lid off various hidden conflicts at the same time as one part of the balancing force disappeared. Zeleza writes (also citing Eghosa E. Osaghae) that 'the total number of conflicts has fallen since the early 1990s— from 33 in 1991 to 24 in 2001 (11 and 7 in Africa, respectively)—but they remain as devastating as ever for the countries and peoples involved. In addition, there are numerous other domestic conflicts involving various forms of civil violence. According to one study, the average level of domestic conflict increased 'from a mean score of 151 during the Cold War period to 235 during the post-Cold War period. Despite the fact that external sponsorship of civil wars has declined dramatically since the end of the Cold War, there has been an increase in civil conflicts around the world'.[2] Between 1998 and 2002, for example, ethnic and civil violence were reported in Nigeria with 5,000 deaths, Liberia with 1,000 deaths, Lesotho with 1,000 deaths, Congo-Brazzaville with 500 deaths and the Central African Republic with 600 deaths.[3]

To counteract this trend, legal frameworks and institutions are being created with the aspiration of coming to grips with the deteriorating Human Rights situation. The leading force behind this development is the UN and its major bilateral supporters.

Human Rights were already consecrated in the UN Charter in 1945, although in general terms. These were later elaborated in the Universal Declaration of Human Rights of 10 December 1948, which divided them into two main categories: (1) economic, social and cultural rights; and (2) civil and political rights. According to Justice Hassan Jallow, a leading African Human Rights specialist, many people now look up supra-national bodies for the protection of their individual and collective Human Rights rather than trusting the State, given the multiple ways in which the latter has failed them in this regard. With the constant repetition and reaffirmation of Human Rights in subsequent instruments, universal and regional, as well as in national constitutions, it is argued that the Universal Declaration, at least its essential principles, has become part of international customary law, binding on all states without their express consent (Umozurike). Two World Conferences on Human Rights have been held, the most significant in Vienna in 1993. A special institution, the UN High Commission for Human Rights, was created in 1994 to look over the work in this field. Three documents now deal with Human Rights on a continental bases: (1) the European Convention on Human Rights, 1950; (2) the Inter-American Convention on Human Rights, 1969; and (3) the African Charter on Human and Peoples' Rights, 1981.

Ample literature exists on the worldwide Human Rights situation after the Second World War as well as on efforts to come to grips with various difficult situations. This is also true regarding Africa. We will mainly refer to that literature and very briefly discuss general developments (Ake, Ankumah, Welch, Umozurike, Viljoen).

Human Rights in Africa

In the traditional African society, although with great disparities between regions and groups of people, a balance was struck between different interests so that Human Rights were taken into account rather well in the society. As Umozurike concludes:

> Traditionally, the rights of full members of the society were fully integrated into the rights of the society as a whole; they were not held against the society but were complementary to societal rights. Human Rights were conceptually linked with the traditions of the people, the observance of which was of immense interest to the people. Thus, Human Rights, at any rate those that were recognised by the community, were effectively enforced, but for the benefit of the members of the society...The rights-clamourer had to be prepared to carry out the obligations that went with them, for rights were intertwined with duties.

In relating individual rights to societal rights, Claude Ake notes:

> We put less emphasis on the individual and more on the collective, we do not allow that the individual has any claims which may override that of the society. We assume harmony, not divergence of interests, competition and conflict; we are more inclined to think of our obligations to other members of our society rather than our claims against them.

The period of the slave trade with its suppression and desecration of Human Rights started the undermining of the traditional balance and the colonial period undermined most of what still remained. Colonialism encouraged racism directly or indirectly. The deconstruction or denigration of African religion, culture, languages and traditions weakened African roots and was partly responsible for the continent's backwardness and underdevelopment. Colonialism denied people their basic right to determine their political, economic and social future (Umozurike).

With the liberation of Sub-Saharan Africa, starting with Ghana in 1957,[4] there were high hopes for the protection and promotion of Human Rights and for the restoration of African dignity. Constitutions and legal systems were adopted, similar to those of the colonial powers, including everything that would allow for a positive development. However, with a few exceptions, the hopes never materialised. On the contrary, many of the practices from the colonial period reappeared, and the democratic development failed, opposition groups were suppressed and military leadership became prevalent. In many places, the rule of law changed to the rule of force. Indeed, the respect for Human Rights reached a low watermark on the continent at the end of the 1970s, with among other things, the prolonged liberation struggles in southern Africa and the prevalence of apartheid in South Africa (Umozurike).

As things worsened, counter-forces developed. As early as in 1961, a first inter-African meeting took place between a number of lawyers giving important recommendations on the improvement of Human Rights in Africa under the title of 'The Law of Lagos'. The recommendations suggested, for the first time, an African Human Rights Charter with a court to which individuals and groups might have recourse. This idea was later developed during professional meetings and later also politically under the auspices of the Organisation of African Unity (OAU). The OAU and its member states were, however, very reluctant to accept the proclamation of individual rights for African people. They justified their reluctance by relying on the domestic jurisdiction principle and the preoccupation with maintaining the African countries' political sovereignty and territorial integrity (Ankumah). After strong pressure from the African public, NGOs and the international community the African Charter was finally adopted by the 18th Assembly of Heads of State and Government of the OAU, in June 1981. The Charter came into force on 21 October 1986.

The African Charter or the Banjul Charter, as it is occasionally called, is composed of four sections, a preamble and three main parts. The first part, Articles 2-30, lists human and peoples' rights and duties. The second part, Articles 31-62, contains the safeguard measures, specifically the establishment and organisation of the African Commission on Human and Peoples' Rights (ACHPR). The third part, Articles 63-68, deals with general administration.

The African Charter reflects, to a great extent, the discourse on Human Rights prevailing internationally at the time of its development but also contains a number of distinctive features, in many ways reflecting the African philosophy of law and conception of Human Rights. The most important of these was the presence of 'peoples' in the title, which heralds group rights or collective rights, among them the rights of people to self-determination, to development and to environmental integrity and the right to freely dispose of natural resources. Another distinctive feature of the African Charter is the importance it gives to economic, social and cultural rights, by putting these so-called 'second generation rights' on an equal footing with civil and political rights. Given the conditions of underdevelopment and poverty that prevail on the continent, this is no small thing, for it makes the so-called second generation rights justiciable, something advocates of 'rights-based approaches to development' should really observe. The African Charter also imposes duties upon the individual towards the State and community. Unlike other Human Rights treaties, many of the individual rights guaranteed by the Charter contain 'clawback' clauses, restricting some rights, for example by providing that a right is subject to law and order in the specific country. This could be construed to mean that the level of protection provided by the Charter is equated to the level of protection provided by domestic law (Viljoen). An example is article 10, which provides that every individual has the right to free association 'provided he abides by the law'.

The Charter took effect on 21 October 1986, after it had been ratified by a simple majority of OAU members as required. Today, 53 states in Africa have ratified or acceded to the African Charter on Human and Peoples' Rights.

The African Commission on Human and Peoples' Rights

The African Charter

The African Charter came into force in 1986 more than 19 years ago. With time it has been established that the Charter contains a number of weaknesses, obstacles which ought to be dealt with (see the studies by Viljoen and Kane below). Commissioners have from time to time analysed these shortcomings and the Commission has discussed these at their meetings. There are different opinions on the wisdom of attempting to bring about a revision of the Charter. One view fears that if member states are given the opportunity, they will bring forward regressive amendments that would weaken rather than strengthen the Charter. Another view (pronounced by many presenters in this anthology) is that the mood and times have changed significantly in the twenty years since the Charter was adopted, and that there are now enough progressive member states to ensure that a revision can be carried out in such a manner as to address the shortcomings and strengthen the Charter. The recent adoption of the protocol on the Court is evidence for this view. It is clear that the Charter will have to be revised at some point.

As regards the interpretation of the different clauses of the Charter the Commission seems to have started cautiously with a conservative, legalistic and careful approach. Over the years with increased experience the interpretations seem to have become broader and bolder. This process has been slow but steady but as noted by Viljoen '...this approach ensured a much more significant role for the Commission than would have been the case if the restrictive wording of the

Charter had been followed literally'. Today the Secretariat in its preparations for the decisions of the Commission on communications increasingly takes care to investigate all possibilities. The work done in this area by both the Commissioners and the Secretariat is of the greatest importance and should be commended. It should be continued and supported because it undoubtedly strengthens the capacity of the Commission to influence the observance of Human Rights in Africa.

The Functioning of the Commission

In contrast to the earlier years of the Commission there appears to have been substantial progress since 1995 on both of the main functions of the Commission, that is: 'Protection' and 'Promotion' of Human Rights. The Secretariat has with its additional staff caught up with the serious backlog of unattended communications and built up an administrative system including proper filing, statistics etc., so that they have reasonable control over the situation. With the increased number of qualified legal officers the preparation of documents to be considered by the Commission is both done on time and is of good quality. A problem pointed out by many is the limited time the Commissioners have at their disposal at each meeting, which only allows for the discussion of very few communications. As they only meet every six months this means considerable – if not extreme – delays of already prepared cases.

The primary aim of the communication procedure before the Commission is, in the words of the Commission itself, 'to initiate a positive dialogue, resulting in an amicable solution between the complainant and the state concerned' (Viljoen). A positive development, in this respect, is the increased participation by state representatives when communications and other matters which concern them are brought up and discussed.

The handling of urgent matters, i.e., taking action on serious Human Rights violations taking place in some countries on a large scale, has to be looked into further. At present the Chairman and the Vice Chairman, in consultation with the Secretary, have the interim Mandate to take any appropriate action during intersessions and report to the Commission at the next meeting. However, if the Commission has any aspirations to having an impact on such cases it has to further develop the special system already in place and delegate additional power to the Chairman and some of the Commissioners and the Secretary.

At the same time as the performance in the carrying out of protective activities has improved considerably the number of communications has not increased. This makes a good case for increased priority setting on the promotional work of the Commission. More promotion should mean more people being aware of their rights and therefore more communications to the Commission.

The Secretariat has developed bold plans for developing these activities further. Again with the staff now in place the Secretariat has divided the member countries among the legal officers who all follow the situation in their countries and prepare for visits to countries which would gain from such visits. The Commissioner going on such a visit should be accompanied by the responsible legal officer, which makes the follow up of the visits much easier. These plans are however dependent on both availability of time for the Commissioners and additional money.

There is no doubt that the Commission must increase its activities in the area of promotion. At the same time the competitive advantage of NGOs in some essential aspects of promotion must be recognised. Particularly local NGOs have to take over in areas where the Commission does not reach. The Human Rights NGOs, both international and local, have been extremely important as partners to the Commission since its start. In fact the NGOs and the Commission have been mutually supportive of each other. The NGOs have a forum where they meet most of the relevant people working with Human Rights in Africa during the Commission meetings and the Commission has been supported, legitimised and constructively criticised by the presence of the NGOs. The pressure of challenges and criticism from NGOs has undoubtedly been an encouraging force in the improvement of the Commission's performance. NGOs have a vital role in continuing to act as a critical watchdog in this respect. The Workshops that have been initiated and financed through ICJ and later the African Centre have contributed to this development and supported the Commission in its work and been a training ground particularly for local NGOs.

The time has now come to work out new ways to involve more and different African NGOs, particularly those coming from the grassroots level, in these activities. The African Centre as well as many others is actively propagating for this to happen. International NGOs have to reassess their ways of working and find new avenues to broaden the involvement of local NGOs and other parties from the African states. They should take great care not to become complacent and stuck in the ways in which they operated in the past despite them having been so successful then. The African Commission has taken this important question into consideration in the Mauritius Plan of Action adopted in October 1996.

Another important basis for the promotional work of the Commission is the requirement in the Charter for reports from the member states. Good reporting will allow the Commission to take up a dialogue with the states on how to improve the legislation and implementation thereof in the field of Human Rights. So far too few member states have presented even their first report (34), even fewer their second or third report. Most of those delivered have been of low quality. Much more work has to be done to induce the states to fulfil their obligations. Preparation of new and simpler guidelines for the reporting; training of staff who are supposed to do the reporting; and pressure through the Heads of State of AU are important measures. Co-operation with the office of the UN High

Commissioner for Human Rights, which also requires states to report on the Human Rights situation in the respective countries is another important venture.

With the aim of highlighting certain important issues, the Commission appoints Special Rapporteurs among the Commissioners. So far four such Rapporteurs have been appointed, one for Summary and Extra-Judicial Executions, one for Prison Conditions, one for Human Rights Defenders and one for the Rights of Women, all with the mandate of investigating and reporting on these investigations. These particular Human Rights issues are especially significant in the current context of many African countries. It is to the credit of the Commission that they have been prioritised in this way. The challenge now is to equip the Rapporteurs with the resources necessary for them to fulfil their role effectively and provide them with the profile that will give impact to their reports.

Confidentiality and Reporting

The requirement for confidentiality in the Charter is one of the areas where over the years the Commission has made increasingly bolder interpretations. Part of the criticism of the lack of transparency in the first years could be refuted by the fact that there was very little to report. Thus in 1994 in only two out of the 52 cases considered during the six years the Commission had been in existence had explicit findings of violations been made. However, since the seventh annual report of the African Commission in 1994, the Commission has become increasingly open. In the past years, an overview on the total process leading to the decisions on communications has been appended to the annual report. This positive development should be further pursued. In particular, the latest annual reports should immediately be published in a readable volume and the plans for a newsletter be implemented and sustained. Furthermore communications being processed should be openly registered and published in, for instance, the Newsletter and on the Commission's website.

The Commission's Structure

The performance of the Commission in its early years was poor. More recently there has been considerable improvement, but a number of fundamental questions remain and, unless they are openly acknowledged and progressively addressed, the Commission will not be able to function as the effective instrument for improving the observance of Human Rights that Africa so urgently requires. As no provision was made in the Charter for geographic, legal or gender representation in the composition of the Commission, the question of nomination and election of Commissioners has become an important issue over the past few years. Although the States nominate Commissioners and the Assembly of Heads of State and Government of the AU decide on their election or re-election, the Secretary and other actors including NGOs have become more active in the process by contacting countries and regions which are under-represented, to make them aware of this fact. On gender balance, efforts are under way (there is now a woman Chairperson of the Commission), and should be continued. The question of incompatibility (i.e. of some of the Commissioners also being full-time, high level government employees) has been raised by many as the most serious problem of the Commission. Here efforts will have to be made to make the nominating states aware of the issue and avoid nominating Commissioners with conflicting interests.

Also, the issue of how much time a Commissioner should be required (and paid for) to work for the Commission must be looked into further. At present the time allowed is demonstrably insufficient (Kane). If the Commissioners are to perform their duties efficiently, both as regards the Commission meetings and the promotional activities, they must be able to set aside enough time. A study on this issue should be made by members of the Commission and the Secretariat leading to a proposal for funding to be sought for that purpose. Another important issue is to make it possible for the Commissioners to also work in their intersessional time. They must be provided with funds and equipment to make this possible.

The lack of resources has been particularly damaging for the work of the Special Rapporteurs. They have not been able to fulfil their important tasks as they have neither time nor resources set aside to implement their work. This has to be looked into further with the aim of finding a proper solution.

The Secretariat

A well-functioning secretariat is a prerequisite for the Commission to implement its important duties. However, in the first years between 1989 and 1994, its performance left much to be desired. Funds available only sufficed for securing one legal officer and one accountant/administration officer plus some support staff, and most often not even these posts could be filled. The quality of administration and accounting was far from satisfactory, leading to complaints by the auditors and to badly prepared Commission meetings as well as low quality documentation. The reliance on short term, often not sufficiently qualified, professional staff from outside Africa and from international NGOs became far too great for an African owned and run organisation.

With the appointment of the new Secretary in 1994, the situation has slowly but steadily improved. Important developments were the appointment of a qualified accountant in 1995 who introduced accountability into the organisation, and Denmark's agreeing to give massive core support to make it possible for the Secretariat to recruit staff within Africa in addition to the staff provided by the regular OAU budget.

The Secretariat, although much still remains to be done in order to improve the efficient running of the operations, is today a relatively well-functioning institution which can perform its duties reasonably well (Baricako). The present number of staff is well suited to perform the duties of the Commission. However, ways have to be found to supply the number of staff employed at present on a longer term basis than today and to adopt a recruitment procedure which ensures the high quality of new recruits. Furthermore, the funds secured to run the Secretariat are far from sufficient, particularly with the new staff on board (Viljoen). Basic funding for running costs, trips etc., must therefore be secured. As has been stated, the same need for vigilance to ensure that all the main languages (e.g. Portuguese and Arabic), cultures and regions are represented at the professional levels of staff in the Secretariat should also be noted. The details for all this have been worked out by the Secretariat in The Strategic Plan for the coming years, which has been approved by the Commission (Baricako).

The African Court for Human and Peoples' Rights

The Commission has been criticised on various grounds. An important element of the criticism relates to the lack of effective enforcement of its decisions due to the non-binding nature of the Commission's findings and the Commission's lack of power to act on its own initiative. This has led to the movement to adopt a Protocol to the African Charter in terms of which an African Court on Human and Peoples' Rights would be established to supplement the Commission's protective mandate (Viljoen).

The Commission which actively participated in the work to prepare for the decision on the Court, welcomed the decision taken by the Heads of State of AU in June 1998. It is too early to predict precisely what impact the Court will have on the work of the Commission. It has been suggested that the Commission will develop—in a sense—as a court of first resort, or first instance, whilst the Court will function more as a Court of Appeal. Whatever becomes reality, everyone would be well advised to learn from the experience with the Commission which shows, firstly, that it will take considerable time before the decision on the Court is ratified and the details of the Court are established and, secondly, the importance of AU really being prepared to set aside the funds necessary to implement the decisions in practice. The risk of having two underfunded and therefore weak and ineffective institutions in this very important field is imminent and should be avoided at any cost.

International Assistance

As can be seen from above the Commission has received some but not sufficient support during its existence (Baricako, Viljoen and Joiner). The support received can be divided into four categories.

(1) The financial contribution of the parent organisation OAU/AU, which has been, as already stated, far from sufficient even to run the Commission at the minimum level originally identified.

(2) Additional contributions to the basic functions of the Commission. A number of bilateral donors as well as NGOs have contributed in different ways by providing interns, temporary staff for the Commission and by arranging workshops and courses on behalf of the Commission. More recently some donors have provided funds for the activities implemented by the Commission itself. Denmark through the Centre of Human Rights as well as directly by Danida is in a category by itself both as regards the amounts involved and the trust they have shown in the Commission. Other major contributors in order of magnitude are Sweden, the EU, the Netherlands and the UN High Commissioner for Human Rights. Gambia also falls within this category covering a substantial part of the local costs such as rent and some of the meeting costs in Banjul. To make this assistance more effective the Danish model (today also implemented by Sweden) should be used by other donors allowing for multi-year agreements and providing for support to specified core activities. It has to be a sustained commitment and although channelled directly to the Commission to be cleared with the AU. The dangers with donor preferences for project rather than core funding should be kept in mind. This easily pushes the institution towards more peripheral activities rather than allowing it to concentrate on its main activities. Special accounts should be opened for each donor or, if agreed, jointly for donors who are willing to collaborate. To make core support easier for donors to accept a special auditor should be appointed by the donors to audit these accounts.

(3) Organisations which provide special services for the Commission and which are themselves largely sustained by donor funding. This is mainly the African Centre (and lately the African Institute in Banjul and AFLA in Accra) which was originally created to assist the Commission to fulfil its objectives, and earlier the African Society which published the Review and recruited staff for the Commission.

(4) Institutions that provide auxiliary services, which support the implementation of certain tasks of the Commission. Here there are a number of international NGOs that arrange training or workshops in order to promote Human Rights issues in Africa. ICJ has been particularly important in this respect, most significantly arranging and financing the workshops, which have taken place in conjunction with the annual Commission meetings. The African Centre with its Pan-African training programme must also be mentioned in this context. When it comes to these activities it would be of great importance to produce a map of the different actors and define in what area they have special competence and competitive advantage. Some specialise in training local NGOs in the use of relevant Human Rights law to air grievances and

how to properly present communications to the Commission, others give training in litigation, others train relevant State officials in the preparation of state reports on Human Rights in their countries etc. As regards future work for all parties and in particular for the Commission it is of great importance to investigate who is doing what and doing it well and how to find ways to co-ordinate efforts in an efficient manner. Again we request the NGOs, particularly the major international NGOs, to assist in finding new ways to make the most of available resources (Forster).

The African Commission in a New Context

With globalisation, democratisation and the new regionalist impulses, the state of Human Rights in Africa has somewhat improved. On the other hand, the HIV/AIDS pandemic, the armed conflicts, widespread and deepening poverty and other scourges of great magnitude still pose formidable challenges for Human Rights. Globalisation itself has brought new challenges for Human Rights protection, as forms of violations become more complex and the location of violators sometimes makes them less easy to apprehend. The social and political environment is therefore in many respects different from what it was when the African Charter on Human and Peoples' Rights was being drafted more than two decades ago.

Justice Hassan Jallow, Under Secretary General of the UN, Prosecutor of the International Criminal Tribunal for Rwanda, and one of the people who drafted the African Charter on Human and Peoples' Rights, points out in his contribution below that with the massive atrocities on the continent, resulting in gross violations of Human Rights, 'many Africans legitimately are losing or have lost confidence in their governments. Many feel that these have failed the people. So people in Africa are looking for institutions "beyond" and/or "above" their national states [such as the ACHPR] for redress'. Human Rights norms do exist; the major challenge is the implementation of these norms. Although there have been some improvements in the governance systems, particularly with the demise of the notorious dictatorial regimes that plagued the continent, and the establishment of pluralistic and participatory political systems, there are still a number of 'non-democratic islands' where repressive laws are still in force, where effective political competition is being undermined, and where the absence of equity and social and economic justice is obvious. The enjoyment of Human Rights in Africa has also been greatly undermined by armed conflict that has, in some cases, led to the destruction of entire ethnic groups and created millions of refugees and internally displaced people. This has made poverty much deeper and even more widespread. The African Human Rights predicament, Justice Jallow argues, is further compounded by the spread of pandemics such as HIV/AIDS and malaria.

In this bleak picture, the work of the ACHPR and the ongoing developments on the continent, many of which are taking place in, around, or are spearheaded by the African Union, stand out as major signs of hope (Kane). These include the entry into force of the Protocol for an African Court of Human and Peoples' Rights on 25 January 2004, the adoption of a Protocol to the African Charter on Human and Peoples' Rights on the Rights of Women, the transformation of the OAU into the African Union (AU) with a stronger, executive Commission, the New Partnership for Africa's Development (NEPAD), the adoption of an African instrument for combating corruption (the African Union Convention on Prevention and Combating Corruption, adopted by the 2nd Ordinary Session of the Assembly of the AU in Maputo on 11 July 2003), and the general evolution towards greater accountability for Human Rights violations, as shown by the proliferation of Truth and Reconciliation Committees (TRCs), and Human Rights Commissions and courts. In this context, Justice Jallow further argues that the ACHPR needs to be strengthened through a number of measures ranging from increased funding of the Commission, through strengthening its status and mandate, enhancing its independence and impartiality, to consolidating and enhancing its activities. Justice Jallow makes a strong appeal for the creation and consolidation of democratic space, a sine qua non for the enjoyment of Human Rights.

> Political governance in Africa should emphasise not only processes (i.e. periodic elections), but must also focus on content, i.e. the pursuit and implementation of the substantive goals of good governance, i.e. social and economic progress. Governments should relentlessly strive to ensure the realisation of all categories of rights and freedoms for all without distinction (...). All these are pointers to the need beyond the preoccupation with Human Rights in the narrow sense to institute and sustain broad programmes of good governance in Africa with a dual focus: on the one hand, creating and supporting the effective functioning of state institutions administering law and justice, mobilising and enhancing integrity in public affairs, curbing maladministration, managing transparent electoral systems, etc., on the other implementing measures for empowerment of the masses through inter alia creating the necessary environment for effective and vibrant civil society and independent media.

In this anthology, leading scholars such as Paul Tiyambe Zeleza also address issues of globalisation, Human Rights and development, emerging issues, new forms of civic engagement, discourses and cultures, and the ACHPR, NEPAD and the African Peer Review Mechanism.

Ibahim Kane discusses the new institutional landscape of the Truth Commissions, Special Courts, and the ICTR. He observes that the African Commission exists in a broad political context, with much of its functioning depending on its relationship and interaction with State parties and the African Union. The new Constitution of the AU and its Peace and Security Council, NEPAD and its

African peer-review mechanism, the African Court on Human and Peoples' Rights, the Conference on Security, Stability, Development and Cooperation in Africa (CSSDCA), also present new opportunities and challenges as partners with whom the Commission shares common goals. While this new landscape has meant increased competition for already existing institutions such as the ACHPR, most authors in this publication stress the new opportunities, which are there to be seized by a well-established, pro-active and open Commission. It is therefore emphasised that right now is a crucial time for the Commission to take its proper place on the African scene and translate policies into actions in favour of the African people.

At the institutional level the parent institution of the African Commission on Human and Peoples' Rights (ACHPR), the OAU, has been transformed into the AU, with a much stronger executive Commission ('Secretariat'). In and around the AU, new institutions have emerged and others are in the making: a Peace and Security Council, an African Court of Human Rights, a Conference on Security, Stability, Development and Cooperation in Africa (CSSDCA) and an African Parliament. To these can be added the International Criminal Tribunal for Rwanda (ICTR), the Special Court in Sierra Leone and a host of new national institutions dealing with Human Rights, such as the South African TRC. The mandates of many, if not most, of the new regional institutions partly overlap with that of the ACHPR. Some of the new institutions will actually be taking over certain functions of the ACHPR. This is the case with the African Court of Human Rights that is going to play the role of interpreting the African Charter. There is therefore a real need to rationalise these institutions and their roles. The ACHPR needs to reposition itself in the new regional institutional landscape, and re-define its mandate. With almost twenty years of existence and active engagement with Human Rights issues, the ACHPR can actually play a leading role in setting the Human Rights agenda on the continent, and in defining the roles of the other institutions as well. It can also play a key role in making the African Peer Review Mechanism (APRM) under the NEPAD framework more effective.

It is quite obvious that the ACHPR can no longer do business as usual, in disregard of the changed context and the presence of other key institutions dealing directly or indirectly with Human Rights in the region. Nor can the ACHPR continue to function with the meagre human and financial resources that it has been coping with over the years, and the low level of autonomy that has so far characterised it as an institution.

About the contributions

This anthology is in three parts, an introductory block including the introductory chapter and the contribution by Commissioner Julia Joiner and Executive Secretary Germain Baricako, followed by the second dealing with the socio-political environment for Human Rights in Africa, highlighting the challenges and opportunities for the protection and promotion of Human Rights, and the third dealing with the structure, procedures, mechanisms, resources and institutional autonomy of the African Commission.

Introductory Block

Julia Joiner discusses in her contribution 'Beyond Commitments, towards Practical Action' how Africa today faces great challenges regarding the Human Rights area. The difference from the past is, however, that today there are organisations and institutions dealing with these challenges, for example the transformation of OAU to AU, the launch of the Pan-African Parliament and the Peace and Security Council. The biggest challenge is to implement the agreements agreed upon during the past years, in Joiner's words: 'to go beyond rhetoric and translate the various commitments into practical action'.

Germain Baricako presents his institution, the ACHPR, which is the only Pan-African organisation mandated to promote and protect Human Rights in Africa, and highlights some difficult questions that the Commission faces, in particular, lack of funds and preparation time for Commissioners, and how the Commission should address emergency situations or receiving the State Reports on time. He insists however that the African Commission has made significant progress in carrying out its mandate.

The Context

Hassan B Jallow presents in his contribution an overview of new challenges and opportunities for Human Rights Promotion and Protection in Africa. The greatest challenge for Africa today is how to make Human Rights a reality in the everyday life of Africans. Jallow states in his paper that it is impossible to focus, in an efficient way, on social and economic expropriation if an environment lacks freedom of speech, a conscience or the effective participation of the population. In this situation, the African Commission has a very important role to play.

Paul Tiyambe Zeleza discusses the challenges of globalisation and democratisation and Human Rights and Development in Africa. He focuses on four central factors (democratisation, globalisation, regionalisation and militarisation) that have had a major impact on African political economies during the last decade. He also deals with the development of Human Rights and finally, he investigates the role of the state in developing Human Rights norms.

Jibrim Ibrahim in his contribution 'Expanding the Human Rights Regime in Africa: Citizens, Indigenes and Exclusion in Nigeria' elaborates on the problem regarding the erosion of citizen's rights. Various groups use the ideology of difference and xenophobia to improve their own citizenship rights at the expense of other groups. 'Social and political actors at national and transnational levels are constructing hierarchies of citizenship that reduce the rights of other Africans', he writes. He illustrates this argument with examples from Nigeria, a multiethnic country.

Challenges Facing the African Commission

Frans Viljoen in his detailed review of the African Commission defines a number of problems that the Commission faces. In his contribution he gives a number of suggestions on how the Commission could be more efficient particularly regarding the procedures for communications, State Reports and Missions and the mechanisms such as Special Rapporteurs, working groups and focal points.

Ibrahima Kane, in his contribution, deals with the relationship between the African Commission on Human and Peoples' Rights and the new organs of the African Union. He sets out to identify the legal obstacles to a clear understanding between the African Commission and the political organs of the African Union by making a comparative analysis of the mandates of the new structures. He also identifies the new opportunities which are opening up to the African Commission and which could enable it to efficiently fulfil the role which the African Charter entrusted to it and prepare the ground 'for dynamic interaction and coordination' with these new structures.

Hannah Forster points out in her contribution the importance of NGO participation concerning Human Rights. NGOs have played a very important role regarding the protection of Human Rights. It is very positive that efforts have been made to strengthen the relationship between the African Commission and NGOs. The African Commission offers a unique and neutral opportunity for all groups working on the ground to bring their constituencies' Human Rights concerns up for discussion. Hannah Forster points out the challenges that NGOs face and suggests a number of actions to make the work of the NGOs more efficient. She also shows how NGOs can strengthen the work of the African Commission.

Conclusions

Many of the issues raised in the chapters in this book have been discussed over the years in other forums, and are therefore not new. As has been noted above, what is new is the context in which they are being discussed today. There is clearly a global moment that favours Human Rights work, although the kinds of issues that need to be addressed have become both more complex, but also, in some respects, more 'basic', given that, it is often the most fundamental human right, the right to life, that is itself under threat, as is the case with the horrendous violence and the scourges like HIV/AIDS prevalent today. More striking, perhaps, is the rapidly changing institutional landscape in Africa and the heavy premium now being put on democracy. The Commission of the African Union and its Chairperson Alfa Oumar Konare with their staff seem to be putting governance,

Human Rights and development issues on the African continent very high on their agenda.

In conclusion, the African Commission has made substantial progress in its almost twenty years of operation and must be seen as an important organ within the African political scene. Much more is however required in order for Human Rights to become an accepted feature of the political process in Africa. It is therefore the duty of all the friends of the African Commission to do their utmost to support the institution so that it can take its proper place among other African regional organisations and work positively for the development of the continent.

Notes

1. Secretary General, Kofi Annan, 21 September 2004, statement delivered to the General Assembly.
2. For a chronology of the developments of Human Rights, see UNDP' Human Development Report, 2000, pp. 8-10 (http://www.undp.org/hdr2000/english/book/ch1.pdf).
3. Zeleza, Paul, 'Human Rights and Development in Africa: New Contexts, Challenges and Opportunities', this volume, chapter 5.
4. Ibid.
5. Liberia obtained its independence in 1848, but remained a rather exceptional and isolated case, with little impact on the political processes on the rest of the continent. Ethiopia regained its freedom after the Second World War, and some countries of North Africa, such as Egypt, also became independent before Ghana. However, Ghana's independence was in many ways a real turning point, partly because of the active role that independent Ghana, under the leadership of Kwame Nkrumah, played in the struggle for freedom in other parts of the continent.

References

Ake, Claude, 1987, 'Human Rights: The African Context', 34 (1-2) *Today*, 41-25.

Ankumah, Evelyn A., 1996, *The African Comminssion on Human and Peoples' Rights*, The Hague: Martinus Nijhoff Publishers.

Ewald, Jonas, Wohlgemuth, Lennart and Yates, Bill, 1998, *An Evaluation of the Three Banjul-Based Human R ights Organisations*, The African Commission on Human and Peoples' Rights, The African Centre for Democracy and Human Rights Studies, The Africa Society of International and Comperative Law.

Heynes, Christof, 1997, ed., *Review of the African Commission on Human and Peoples 'Rights*: 21 October 1986 to January 1997, Human Rights Law in Africa.

Umozurike, U. Oji, 1997, *The African Charter on Human and Peoples 'Rights*, The Hague: The Raoul Wallenberg Institute Human Rights Library: Martinus Nijhoff Publishers.

Viljoen, Frans, 2001, *Evaluations and Reviews of Partnership Programmes* No. 17, 2001, Final Evaluation Phase 1 (1996–July 2000), Strengthening the Core Activities and Secretariat of the African Commission on Human and Peoples' Rights, Copenhagen: The Danish Centre for Human Rights.

Chapter 2

Beyond Commitments,
Towards Practical Action

Julia Dolly Joiner

Seventeen years ago when the African Commission on Human and Peoples' Rights was established, Africa was still a continent where the human rights record was among the worst in the world. Largely influenced by the politics and policies in the Cold War era, the continent became a testing ground for new ideologies and weapons. Dictatorship and impunity became the order of the day while the rights of the citizenry were constantly being trampled upon without international condemnation.

Today, the human rights landscape has dramatically changed. Internal and external developments have created new challenges and as well as opportunities for the African Commission and the enhancement of human rights on the continent.

The Constitutive Act of the African Union (AU) has underscored the centrality of the promotion and protection of human rights throughout the continent. Since its inception, the AU has recognised these challenges and opted to systematically address them by exploiting Africa's own resources to the fullest and working in close partnership with the rest of the international community.

The multifaceted challenges of human development in general and human rights in particular, that Africa is confronted with today, are indeed daunting. Armed conflicts, corruption, dictatorship, unconstitutional changes of government, and terrorism add to impoverishment and underdevelopment and constitute serious challenges to the promotion and protection of human rights on the continent. As conflicts spread from country to country, there is lesser and lesser safe refuge for the millions of people who become displaced everyday. HIV/AIDS and other tropical diseases compound this situation while political instability jeopardises any effort to reduce poverty.

To face these contemporary challenges, the continent is today endowed with a consensual platform made up of specific institutions and instruments dealing with human rights, gender equality, peace, development and poverty. Needless to say, bold steps are to be taken and it is through the implementation of these vital instruments and indeed the effective operation of its organs that the African Union will make headway in the advancement of human rights on the continent.

Two core documents are essential to the policy statement of the African Union's human rights agenda—the Grand Bay (Mauritius) Declaration and Plan of Action, adopted in April 1999, and the Kigali Declaration adopted in May 2003.

The African Union Commission is working towards the implementation of the roadmap on the promotion and protection of human rights in conjunction with the African Commission and specific attention is being given to four mutually reinforcing areas, namely: capacity building within the AU human rights system and Member States, advocacy for more effective realisation of human rights, promotion of a culture of respect for human rights across the continent, and lastly, through taking appropriate political and logistical actions to strengthen the human rights mechanism.

The transformation of the OAU into the AU and the recent launching of some of its key organs also hold immense potential of significantly impacting on the continent's human rights landscape.

The Pan-African Parliament, launched on 18 March 2004 and the Peace and Security Council, inaugurated on 25 May 2004, constitute recent initiatives to promote democratic principles, good governance, human rights, peace, security and stability in the continent. These organs will no doubt provide the African Commission the opportunity to broaden its reach on human rights.

In addition, African leaders have committed themselves through the NEPAD to delivering pluralistic states with transparent administrations, effective institutions and sound regulatory frameworks, all underpinned by the rule of law and with an innovative inter-state peer review mechanism. The African Peer Review Mechanism offers yet another opportunity for the Commission and indeed the continental human rights network to expand its scope.

The African human rights framework, which has been evolving progressively from and around the African Charter on Human and Peoples' Rights, now also includes specific instruments related to the rights of children and women. The

African Charter on the Rights and Welfare of the Child, which came into force in November 1999, and the Protocol to the African Charter on Human and Peoples' Rights, relating to the Rights of Women, which was adopted in Maputo last year, together represent invaluable instruments in our pursuit and enhancement of the basic tenets of human and peoples' rights. Advocacy for the ratification of the latter is being actively pursued.

A recent milestone is the entry into force of the Protocol to the African Charter on Human and Peoples' Rights Relating to the Establishment of the African Court on Human and Peoples' Rights, following the recording of the critical threshold of fifteen ratifications on 25 January 2004. Preparatory activities have been initiated for the establishment of the Court which, when operational, will represent an effective means of strengthening the regional mechanism for the protection of human rights in Africa.

I alluded to these initiatives to introduce and buttress the point that the real human rights challenge we face on the continent today is the practical application of commitments undertaken. After over fifty years since the inception of the United Nations Organisation and forty years after the creation of the Organisation of African Unity, the world, and Africa in particular, is equipped with enough Treaties, Protocols, Charters and Declarations to realise respect for the sanctity of the human being. Many African countries have ratified a number of regional and international human rights instruments, but have failed to translate their provisions into practical realities. In a message to an All-Africa Conference on Law, Justice and Development held in Nigeria in 2003, the Secretary General of the United Nations has been quoted saying that:

> It is not enough for States simply to give their consent to be bound by treaties, or to take action only to give the appearance of compliance. States must respect and implement the obligations embodied in the treaties, norms and laws.

The history of modern Africa is littered with failed institutions and initiatives and it is time that attention is focused on delivery and accountability. The ongoing, active engagement with civil society, including the setting of goals and targets and the monitoring of progress, is one good medium through which aspects of that apparent inertia can be overcome. Indeed, it is true that the same process of engagement will also help civil society understand the constraints under which governments are acting and perhaps refocus demands to more deliverable outcomes.

The Constitutive Act of the African Union provides for a broad range of human rights principles that were not reflected in the Charter of the Organisation of African Unity. These principles coupled with the two policy documents referred to earlier, the emphasis on democratic pluralism, the dynamics of civil society and the emergence of a core mass of leadership committed to the promotion and protection of human rights, should give the African Commission the space and opportunity to manoeuvre and expand the African human rights landscape.

Being the pioneer African human rights body and the only one within the African Union structure, the opportunities offered the African Commission must be fully exploited and effectively utilised if we are to establish a genuine human rights culture and make human rights central to the work of the African Union and all its organs.

The African Commission has to seize the opportunity provided by this conducive environment to be proactive and initiate ground-breaking policies and take decisions that would shape the course of human rights in Africa.

I cannot conclude without making an admission though. The African Commission as it stands today lacks the requisite human, material and financial resources to fully respond to the numerous human rights challenges arising from a growing number of countries on the continent. The need to strengthen this institution has been fully recognised and it is our hope that through our consultations, concrete proposals will be formulated in this direction, to enable the continental body to become a credible partner in promoting political change across the continent.

Building an effective regional human rights protection system also requires both the political will of Member States and the involvement of civil society. I dare say that the will to realise human rights for all is the motivation of the African Union. The will to build partnerships and inclusive societies is evident when looking at the plethora of instruments that have been signed and ratified. The big challenge, however, that will make all the difference, is now to go beyond rhetoric and translate the various commitments into practical action!

It is the African Union Commission's expectation that international interaction will further enhance our motivation and contribute towards the building of a society in which people live with hope.

Chapter 3

Institutional Consolidation of the African Commission on Human and Peoples' Rights: Challenges and Progress Made

Germain Baricako

Introduction

In the eighteen years or so of its existence, the African Commission on Human and Peoples' Rights (ACHPR) has had to confront a lot of challenges. Notwithstanding these challenges, it is fair to say that there has been considerable improvement in the work of the African Commission over the years. The fact that the African Commission has become one of the leading human rights bodies in the world today attests to the progress made in the building and consolidation of the institution. Therefore the African Commission's progress provides a wealth of experience that justifies the presentation of the institution: its mandate, composition and functioning, main activities, place and role in the new institutional environment of the African Union, and the perspectives contained in the Strategic Plan. This chapter identifies the main actors and partners of the abovementioned institutional development process, the strengths and weaknesses of the African Commission, the challenges currently facing the institution, and the relationships and interactions with State Parties, the African Union and its newly established organs.

Presentation of the African Commission on Human and Peoples' Rights

The Commission is composed of eleven members, called Commissioners and shall not include two nationals from the same State. They must be of the nationality of a state party to the African Charter and be chosen 'from amongst African personalities with the highest reputation, known for their high morality, integrity, impartiality and competence in matters of human and peoples' rights; particular consideration should be given to people having legal experience'. They serve in their individual capacities and should be free from improper influence and bias (Ankumah 1996). However, some Commissioners hold high government positions which might lead to conflicts of interest. Today, five out of the eleven are women, including the Chairperson of the ACHPR.

Commissioners are elected by the Assembly of Heads of State and Government of the AU for a six-year period and may be re-elected. The Commission elects its Chairman and Vice-Chairman for a two-year period and they are eligible for re-election. The Commissioners have so far all been lawyers or diplomats. The Commission adopted its Rules of Procedure in 1988 and amended them in 1995. The 120 Rules are intended to make the Commission a 'rational and functional effective organisation'. The functions of the Commission can be divided into two main categories: promotional and protective activities.

Mandate and Functions of the African Commission on Human and Peoples' Rights

Created by virtue of Article 30 of the African Charter[1] on Human and Peoples' Rights, the Commission[2] is mandated (Articles 30 and 45 of the Charter) to:
(i) Promote human and peoples' rights by:
 • collecting documentation, carrying out studies and research on African problems in the area of human rights, organising seminars, workshops and conferences, disseminating information, supporting national and local bodies engaged in the defense of human and peoples' rights and, if need be, advising or submitting recommendations to State Parties;

 • formulating and drafting principles and rules which would allow the resolution of legal problems relative to the enjoyment of human and peoples' rights and fundamental freedoms;

 • co-operating with other African or international institutions engaged in the promotion and protection of human and peoples' rights;

(ii) Guarantee the protection of human and peoples' rights under the conditions stipulated by the Charter;
(iii) Interpret any provision of the Charter at the request of a State Party, an institution of the OAU, (now the AU), or of an African organisation recognised by the OAU, (now the AU);

(iv) Execute all other duties which may be entrusted to it by the Assembly of Heads of State and Government.

Promotional Activities

The major actors, when it comes to the promotional activities, are the Commissioners. They are expected to carry out these activities. Their task is immense since each Commissioner is only working part-time for the Commission and is responsible for four to six countries. Therefore, they have to find ways to work with other organisations.

In accordance with Article 62 of the Charter, each State Party is required to present periodic reports on the status of human and peoples' rights every two years, for which the Commission has issued detailed guidelines. These reports are then discussed during the bi-annual sessions where States' delegates are present. NGOs from the country in question are also invited to give their comments (shadow reports), which allow interesting discussions.[3] Unfortunately, very few countries submit their reports on time[4] (see Viljoen in this book for more details). The Secretariat reminds State Parties to submit their reports on a quarterly basis. The Secretariat maintains and updates a status of submission of reports by State Parties. This status is sent along with the reminders. In order to facilitate the work of the Commission, the Secretariat summarises the reports and prepares questionnaires thereto. Because of insufficient funds, the Secretariat cannot translate States' reports into other working languages. Only summaries and questionnaires are translated and reproduced for Commissioners who do not understand the original language in which reports are submitted. It should be noted that a constructive dialogue between the African Commission and Member States comes about through the presentation of periodic reports. Overtime countries are showing more interest and willingness to present their reports. Some countries, which encounter difficulties in drafting their reports spontaneously, seek assistance from the Commission.

A cornerstone for the promotional activities is the openness of the work of the Commission and the publication of its results. States' periodic reports are to be published with the concluding observations of the Commission and the eventual comments of the States concerned. Reports on promotion missions are made public after their adoption by the Commission. The Annual Activity Reports are also published after their consideration by the Assembly of Heads of State and Government.[5] The Final Communiqués issued at the end of each session are more detailed and more informative than before. Press releases issued before, during, after the sessions and on various other occasions contain useful information.[6] Finally, the African Commission publishes a newsletter and operates a website (www.achpr.org). The publication of the newsletter[7] was stopped in 2000 due to a lack of technical support and funding. As part of its promotion activities, the African Commission has adopted quite a large number of recommendations, resolutions and guidelines[8] with the view of clarifying some human rights concepts, addressing some worrying situations and proposing to States Parties and other actors concerned ways and means of fulfilling their obligations. In this way, the African Commission has done very useful interpretation work. Indeed, people can understand better the scope of their rights; for their part, States have a better knowledge of their obligations and the legitimate expectations of the beneficiaries of the rights in question.

Protective Activities

In order to protect the rights and freedoms enshrined in the Charter, the Commission investigates and makes recommendations about communications from individuals as well as from State Parties. The protective activities thus principally consist of receiving communications and acting on them in accordance with the prescriptions of the Charter.

Submission of Communications

The Secretariat receives and registers a communication before forwarding it to the members of the Commission. The communications are assigned numbers in the permanent register and summarised by the Secretariat.

According to Article 55 of the African Charter, 'a communication shall be considered by the Commission if a simple majority of its members so decide'. At this stage, the Commission decides to be seized of a communication. Parties are informed accordingly. In practice, the decisions are taken by consensus. No communication concerning a State, which is not party to the Charter, shall be received by the Commission. Moreover, the communication must deal with specific breaches of the African Charter. The facts presented in the communication must furthermore be coherent, understandable and clear. The Commission may request the author of a communication to clarify it and supply the Commission with additional information. In practice, the Secretariat is mandated to write to the author if the communication is incomplete to request further clarifications. The examination begins with the Rapporteur (one of the Commissioners), who orally presents the communication to the other members of the Commission. The designation of a Rapporteur is done by the Secretary in consultation with the Chairperson. At the 15th Ordinary Session, March 1994, the Commission decided to apply the principle of not assigning communications to a Commissioner from the State against which complaints have been made. In the interest of continuity and efficiency, the Rapporteur remains the same throughout the procedure.

Admissibility

All communications shall be brought to the knowledge of the State concerned prior to any substantive consideration, meaning prior to the decision on admissibility. The concerned State is to react and submit its information and observations. The Commission continues with the consideration on admissibility, if the State does not respond in writing within a reasonable time. The first requirement for admissibility is that local remedies are exhausted unless it is obvious that this procedure is unduly prolonged. This rule is essentially defending the State's sovereignty, since it is founded in the principle of first allowing the State to redress the matter within the national judicial system. This rule has been the most frequent reason for declaring a communication inadmissible by the Commission. Both the African Charter and the Rules of Procedure do not say much on the question of remedy. In practice, however, the Commission has considered that it has competence to decide on the availability and efficiency of local remedies and has done so in a number of cases.[9] A second requirement is that a communication shall be compatible with the Charter of the OAU, now the Constitutive Act of the AU, and the African Charter and fall within the competence of the Commission. A further requirement is that the communication shall be submitted, 'within a reasonable period from the time local remedies are exhausted or from the date the Commission is seized of the matter'. Furthermore, the Commission does not deal with cases which have been settled in accordance with the principles of the Charter of the United Nations, or the Charter of the OAU, now the Constitutive Act of the AU, or the provisions of the African Charter. The 'victim requirement' involves communications to be submitted by any individual who alleges that he or she has been a victim, or they may be submitted in his or her name. Any African or international NGO may submit communications on behalf of the victim. Practice shows that communications have to a very large extent been submitted by NGOs. Communications shall not be 'written in disparaging or insulting language', directed against a State or the institutions of the OAU, now the AU. The Commission has not, however, referred to this in any communication dealt with. By declaring a communication admissible, the Commission undertakes to ascertain the facts and places itself at the disposal of the parties with the view of securing an amicable settlement. This procedure has developed from the practice of the Commission since both the African Charter and the Rules of Procedure are silent on amicable settlement of individual communications. In consequence, the amicable settlement process has a flexible and informal character. Articles 48 and 52 of the Charter refer to amicable settlement of interstate communications.[10] An inadmissibility decision is considered as a final decision and the Commission submits it to the Assembly of Heads of State and Government of the AU in its Annual Activity Report. An admissible communication must be brought to the knowledge of the State concerned and the author. The time limit decided for submissions of the State after the communication has been declared admissible is three months. When necessary, reminders are sent to the State with a new time limit of three months. If it becomes obvious to the Commission that Parties are not cooperating, it makes a decision on the basis of available documentation.

Consideration of the Merits of a Communication

Like the procedure concerning seizure and admissibility, the examination of merits takes place in closed sessions. The Commission shall inform the State concerned and the author of the communication about its readiness to consider the substantive issues of the communication and give them the opportunity to make oral or written presentation. The decisions of the Commission state the facts, the procedure and whether the Commission finds the facts presented to be a violation of the African Charter or not. It is worth noting that the African Commission has made significant progress with regards to the quality of its decisions on communication.

Since 1995, the African Commission has been able to adopt decisions on communications with a full account on the procedure and the reasoning on the merits. The decisions on merits are notified to the author and the State concerned just after the sessions during which they have been made. Parties are also informed that such decisions cannot be made public before the Annual Activity Report containing them is considered and adopted by the Assembly of Heads of State and Government. The ACHPR endeavours to follow up the implementation of decisions by the States concerned during field missions or whenever opportunity arises. By the end of year 2004, the African Commission has received 298 communications and has already disposed of 41 cases; 257 files are still pending before the African Commission.

Emergency Situations

A very difficult question the Commission has tried to deal with is how to address cases revealing emergency situations, i.e. when a situation presents the risk of further human rights violations or when the life of the victim is in danger. The Charter requests the Commission to submit, by letter to the Chairman of the Assembly of Heads of State, such cases for further action. But the Commission has adopted a creative approach in its interpretation of the Charter by using interim measures, allowing the Commission to resort to any appropriate method of investigation and to contact Member States directly rather than through the AU. During the sessions, the Commission takes any appropriate action. In between sessions the Chairperson of the ACHPR is mandated to initiate any appropriate action in consultation with the Vice-Chair and the Secretary to the Commission and to report to the ACHPR at the following session. Furthermore, the Rules of Procedure permit the Commission to suggest application of interim measures to States to avoid irreparable prejudice pending the examination of a complaint. In emergency situations, the Commission has the mandate to send missions to the State concerned for fact finding and in-depth studies. Although it has had difficulties in persuading States to accept missions, a number of such missions have been undertaken (Mauritania, Togo, Senegal, Nigeria and lately Zimbabwe and Sudan) and were successful.

In view of some shortcomings of the African Charter, the African Commission has taken initiatives aimed at strengthening the current system with regards to its protective mandate and the better protection of women's rights. However, observers have considered that the African Commission was too secretive about its protective activities (Viljoen ibid). They criticised the fact that the protective work of the African Commission remained hidden from public view and scrutiny on the grounds that a restrictive interpretation of confidentiality is problematic as publicity and its resultant shame, have major deterrent effects on prevention of future human rights abuses (Ankumah, 1996). But due attention is to be paid to the provisions of Article 59 (1) of the Charter which are very clear about the confidentiality requirement. Furthermore, the African Commission has been trying to disclose and disseminate non-confidential information like the list of communications, names of parties as well as the current state of the files (seizure, admissibility, merits). The decisions are part of the Annual Activity Reports submitted to the Assembly of Heads of State and Government of the AU. The activity reports are published after their adoption by the said Assembly (Articles 59, 2 & 3 of the Charter).

Unlike other regional and global human rights bodies, the Commission does not have a formal follow-up mechanism to ensure implementation of its recommendations and decisions. When the Assembly of Heads of State and Government of the African Union (AHG/AU) adopts the Commission's Annual Activity Report, the Commission publishes the report but cannot follow it up closely to ensure that the recommendations contained therein are implemented. This is mainly because the Commission does not have an enforcement mechanism. This has been very frustrating, especially for the victims who have to pursue the execution of the decisions on their own. At present, the Commission's follow up is carried out through Notes Verbales, during field missions and during its ordinary sessions when State delegates are present. In view of the results achieved, this approach has proved to be unsatisfactory.

Functioning of the African Commission

The Commission meets twice a year for fifteen days. At the given moment, the duration had been temporarily reduced to ten days, due to lack of funds. The balance between open and closed meetings at the sessions varies with the items on the agenda. The working languages of the Commission are English, French and Arabic. During the intersession, some Commissioners are engaged in their professional business and it is sometimes difficult for them to spare time for the Commission's activities. They do not get time to read working documents for sessions. Due to lack of preparation, discussions are unduly prolonged. Some

Commissioners cannot attend sessions up to the end. As a consequence, during Ordinary Sessions, the very heavy agenda hardly gets exhausted. To this date, there are about nineteen pending Mission Reports for consideration and adoption as well as communications which are ready and waiting for consideration and decisions. In view of the high number of the Mission Reports and the urgency to consider and adopt them in order to forward them to the State Parties visited, the African Commission had decided to hold an Extraordinary Session but due to lack of funds the Session could not be held. Members of the Commission are really concerned about this situation. Some Commissioners are of the view that arrangements should be made in order to alleviate the workload for members employed in public service and to have a permanent chairmanship.

Since the 15th Session, the Commission has demonstrated an open attitude.[11] The Commission has put in place an observer status system for NGOs and other partners. Over the years a great number of organisations have applied for and been granted such observer status (319 in November 2004) and thus developed a close working relationship with the Commission. In fact, NGOs have become major partners at the bi-annual meetings, providing both useful information and assistance in implementing the tasks of the Commission. Since 1991, the International Commission of Jurists (ICJ), later taken over by the African Centre for Democracy and Human Rights Studies, has organised and financed workshops for NGOs just before the sessions. These workshops have become very important; they allow the members of the commission to interact with the NGOs and vice versa. The NGOs also participate in the public sessions of the Commission and make substantial contributions. Over the years, partners have shown growing interest in the work of the Commission. In 1999, the Commission reviewed its criteria for granting observer status in order to make this relationship more efficient for all stakeholders. In view of the importance that NGOs attach to their collaboration with the African Commission, they have resolved to reflect on ways for strengthening and rationalising their partnership with the latter. They have yet to conclude this reflection and submit their proposals to the Commission.

The African Commission has observed that while some NGOs are very dynamic and contribute greatly to its work, quite a large number of them have just been granted observer status and disappeared. They do not submit their activity reports and have lost contact with the Commission. The latter has therefore decided to impose sanctions on NGOs which do not comply with the criteria. Sanctions go from a warning to loss of observer status.

With regards to National Human Rights Commissions, the African Commission is encouraging States Parties which have not yet done so, to create these Commissions and make available adequate resources for their smooth and independent functioning.

Special Rapporteurs and Working Groups

In order to pay adequate attention to some important human rights issues, the African Commission has resolved to establish special mechanisms, i.e. a special Rapporteurship and working groups. So far Special Rapporteurs are appointed from within the Commission. But appointing non-members of the African Commission when necessary is also envisaged. To date, the African Commission has six Rapporteurs and two working groups.[12] Unfortunately, these mechanisms encounter difficulties in their functioning due to inadequate resources. Some partners are assisting in this regard.

The Secretariat of the African Commission

The Secretariat to the Commission has since 12 June 1989 been located in Banjul. Apart from the Secretary to the Commission, the staff[13] is supposed to consist of two legal officers, one documentalist, one accountant/administrator, one bilingual secretary, one filing clerk as well as support staff and security. Thanks to the assistance of the partners of the Commission, the current composition of the staff is as follows: Secretary to the ACHPR, Finance and Administration Officer, Documentation and Information Officer, Public Relations Officer, Legal Officers (five), Policy and Planning Officer and Support Staff.

The main mission of the Secretariat is to assist the Commission in effectively carrying out its mandate, by handling all the technical and administrative work such as:

- preparing complaints against State Parties of human rights abuses to the Commission for consideration;

- receiving and preparing state reports to be examined by the Commission;

- processing working documents for the session;

- carrying out necessary arrangements in connection with the organisation of the sessions;

- preparing for the promotion activities; and

- raising funds for the activities of the Commission.

The Secretary to the Commission is responsible for the management of the Secretariat under the general supervision of the Chairperson and should particularly:

- assist the Commission and its members in the exercise of their functions;

- serve as an intermediary for all the communications concerning the Commission;

- be the custodian of the archives of the Commission; and

- bring issues immediately to the knowledge of the members of the Commission.

One cannot over-emphasise the crucial role of the Secretary to the Commission and the Secretariat, considering the Commission's limited time for the execution of its activities.

The OAU was the founding organ of the African Commission and its successor, the AU, plays a vital role in the work of the Commission. The AU is supposed to bear the cost of the operation of the Commission and of the Secretariat. However, the funding from the AU is not sufficient, and has never covered the cost for the minimum staff required to run the Secretariat, nor the funds needed for the activities of the Commission. NGOs and international development agencies have therefore over the years been asked to fund various parts of the work of the Commission and its Secretariat.

In accordance with the terms of Article 41 of the African Charter on Human and Peoples' Rights, 'the Secretary General of the Organisation of African Unity appoints the Secretary to the Commission and also provides the staff and means necessary for the effective discharge of the duties attributed to the African Commission. The Organisation of African Unity bears the costs related to this staff and means and services'. The Commission of the African Union inherited this responsibility which it has to bear from the budgetary contributions of Member States. Due to the limited resources of Member States, the funds allocated to the African Commission by the AU fall far short of the essential requirements of this institution. This gives rise to the need to seek external or extra budgetary resources. In this regard, the African Commission has established fruitful co-operation relations with external partners, in particular with the Nordic countries through the Danish Human Rights Institute and the Swedish Agency for International Development and Co-operation. NORAD, (Norwegian Agency for Development Cooperation) funded at one point the activities of the Special Rapporteur on Prisons and Conditions of Detention in Africa, through Penal Reform International (PRI).

The African Court on Human and Peoples' Rights[14]

The idea of an African Court was first raised in 1961 during the first discussions on the African Charter. It was put aside, due to lack of adequate political support, when the African Charter was adopted. In July 1994, the Assembly of Heads of State and Government of the OAU adopted the resolution AHG/Res.230 proposed by the ACHPR requesting the Assembly to reflect on the possibility of establishing an African Court on Human and Peoples' Rights. Against this background, African experts first met in Cape Town, South Africa, in September 1995, where they drafted a Protocol. It took some time before member states reacted to the draft with comments and observations. Experts held another meeting in Nouakchott, Mauritania, in April 1997. The draft Protocol went through a final reading in Addis Ababa, Ethiopia, in December 1997. After endorsement by the OAU's Council of Ministers on 27 February 1998, it was finally adopted in

Ouagadougou in June 1998. It was immediately signed by thirty-one Member States. The Protocol entered into force on January 24, 2004, 30 days after the fifteenth Member State had deposited its instrument of ratification with the Chairperson of the AU Commission.

The Court comprises eleven judges, with a six-year mandate renewable once. Except for the President (and the registrar) they will sit on a part-time basis, at least initially, in order to cut down costs. The appointment process and the judges' independent status will be similar to those applying to the Commission. The Court elects its President and Vice-President for a two-year mandate, renewable once. According to the Protocol, the Court 'shall complement[15] the protective mandate' of the Commission. Its jurisdiction[16] is potentially wide, extending to all cases and disputes submitted to it concerning the interpretation and application of the Charter, the Protocol instituting the Court, 'and any other relevant Human Rights instrument ratified by the States concerned'. In addition to interpretative powers, the Court may also provide advisory opinions.[17] It will determine its own rules of procedure.[18] The African Commission, litigants, defendants and States are all granted access to the Court,[19] as are 'African intergovernmental organisations'. However, access to the Court by NGOs and individuals is contingent on Member States' special acceptance.[20] In this regard, the African Court will take one step backwards compared to the Commission. The Court must 'conduct its proceedings in public'.[21] This means that the evidence and the opposing argument debate get public exposure. The Court's duly motivated judgment must similarly 'be read in open court'.[22] These two provisions contrast with the confidentiality prescribed by Article 59 of the African Charter. However, no publicity is provided for the Court's annual report, whereas it is specifically required to mention whether any Member State has failed to comply with a Court judgement.[23] But nothing prevents the Court from publishing its decision. The judgment of the Court is final and must be rendered within three months after deliberations are completed.[24] The Court must transmit judgments to AU Member States, the African Commission and the AU Council of Ministers.[25] In the event of a violation, the Court must provide for remedies, including 'the payment of fair compensation or reparation'. The Court may also prescribe provisional measures 'in case of extreme gravity and urgency, and when necessary to avoid irreparable harm to persons'.[26] The major difference from the Commission is that the Court's judgments are binding and final and the AU Council of Ministers monitors their execution 'on behalf' of Heads of State. This is a very important step forward in the strengthening of the African human rights system.

The Protocol on the Rights of Women in Africa

In view of the fact that article 18 of the African Charter does not provide adequate protection of the rights of women, the African Commission proposed to the OAU Assembly of Heads of State and Government, which agreed[27] that it draft a Protocol on the Rights of Women. The African Commission played a key role in the drafting process of this Protocol. At its second Summit in Maputo, Mozambique in July 2003, the African Union adopted the Protocol on the Rights of Women in Africa. This Protocol is the first regional human rights instrument in Africa to specifically address women's rights. Since then, the African Commission together with its partners and other stakeholders has engaged in sensitisation campaigns to encourage the quick ratification and entry into force of the Protocol. The Protocol will enter into force upon ratification by fifteen States. As of December 2004, only nine States had ratified the Protocol.[28]

Place and Role of the African Commission on Human and Peoples' Rights in the New Institutional Environment of the African Union

The Constitutive Act of the African Union (AU) gives great importance to human rights. Indeed, the Constitutive Act reaffirms, in its preamble, the resolution of Member States to promote and protect human and peoples' rights, to consolidate democratic institutions and culture, and to guarantee good governance and the rule of law. Also, according to Article 3, the AU undertook to 'promote and protect human and peoples' rights in conformity with the provisions of the African Charter on Human and Peoples' Rights and of other pertinent instruments relating to human rights'. In article 4, the importance of 'respect for democratic principles, human rights, the rule of law and good governance' is stipulated. Within the framework of these same principles, the Constitutive Act invites Member States to promote equality between men and women as well as social justice in order to guarantee equitable economic development, just as it condemns and rejects impunity and unconstitutional changes of Government. Human rights issues in the Constitutive Act are dealt with in a more detailed and committed manner than was the case in the Charter of the Organisation of African Unity. It should also be noted that the various organs of the African Union recognise the important role of the African Commission within the African Union. This, in effect, confers a role and position of privilege on the African Commission on Human and Peoples' Rights within the new political and institutional set up of the AU. It is for this reason that, in July 2003, in Maputo, Mozambique, the Assembly of Heads of State and Government, by Decision Dec. Assembly/AU/7 (II), requested the African Commission on Human and Peoples' Rights 'to pursue the reflection, in close collaboration with the Commission of the African Union, on the establishment of more dynamic interaction and co-ordination with the various organs of the African Union in order to strengthen the African mechanism for the promotion and protection of human and peoples' rights'.

The AU organs, institutions and services that the Commission has to interact with are mainly:

- The Department of Political Affairs;

- NEPAD and the African Peer Review Mechanism;

- The Conference on Security, Stability, Development and Cooperation in Africa (CSSDCA);

- The Peace and Security Council;

- The African Committee of Experts on the Rights and Welfare of the Child;

- The Gender Directorate;

- The Pan African Parliament.

The involvement of the Commission in the work of the organs and institutions of the African Union will necessarily generate a large volume of additional activities. It should therefore be re-organised and adequately equipped to face these new duties added to its original activities.

The Strategic Plan of the African Commission (2003–2006)

Introduction

In order to orient its work towards better perspectives for the promotion and protection of human and peoples' rights in Africa, in accordance with the relevant provisions of the African Charter on Human and Peoples' Rights, the African Commission adopted, during its 33rd Ordinary Session held from 15 to 30 May 2003 in Niamey, Niger, a Strategic Plan for the period 2003–2006. After the Mauritius Plan of Action (1996–2001), prepared and implemented with the assistance of the Danish Centre for Human Rights, the planning process was pursued and reviewed during 2002. The current Strategic Plan is intended to build the capacity of the Secretariat of the African Commission to enable it to provide all the necessary support to the Members of the African Commission for the effective discharge of their duties in accordance with their mandate as defined under Article 45 of the Charter.

It is divided into 5 parts:

- The first part identifies the African Commission's objectives, vision, philosophy, values and mission and determines the key areas;

- The second part relates to the key result indicators presented in table format;

- The third part deals with results achieved within the Mauritius Plan of Action and projections for coming years;

- The fourth part breaks down each key result area into a certain number of objectives and subsequently lists related Plans of Action;

- The fifth part provides a cost overview for the implementation of the said Action Plans.

(1) Vision

The vision of the African Commission is to be a leading and efficient institution in the implementation of the African Charter, through better promotion and protection of all rights and freedoms enshrined in this instrument.

(2) Philosophy and Values

The philosophy and values of the African Commission are expressed in the African Charter. Furthermore, note should be taken of the reference in the preamble to the OAU Charter which stipulates that 'freedom, equality, justice and dignity are essential objectives for the achievement of the legitimate aspirations of the African peoples'. This reference also reaffirms the commitment to promote international co-operation having due regard to the Charter of the United Nations and the Universal Declaration of Human Rights. These values are clearly reiterated in the Constitutive Act of the African Union.

(3) Mission of the African Commission and Its Secretariat

The Mission of the African Commission is to promote and protect human and peoples' rights in Africa. In providing the administrative, technical and logistical support to the Members of the Commission, the Secretariat enables the Commission to fully discharge its mandate as a leading institution for the protection and promotion of human rights in Africa.

In consequence, the Secretariat:

- provides technical support for consultative and follow-up activities of the Commission and all other support required by the Commissioners for the execution of their mandate;
- disseminates results of the work of the Commission;
- facilitates the promotion of the African Charter;
- builds networks with human rights organisations and facilitates activities between them; and
- procures the required resources for the fulfilment of the Commission's mandate.

The Secretariat has divided its activities into the following main areas:

- Support to the Bureau of the African Commission, comprising the Chairperson and the Vice-Chairperson, and support to the individual Commissioners in tasks assigned to them;
- Dissemination of relevant material resulting from the work of the African Commission both as a collegial body and through the various functions exercised by its members;
- Promotion of the African Charter through general support, publishing and special activities;
- Networking at the global, continental, regional and national levels;

- Institutional support for the fulfillment of its mission and for putting in place the necessary mechanisms for co-operation with other human rights organisations. While the provision of the various resources is ultimately the responsibility of the AU, the Secretariat is directly charged with the accountability and management of these resources, once obtained, and with procurement of alternative sources of funding when required.

Due to the limited human, material and financial resources currently available, it is not realistic for the Secretariat to try to undertake all the defined tasks. Thus, the Secretariat should prioritise its work.

The work of the Secretariat can be divided into three categories as follows:

- Tasks that the Secretariat must execute in order for the African Commission to fulfil its mandate;

- Tasks which provide support for the work of the African Commission and which improve its performance. These tasks can be undertaken by other institutions or organisations, but, in view of its mandate, the African Commission has a special obligation to supervise and monitor the follow-up of their correct fulfillment (essentially promotional tasks) to the extent that is has resources for this purpose;

- Other tasks which guarantee the promotion of the African Charter.

The Secretariat has accorded priority to its primary mission, i.e. to the tasks of the first category and to those of the second which could significantly improve the results of the first. This relates to the missions (including rapid intervention missions), the processing of communications, the consideration of State reports and the organisation of sessions. Adequate support should also be provided for Special Rapporteurs. Furthermore, the Secretariat should be able to draft all the working documents of the Commission, to produce the Annual Activity Reports and Newsletters regularly and on time, and to provide the required support for the Bureau and the Commission as a whole.

Finally, the Secretariat should be sufficiently equipped for the timely preparation of a Five-Year Plan.

Conclusion

The African Commission is unique in that it is the only Pan African mechanism mandated to promote and protect human rights on the continent and as such has the capacity to take very progressive steps to carry out its mandate. It has emerged as one of the most flexible regional bodies in the protection of human rights, especially in view of the fact that it entertains complaints from individuals and NGOs from all over the world regarding infringement of human rights in Africa. This *actio popularis* approach gives credence and generous access to the Commission to anyone who has an interest in human rights, whether he/she is a victim or not. The African Charter thus provides the Commission with wide room for interpretation and the discharge of its mandate. The Commission has made progress in creating a culture of human rights on the continent and contributed in developing international human rights jurisprudence. In this regard, the Commission has made positive progress in issuing landmark decisions on communications.[39] For example the decision on the SERAC case[30] against Nigeria on the role of the State in providing socio-economic rights has been hailed worldwide as a precedent for international and domestic courts on the socio-economic rights of a people. The Commission recognised the rights of 'peoples' and even recommended compensation for the victims. The Commission has also been able to prevent States from taking certain actions while awaiting its decisions, through its urgent appeals mechanism. In spite of the lukewarm attitude of certain States about the efficacy of the Commission, it remains a fact that the latter has been able to implant the subject of human rights in the agenda of political leaders on the continent. The Commission has also improved its relationship with other organs of the African Union and partners and is involved in their activities. For example the Commission has been holding joint seminars and workshops with international and NGOs on pertinent issues concerning human rights in Africa. The Commission has been actively involved in the preparation and lobbying for the adoption of Protocols to the African Charter, specifically the Protocol to the Charter Establishing an African Court on Human and Peoples' Rights and the Protocol on the Rights of Women in Africa. In so doing, the African Commission is making important steps towards contributing to the strengthening of the African human rights system. The above-mentioned Strategic Plan, if properly funded and implemented, will undoubtedly guarantee improved output and enhanced visibility of the African Commission on Human and Peoples' Rights through the achievements that it would be able to show. At the same time, the Secretariat would get adequate means to enable it to improve its performance in the provision of technical, administrative and logistical support for the Members of the Commission.

Notes

1. Adopted in June 1981 in Nairobi, Kenya, by the Assembly of Heads of State and Government of the Organisation of African Unity (OAU), currently the African Union (AU), and entered into force on 21 October 1986.
2. Set up on 2 November 1987 in Addis Ababa, Ethiopia, after the election of its 11th members by the 23rd Ordinary Session of the Assembly of Heads of State and Government of the OAU, held in July 1987.
3. During the consideration of States' reports, only the Members of the Commission and the Delegates presenting the report participate in the discussion.
4. Seven States Parties have submitted all due reports, thirteen States Parties have already submitted some reports but have some overdue reports, eighteen States Parties have never submitted their reports.

5. Article 59 of the Charter.

6. For example: African Human Rights Day, Commemoration of the Rwanda Genocide, International Women's Day, etc.

7. The Late Chairman Emeritus of the ACHPR, Isaac Nguema was coordinating the contribution of articles and the processing of the Review which was published with the funding of the Netherlands Government and the technical support of the African Society on International and Comparative Law. The African Commission paid tribute to Professor Isaac Nguema, who was a Member of the African Commission since its inauguration in November 1987, by conferring upon him the unique title of 'Chairman Emeritus of the African Commission on Human and Peoples' Rights' for his sterling advocacy for human rights throughout the continent. Commissioner Nguema also served as Chairman of the Commission for three terms.

8. The resolutions, recommendations and guidelines are posted on the ACHPR's website.

9. See communications:
   - Communication 39/90 - Annette Pagnoule pour le compte de Abdoulaye Mazou c/Cameroun.
   - Communication 103/93 - Alhassane Aboubacar c/Ghana.
   - Communications 147/95 & 149/96 - Dawda Jawara c/ Gambia.
   - Communications 25/89, 47/90, 56/91 and 100/93 - Free Legal Assistance Group, Lawyers' Committee for Human Rights, Union Internationale des Droits de l'Homme, Les Témoins de Jéhovah c/ RD Congo.

   - Communication 71/92 - Rencontre Africaine pour la Défense des Droits de l'Homme c/Zambia.

   - Communication 74/92 - Commission Nationale des Droits de l'Homme et des Libertés c/Tchad.

10. See also Rule 98 of the Rules of Procedure.

11. The partners are consulted about the agenda of the sessions and they make necessary proposals thereto. The Final Communiqués of the sessions are more detailed and informative than before. More interns are hosted at the Secretariat.

12. Special Rapporteurs: Extrajudicial, Summary and Arbitrary Executions; Prisons and Detention Conditions; Rights of Women; Refugees and Internally Displaced Persons (IDPs); Human Rights Defenders; Freedom of Expression; Working Groups on: Indigenous Populations/Communities; Prevention and Prohibition of Torture.

13. This is the structure of the Secretariat as adopted by the AU.

14. This chapter does not refer to the recent developments after the Assembly of the AU decision in July 2004 to merge the ACHPR Court with the ACJ.

15. Article 1.

16. Article 2.

17. Article 4.
18. Article 33.
19. Article 5, (1) & (2).
20. Articles 5, (3) & 34 (6)
21. Article 10 (1)
22. Article 28 (5)
23. Article 31
24. Article 28 (1)
25. Article 29
26. Article 27
27. See resolution of the Assembly AHG/Res. 240 (XXXI).
28. Mali, Senegal, Comoros, Djibouti, Rwanda, Lesotho, Namibia, South Africa and Libya.
29. See Chidi Anselm Odinkalu & Camilla Christensen, 'The African Commission on Human and Peoples' Rights: The Development of its Non-State Communications Procedures', 20 *Human Rights Quarterly,* 278 (1998).
30. Communication 155/96 The Social and Economic Rights Action Center and the Centre for Economic and Social Rights, Nigeria.

Chapter 4

New Challenges and Opportunities for Human Rights Promotion and Protection in Africa

Hassan Bubacar Jallow

Introduction

One of the greatest and ever pertinent challenges to Africa in our time is how to make human rights a reality in the day-to-day lives of our people through Africa's premier regional human rights institution, the African Commission on Human and Peoples' Rights. The enjoyment of human rights by everyone on the continent, regardless of sex, gender, race, ethnic origin, nationality, citizenship, language, economic status, religion, creed, etc., has been and continues to be the greatest aspiration of the African people. Indeed this is an aspiration of the entirety of humanity as expressed by the Universal Declaration of Human Rights[1] and as reiterated in a multiplicity of global and regional human rights treaties, including the African Charter on Human and Peoples' Rights,[2] the anchor of the African regional human rights system. The yearning and thirst for the enjoyment of human rights is even more profound among the people of Africa, a continent where the human rights situation has been and continues to be very precarious.

The quest for the enjoyment of human rights and freedoms in Africa has a deep and longstanding historical resonance. Africa was the theatre of massive and widespread atrocities committed against the African people during both the slave trade and colonial periods. The quest for human rights and freedoms was a fundamental goal of the fathers of independence, and has remained the greatest aspiration of the African people.

Regrettably, post-colonial Independent Africa has witnessed and continues to witness atrocities being committed against the African people by or with the complicity of their own African governments. Widespread poverty, conflict, insecurity, the AIDS/HIV pandemic, among others, have ravaged the African continent, while the exacerbation of ethnicism has culminated in genocide and massive atrocities, including widespread acts of sexual violence.

The African Commission on Human and Peoples' Rights is the premier and specialised inter-governmental human rights institution within the larger African regional system.[3] An examination of the functioning of the Commission and the African regional system in general with a view to identifying ways and means of enhancing their efforts to change the human rights practices of African states and for dealing with various cases not effectively addressed at the national level, are extremely important. It is also imperative in the light of the new challenges to good governance and human rights.

Defining the Challenges

In the past half-century since the inception of the international human rights revolution, the international community can point to fundamental achievements in the area of human rights. Worthy of note is the issue of international human rights norms. The international community has adopted extensive human rights norms and standards, embodied in both global and regional instruments, with the result that a lack of human rights norms and standards no longer constitute a major challenge.[4]

Within Africa, the African Charter on Human and Peoples' Rights,[5] the anchor of the African regional systems, has been ratified by all members of the African Union. The Charter is very rich in the area of human rights, encompassing under one roof all categories of human rights (civil and political, economic, social and cultural, as well as group or solidarity rights) that must be implemented by all states parties. The Charter's approach to individual and collective rights and the concept of individual duties in the context of human rights are worthy of note.

The major challenge in Africa as in the rest of the world is the implementation of human rights norms so that human rights have a meaning in the daily lives of the people. But there are other challenges, old and new, that continue to undermine the implementation and enjoyment of human rights in Africa. Today, at the dawn of the twenty-first century, Africa is once again at a crossroads. While diminished in numbers, dictatorial and abusive governments, representing the 'classic category' of challenges to human rights in Africa, have not entirely disappeared. This and other longstanding categories are compounded by what may be termed 'new' human rights problems.

Repressive laws and practices and other challenges to Sustainable Democratic Governance

Since the establishment of the African Commission, and particularly over the last ten years, Africa's political landscape has witnessed important advances. Many member states of the OAU/AU have established more pluralist and participatory political systems. Repressive dictatorships in Africa have generally diminished. Positive changes in hitherto notorious dictatorial and abusive regimes must be applauded. The demise of military regimes and the general progress towards good governance is quite remarkable. Undoubtedly the adoption of the Charter and other human rights instruments as well as the work of the Commission and other human rights bodies have contributed significantly to such progress. However, some pockets of repression and malgovernance still remain.

There is a need to consolidate and improve upon the progress made and ensure sustainable and substantive democratic governance, i.e., governance that respects not only processes (free and fair periodical elections), but also provides a vehicle to deliver social and economic justice.

The Commission's efforts not only in ensuring that the practices of African governments are compatible with their human rights obligations under the African Charter, but also in promoting democratic governance, including denouncing military regimes, observing elections and promoting participatory democracy,[6] are indispensable.

Conflicts, Refugees, and Internally Displaced Persons

Whilst the principal concern in the years pre-dating the Charter and for sometime thereafter appeared to be violations of individual civil and political rights, the challenges now confronting us appear to be targeted at groups - ethnic minority groups or others.

The enjoyment of human rights in Africa has been greatly undermined by armed conflict. Inter-state and intra-state conflicts in Africa pose one of the greatest challenges to the global/United Nations and regional efforts to ensure global peace, human rights, prosperity and development in Africa. Rwanda, the DRC, Uganda, Sierra Leone, Liberia, Angola, Mozambique, the Sudan have all during these past two decades, epitomised some of the worst humanitarian tragedies of modern times.

In a great majority of conflicts, as the UN Secretary-General has noted in his Report to the UN Security Council on the Causes of Conflict (1998), '[the] main aim increasingly is the destruction not just of armies, but civilians and entire ethnic groups'.[7] The exacerbation of ethnicism has created tensions and conflicts, culminating in genocide and massive atrocities, such as in Rwanda in 1994.

Conflict in Africa has created tens of thousands of refugees or internally displaced persons. Over five million of the world's seventeen million refugees are in Africa, and the continent contains about fifteen million of the world's twenty-five million internally displaced persons.[8]

While the causes of conflict in Africa are diverse and complex, there are common denominators and linkages amongst them. The lack of respect for human rights and the rule of law, inequitable distribution of resources, the repression, marginalisation and exclusion of large segments of society from political participation, and an environment of malgovernance characterised by lack of accountability and transparency, have all been contributory factors. The inability and lack of capacity of African regional institutions to halt the conflicts on the one hand and often the apathy of a world which had the capacity, but lacked the will to act, as in Rwanda in 1994, on the other, have left thousands of African civilians at the mercy of ruthless governments and warlords.

Poverty

While Africa is potentially one of the richest continents in terms of natural resource endowment,[9] many of its peoples live under absolute poverty.[11] Large segments of the African population continue to live under very difficult conditions.

Lack of access to basic social services, including education and health, coupled with hunger, malnutrition and infant mortality, are more acute in most countries of Africa than in the rest of the world. Poverty and deprivation are a challenge to human rights; they are indeed a violation of people's rights to a decent living.

The causes of Africa's continuing cycle of economic failure and widespread poverty and deprivation are diverse.

While 'external' causes for Africa's crises are significant, even more salient are the 'internal' ones, notably the ineptitude, corruption and mismanagement of our communities. The plundering of public resources by officials of countries most of whose peoples live below the poverty line continues to be a major problem. Corruption is undoubtedly a key element in economic under-performance and deprivation.

But the social and economic deprivations of our peoples cannot be addressed effectively in an environment lacking freedom of speech, conscience, the effective participation of the populace in political affairs, their right to dissent and promote alternatives to those in power.

Health/HIV/AIDS

Compounding the African human rights condition is the prevalence of disease. The HIV/AIDS pandemic in particular has seriously ravaged the continent more than any other part of the world. Other communicable diseases, including malaria and tuberculosis, present a significant threat to the lives and well being of millions of people in Africa. They also pose a threat to the future.

The problem of disease has seriously undermined the right to health recognised in various international human rights treaties as well as the Constitution of the World Health Organisation (WHO).

Prospects and Opportunities

Redressing the African human rights predicament is an uphill task that calls for the constant mobilisation and reinvigoration of the entire African regional system within which the African Commission operates. The recent developments in the African regional system, including the entry into force of a Protocol for an African Court on Human and Peoples' Rights, the adoption of a specific African instrument for the protection of the rights of women in Africa, an African instrument dealing with corruption, the transformation of the Organisation of African Unity (OAU) into the African Union (AU) with a strong commitment to promoting human rights and justice, the New Partnership for Africa's Development (NEPAD), among others, enhance the promise, prospects and opportunities for human rights in Africa. Instances of joint action and closer cooperation between the African regional system and the United Nations further enhance opportunities for more effective responses to serious human rights crises on the continent.

In order for the above developments to have meaning in Africa, there is a need to adopt a greater human rights perspective on the functioning of the entire African regional political system. The entire African system should bring a human rights and good governance perspective to economic integration, to development, peace, security. More consistent, concerted and deepened cooperation between the African system and the United Nations in responding to serious human rights crises in Africa is also important.

Building on the progress and foundations established by the African Commission

Since its inception to date, the African Commission on Human and Peoples' Rights may be credited for laying important foundations and for a remarkable progress in the promotion and protection of human rights in Africa. This modus operandi has transformed the Commission into an important instrument for the protection and promotion of human rights in Africa, and thus providing an significant promise for redressing the current African human rights predicament.

Enhancing the Functioning of the Commission

There is a need, however, to improve the functioning of the Commission in order to place it in a better position to meet the current human rights challenges in Africa. Less secrecy/confidentiality in its mode of operation, and greater openness/transparency and publicity will enhance the impact of its work and dispel a popular perception of its alleged ineffectiveness. Adequate funding of the Commission is imperative. For several years to date, the Commission's work has been constrained by lack of sufficient funds, and the Commission has had to rely on external sources. The part-time nature of the Commission restricts its effectiveness. There is an urgent need to introduce a full-time element in the functioning of the Commission. There is also an urgent need to increase the ordinary sessions of Commission. So also the promotional activities of the Commission.

African states should prioritise the financing of human rights activities within the African system.[10]

Independence and Impartiality of the Commission

The mandate of the Commission requires that the Commissioners are independent and impartial, and that there is a separation of powers between the Commission and those states party to the Charter.

Any perceived conflict of interest by the public undermines the effectiveness of the Commission in holding governments accountable. A strong perception of independence and impartiality among the public towards the Commission constitutes one of its strongest assets. Such a perception threatens to be undermined by the membership of government officials in the Commission. The practice should be discontinued.

The African Court on Human and Peoples' Rights

The establishment of the Court heralds a new step, demonstrating the intention of African states to give more meaning to the spirit of the African Charter. There is an urgent need for states to nominate and elect judges in order for the Court to become functional. African governments that have not yet ratified the Protocol need urgently to do so to ensure that people across Africa can benefit from the Court.[12] It is important that African governments provide sufficient resources and funding both to the Court and the Commission in order to enable them effectively establish a constructive and complementary role in the protection and promotion of human and peoples' rights in Africa.

Whilst the establishment of the Court is a welcome development, a note of caution must be made. There is little point in having a Court if it is to suffer the lack of resource support which has so far gravely undermined the work of the Commission. It is imperative that both institutions are fully resourced to operate effectively.

The efforts by the AU to develop and implement a mechanism to deal with conflict are worthy of note. In July 2001, the Assembly of Heads of State and Government adopted a decision recognising the Mechanism for Conflict Prevention, Management and Resolution (MCPMR) as an organ of the AU. Under Article 22 of the Protocol Relating to the Establishment of Peace and Security

Council of Africa, a Security Council has replaced the Central Organ of the MCPMR.

The Protocol on the Rights of Women and the Charter on the Rights and Welfare of the Child

Complementing efforts to realise human rights in Africa are two recently adopted instruments for the protection of women and children, the Protocol to the African Charter on Human and Peoples' Rights on the Rights of Women[13] and the African Charter on the Rights and Welfare of the Child.[14] The former has not yet entered into force, while the latter entered into force on 29 November 1999.

The Protocol on the Rights of Women once it comes into force promises to address the longstanding and widespread abuse of women in Africa both in the public and private spheres. The Protocol obligates states to embrace a gender perspective in their policy decisions, legislation, developmental plans and activities in order to ensure the overall well being of women.[15] Extending over a wide area, the Protocol enshrines provisions for the elimination of all forms of discrimination against women in all spheres. Couched in detailed and creative language, the Protocol not only draws on the UN Convention on the Elimination of All Forms of Discrimination Against Women,[16] but moves beyond to address problems particularly inflicting the African women.[17] The African Commission is mandated to supervise the implementation of the Protocol pending the establishment of an African Court.[18]

The African Charter on the Rights and Welfare of the Child also provides a strong promise in ensuring the protection of the rights of children in Africa. The Charter is normatively rich. It encompasses thirty-one rights and duties intended to address the critical situation facing children in Africa due to unique factors obtaining on the continent, including socio-economic, cultural, traditional and developmental circumstances, armed conflict, natural disasters, poverty, exploitation and hunger. Underpinning the rights of the child in the Charter are four core values or principles, namely, non-discrimination (art. 3 and 36); the best interest of the child (art. 4); the right to life, survival and development (art. 5); participation of the child, which is subdivided into respect for the child's views (art. 7), and provision of information to children and promotion of their participation (art. 4, 7 and 12). The Charter is not only inspired by the UN Convention on the Rights of the Child,[19] but also moves beyond to enrich the protection of children in Africa. It thus encompasses some entirely new additions to the child rights arena and other drafted to offer a higher level of protection.[20] The Charter establishes an African Committee of Experts on the Rights and Welfare of the Child to promote and protect the rights of the child, and monitor state compliance with their obligations under the Charter.[21]

There is an urgent need for states to ratify the Protocol on Women in order for it to come into force. The African Commission and the future Court need to act more actively and creatively to ensure that the plight of African women is addressed as a matter of urgency and priority. Similar approaches are called for in the implementation of the African Charter on the Rights of the Child. There is an urgent need for the Assembly to recognise the Committee as an independent organ of the AU.

The Human Rights Promise of the AU and Recent Developments in the African System, such as NEPAD, the Mechanism for Dealing with Conflict and an African Instrument against Corruption

The transformation of the OAU into the African Union enhances the promise of the African system to more effectively deal with the human rights and governance challenges on the continent. Compared with the OAU Charter, the Constitutive Act of the AU provides a much stronger framework for supporting human rights and democratic governance.

The Constitutive Act, by establishing a strong framework for effective economic integration in Africa, lays an important foundation for a successful enforcement of human rights. Effective economic integration may not only lead to expanded markets and related benefits, but also enhanced socio-economic, environmental and security interdependence among member states. In the absence of a regional police force or army to enforce state compliance with their human rights obligations, intergovernmental institutions have to rely more on shame and pressure mechanisms such as economic sanctions, the severance of diplomatic relations, sport and other ties with the recalcitrant states. The interdependence promoted by the AU is instrumental in the effective deployment of these mechanisms.

The Act of the Union provides a richer human rights base than the OAU Charter. The Act extensively incorporates human rights as one of the objectives and principles and makes explicit reference to the African Charter, the Universal Declaration of Human Rights and other relevant human rights instruments in this regard.[22] The Act recognises the indispensability of good governance in the realisation of human rights and other objectives and principles of the Union. It thus expresses a determination to promote democratic principles and institutions, popular participation, the rule of law and good governance.[23] The promotion of gender equality, the promotion of social justice and balanced economic development, the respect for the sanctity of life, the condemnation and rejection of the culture of impunity, political assassination and acts of terrorism and the rejection of unconstitutional changes of government, are important principles of the Union.[24] The implementation of these principles enhances the promise for the realisation of human rights in Africa.

While retaining the principles of respect for state sovereignty and sovereign equality of states, the Act curtails state sovereignty in the interest of human rights and good governance. It thus creates the right of the Union to intervene in a member state pursuant to a decision by the Assembly in respect of grave circumstances, namely genocide, war crimes and crimes against humanity and the right of member states to request intervention from the Union in order to restore peace and security.[25] The Act also condemns and rejects unconstitutional changes of government. An even handed implementation of these clauses creates greater promise for the realisation of human rights and democratic governance in Africa.

In terms of enforcement of its objectives and principles and the participation of the people of Africa in its activities, the AU makes remarkable strides. Unlike the OAU Charter which invested virtually all authority in the Assembly, the AU Statute creates multiple sources of authority. It invests authority not only in the Assembly, but also in others, including 'democratic' and judicial institutions, namely the Parliament and the Court respectively. The participation of the people of Africa in the election of members of the Union's Parliament[26] and allowing different social and professional groups of member states in the functioning of the Economic, Social and Cultural Council,[27] establish important avenues for the people and civil society in Africa to be involved in championing the cause of human rights and democratic governance within the Union.

Although the Act of the AU expressly refers to the African Charter on Human and Peoples' Rights, and also creates various institutions, it is silent on the place and role of the African Commission, the future Court and the Committee on the Rights and Welfare of the Child, as well as their relationship with other organs of the Union. There is an urgent need to incorporate the African human rights mechanisms into the structure of the AU.

The efforts by the AU to develop and implement a mechanism to deal with conflict are worthy of note. In July 2001, the Assembly of Heads of State and Government adopted a decision recognising the Mechanism for Conflict Prevention, Management and Resolution (MCPMR) as on organ of the AU.[28] Under Article 22 of the Protocol Relating to the Establishment of Peace and Security Council of Africa, a Security Council has replaced the Central Organ of the MCPMR. An analysis of the working of this Council so far raises hope that with continued effort and goodwill by member states the African Union can more effectively deal with conflict.[29]

The New Partnership for Africa's Development (NEPAD), a broad policy framework for development programming drafted by several African Heads of States, and launched in 2001, is also worthy of note. As a programme of the AU, NEPAD's primary objectives are to champion the challenge to eradicate poverty in Africa, establish stable peace and security conditions, promote the role of women in all activities, and ensure sustainable growth and development.[30] Respect for human rights is also emphasised.[31] NEPAD identifies peace, security, democracy and political governance as prerequisites for sustainable development.

No doubt, the realisation of these objectives is relevant to the enjoyment of human rights in Africa. It is important in the implementation of these objectives that a human rights perspective is adopted. NEPAD provides for the development of an African Peer Review Mechanism, which will also deal with human rights issues.[32]

Enhanced joint action and closer cooperation between the United Nations and the African regional system in responding to African human rights catastrophes, are also important.[33] The adoption by African member states of an instrument to deal with corruption[34] is also a significant development. Combatting corruption in public offices in Africa is urgently called for in order to ensure greater integrity in public life as well as transparency and accountability.

Conclusions

The challenges to human rights in Africa are multifaceted and very serious. The above survey however, demonstrates that existing foundations laid and the positive changes and progress realised by the African Commission on Human and Peoples' Rights and the recent developments on the continent provide greater hope that the challenges to the enjoyment of human rights in Africa may be more successfully addressed than they have been in the past.

Efforts should be enhanced to promote and consolidate a rights and democratic governance consciousness and ensure the domestication of these values within African states.

Greater efforts by the Commission are needed to ensure deepened linkages and cooperation between the Commission and national institutions, such as courts, parliaments or national assemblies, human rights commissions, bar associations, human rights NGOs, etc.[35] This is important in ensuring that the work of the Commission can have a more direct impact on the functioning of national institutions.

The jurisprudence of the Commission provides potentially a rich source for strengthening national legal systems, particularly in the interpretation and application of constitutional human rights guarantees. But there continues to be a serious gap in the flow of information from the Commission to national judiciaries, bar associations and other institutions which could benefit immensely from such jurisprudence. Unless this gap is bridged, the prospects of reliance by national judiciaries and legal practitioners on the jurisprudence of the Commission - an important step in ensuring that the rights in the Charter as interpreted by the Commission are controlling at the national level—remain very distant. The African Charter and the jurisprudence which has emanated from it have the greater potential to constitute the new constitutional law for Africa, if and only if, it were to be disseminated and relied upon by national institutions.

It is imperative that states create and consolidate democratic space which is a sine qua non for the enjoyment of human rights. Democratic space is required to enable people to participate in the public affairs of their community, influence policy decisions and choices and make governments accountable to the governed for all their actions.[36]

The creation and sustenance of democratic space rests on various elements, including allowing people freely to choose their leaders, respect for the constitution and the rule of law, political pluralism which allow free and fair competition for political offices as well as the possibility for peaceful, periodic and constitutional transfer of power. The creation and enforcement of transparent and even-handed electoral systems is important.

To be effective, political pluralism should go hand in hand with 'equality of arms', in the nature of a level political field, funding and access to the media. Nurturing and consolidating a culture of tolerance and the respect for and the protection of dissenting views, notably political views of the members of the opposition, are imperative.[37] Good governance is not only about majorities; it involves the protection of all, including minorities such as those in the opposition. The right to free speech and dissent rests on the existence of an independent private media—both in print and particularly on radio, given literacy levels in Africa. The establishment of independent civil society organisations and the creation of the democratic space for them to operate effectively must be nurtured to diffuse the over-centralisation of power and authority, empower the ordinary citizenry and thereby reduce the risks of abuse of centralised authority.

Peace and progress depend so much on an environment where justice and respect for the rule of law prevail. The strengthening of national judicial institutions to make them more effective, relevant, independent and impartial, is an indispensable foundation for a system's justice.

Political governance in Africa should emphasise not only processes (i.e. periodic elections), but must also focus on content, i.e. the pursuit and implementation of the substantive goals of good governance, and social and economic progress. Governments should relentlessly strive to ensure the realisation of all categories of rights and freedoms for all without distinction. There is an urgent need for the promotion of integrity in public office and the eradication of corruption. Corruption continues to sap and destroy the very fabric of government and society and contributes to the widespread poverty and deprivation in Africa.[38] The adoption of an African instrument against corruption should urgently be followed with effective monitoring to ensure that African governments put in place or operationalise and boost existing institutions and procedures for the eradication of corruption and for enhancing integrity in public life.

All these are pointers to the need to proceed beyond the preoccupation with human rights in the narrow sense to institute and sustain broad programmes of good governance in Africa with a dual focus: On the one hand, creating and supporting the effective functioning of state institutions administering law and justice, mobilising and enhancing integrity in public affairs, curbing maladministration, managing transparent electoral systems, etc.; on the other implementing measures for empowerment of the masses through inter alia creating the necessary environment for an effective and vibrant civil society and independent media. Such a governance strategy will build capacity at the national level to reduce, control and where they occur provide effective national remedies for human rights violations. An important element of the AU's actualisation of its commitment to human rights promotion and protection should be to devise and deliver a credible governance programme in partnership with the African Commission on Human and Peoples' Rights, the United Nations system as well as other bilateral or multilateral agencies. The African Commission particularly should have a lead role in this programme, thus enabling it to deal not only with individual allegations of violations of human rights but also engage more effectively in promotional and preventive strategies.

I hope that some years hence historians can look back to this conference and recognise it as a major turning point in the future of human rights and good governance for the peoples of Africa.

Notes

1. Adopted 10 December, 1948, G.A. Res. 217A (III), U.N. Doc. A/810, at 71.
2. Adopted June 1981, OAU Doc. CAB/LEG/67/3/Rev. 5 (1981); entered into force 21 October 1986. (Hereinafter 'the African Charter').
3. Institutions created by existing sub-regional arrangements in Africa which are closer to states than the African Commission on Human and Peoples' Rights are not principally human rights systems but merely contain an additional human rights dimension. These systems are principally concerned with economic development, although they refer to the protection of human rights in accordance with the African Charter on Human and Peoples' Rights. See for example the *Treaty of the Economic Community of West African States (ECOWAS)*, Art. 4(g), and *Treaty of the African Economic Community (AEC)*, Art. 3(g). Notwithstanding their principal function, it is recommended that to have full meaning, these sub-regional arrangements should embrace a human rights-based approach to economic development. The African Commission on Human and Peoples' Rights can play a major role in this project.
4. See Kofi A. Annan, 'Strengthening United Nations Action in the Field of Human Rights: Prospects and Priorities', 10 *Harvard Human Rights Journal* 1 (1997). This does not suggest that the need for adoption of new norms or the elaboration of existing ones does not exist at all or that such need may not emerge in the future. New and ongoing developments, for instance in the areas of global and regional trade, environment, science and technology, globalisation, create challenges to human rights and the environment. These new challenges may call for a continuous reevaluation of existing human rights norms to determine whether or not, if

existing norms are fully implemented, they provide the necessary protection against a specific threat to human rights, human dignity and well-being. See generally Dinah Shelton, 'Challenges to the Future of Civil and Political Rights', 55(3) *Washington & Lee Law Review* 669, 671 (1998); G. W. Mugwanya, 'Human Rights in Africa: Enhancing Human Rights Through the African Regional Human Rights System' (2003) at 2.

5. Adopted June 1981, OAU Doc. CAB/LEG/67/3/Rev. 5 (1981); entered into force 21 October 1986.

6. The Commission has observed elections in several countries, including Mali, Gambia, Zimbabwe and Madagascar. It has adopted various resolutions denouncing military coups and promoting participatory democracy. See for example 'Resolution on Electoral Processes and Participatory Governance', AHG/207(XXXII); 'Resolution on the Human Rights Situation in Africa', adopted at the 16th Session of the Commission; 'Resolution on the Military', adopted at the 16th Session; Resolutions on Nigeria and the Gambia (both reprinted in African Society of International and Comparative Law: Report on the 161st Session, 1996), condemning forcible military take-overs of civilian governments as a repudiation of the individual's right to participate in government and the right to self-determination.

7. United Nations Secretary-General's Report to the United Nations Security Council on Conflict, supra, para. 3.

8. See United Nations High Commission for Refugees, The State of the World's Refugees, Annex 1-1, UNHCR (1993); Analytical Report of the UN Secretary-General on Internally Displaced Persons, E/CN.4/1992/3 (UN, 1992).

9. Africa hosts about thirty percent of the planet's mineral reserves, including forty percent of gold and sixty percent of cobalt. It has proven oil reserves of 75.4 billion barrels, which is seven percent of the world's total. See Office of the Chairperson of the African Union Commission, supra, at 11.

10. See Hassan B. Jallow, 'Poverty Alleviation: The Imperative of Democratic Space',' in *Law, Justice and Governance* (Selected Papers of Hassan B. Jallow), (1998), at 148.

11. At the 13th Commission's Session soon after the adoption of its first Programme of Action, the Commission drew the attention of the OAU Assembly to the 'very alarming situations [...] in terms of logistics'. See Sixth Annual Activity Report of the Commission, 1992-93, at 7.

12. So far, only fifteen countries have ratified the Protocol, namely: Burundi, Algeria, Côte d'Ivoire, Gambia, Uganda, South Africa, Togo, Burkina-Faso, Libya, Lesotho, Mali, Mauritius, Rwanda, Senegal and the Union of the Comoros.

13. Adopted by the 2nd Ordinary Session of the Assembly of the African Union on 11 July 2003.

14. OAU Doc. CAB/LEG/24.9/49 (1990), entered into force 29 November, 1999.

15. Art. 2 of the African Protocol on the Rights of Women.

16. G.A. Res. 34/180, UN GAOR, 34th sess., Supp. No. 46, UN Doc. A/RES/34/80, entered into force 3 September, 1981. For an analysis of the Convention, see generally G. Mugwanya, 'Augmenting the Struggle for Gender Equality in Uganda: A Case for the Domestication of International Human Rights Standards', 19 Netherlands Quarterly of Human Rights 235, 243-250 (2001).

17. For instance, the Protocol explicitly calls for the legal prohibition of female genital mutilation (Art. 5-b); the prohibition of all forms of violence against women including unwanted or forced sex, whether it takes place in private or public (Art. 4-2); it recognises the rights of particularly vulnerable groups of women including widows, the elderly, disabled women, and women in distress. The latter category includes women from marginalised population groups and pregnant or nursing women in detention (Arts. 20-24). The Protocol also guarantees women the right to self-protection and to be protected against sexually transmitted infections, including HIV/AIDS (Art. 14(1)(d). It also endorses affirmative action to promote the equal protection of women with men (Art. 9). The Protocol provides for the right to peace and recognises the right of women to participate in the promotion and maintenance of peace.

18. In addition to providing reports on the measures taken to give effect to the Protocol, states undertake to adopt all necessary measures and in particular shall provide budgetary and other resources for the full and effective implementation of the rights in the Protocol. They also undertake to provide remedies to any woman whose rights are violated. See Arts 25 and 26 of the Protocol.

19. UN Convention on the Rights of the Child, G.A. res. 44/25, annex, 44 UN GAOR Supp. (No. 49) at 167, U.N. Doc. A/44/49 (1989), entered into force 2 September 1990.

20. See e.g. Art. 11(6) (protection of pregnant girls to enable them to complete interrupted education; pregnancy not to be a legitimate ground of discrimination); Art. 21 (protection against harmful social and cultural practices); Art. 22(2) (increases protection of children up to eighteen years. They are not to take a direct part in hostilities and shall not be recruited into the army. States are to take necessary measures to ensure this. The UN Convention on the other hand requires states to take feasible measures to ensure that children below fifteen years do not take direct part in hostilities, but leaves room for children between fifteen and eighteen years to be recruited into armed forces under Art. 38); Art. 23(4) (the protection of refugee children applies mutatis mutandis to internally displaced children whether through natural disaster, internal armed conflict, civil strife, or breakdown of economic and social order); 24(a) (obligating states to establish competent authorities in the area of adoption if none are in place); Art. 26 (protection against apartheid and discrimination); Art. 14(2) (broadens the range of people who must be informed and supported in the use of basic knowledge to include not only parents and children, but also community leaders and workers).

21. Art. 32 of the African Charter on the Rights and Welfare of the Child. The Committee is invested with a broad promotional mandate equivalent to that of the African Commission. Art. 42 (its protective mandate).
22. Constitutive Act of the AU, preamble, and Art. 3(h).
23. Ibid., Art. 3(g).
24. Ibid., Art. 4.
25. Ibid, Art. 4(h) & (j).
26. Ibid., Art. 17.
27. Ibid., Art. 22.
28. See OAU Decision on the Implementation of the Sirte Summit Decision on the African Union, 37 Ordinary Session of the Assembly of Heads of States and Government, July 2001, AHG/Dec 1 (XXXVII).
29. See for example Peace and Security Council, Report of the Chairperson of the Commission on the Situation in the Sudan (Crisis in Darfur), 5th Sess. 13 April 2004, Addis Ababa, PSC/PR/2(V); Peace and Security Council, Report of the Chairperson of the Commission on the Establishment of an AU Liaison Office in Liberia, 4th Sess. 6 April 2004, Addis Ababa, PSC/PR/3(IV); Peace and Security Council, Report of the Chairperson of the Commission on the Situation in Côte d'Ivoire, 5th Sess. 13 April 2004, Addis Ababa, PSC/PR/3(IV) Peace and Security Council, Report of the Chairperson of the Commission on the Situation in the DRC, 5th Sess. 13 April 2004, Addis Ababa, PSC/PR/4(V).
30. Office of the Chairperson of the African Union Commission, supra, at 10-14.
31. The New Partnership for Africa's Development, Declaration on Democracy, Political, Economic and Corporate Governance, AHG/235(XXXVIII), Annex I, sects. 10 and 13.
32. See The New Partnership for Africa's Development, African Peer Review Mechanism, AHG/235 (XXXVIII), and Annex 2. It provides for the appointment of a Panel of Eminent Persons to conduct peer reviews of member states also in respect of democracy and political governance.
33. See generally United Nations Secretary-General's Report to the United Nations Security Council on Conflict, supra.
34. See African Union Convention on Prevention and Combatting Corruption, Adopted by the 2nd Ordinary Session of the Assembly of the African Union, Maputo, 11 July, 2003.
35. In this regard, enhancing the Commission's promotional activities is important. The Commission's success, including dealing with NGOs, is noteworthy, but more needs to be done, particularly with regard to the Commission's interactions with national courts, parliaments or national assemblies and bar associations. There is a need for follow-ups of several resolutions passed by the Commission to ensure that they are implemented. These include Resolutions on Judicial Independence and the Role of the State, the Judiciary and the Bar in Integrating and Incorporating

the Charter and International Human Rights. See G. Mugwanya, 'Human Rights in Africa', supra, 310-311.

36. See generally Hassan B. Jallow, 'Poverty Alleviation: The Imperative of Democratic Space' supra, at 148 151.

37. Ibid., at 150-151. 92.

38. Ibid., at 150.

Chapter 5

Human Rights and Development in Africa: New Contexts, Challenges and Opportunities

Paul Tiyambe Zeleza

Introduction

The contexts, challenges and prospects for human rights in Africa have changed quite considerably in recent years. Human rights discourses find favour in both political and popular circles, among the ideologues of the state and the interlocutors of civil society, a tribute to the enduring and unfulfilled yearnings for more humane societies deeply rooted in African collective memories and social psyches, and to the remarkable changes that have already taken place in Africa's human rights landscapes. Contemporary Africa is a complex tapestry of contrasts in which human rights, as rhetoric and reality, has never been more pronounced and yet remains precarious as claims for and contestations over these rights persist and take new forms.

Today, more people enjoy more rights than ever before, but more people are also more aware of the limitations of Africa's human rights regimes. Indeed, as the promoters of human rights have proliferated, so have the perpetrators of abuses among state and civil society actors. The state no longer has a monopoly on vice, if it ever did, no more than civil society has a monopoly on virtue in the protection of human rights; both are as likely to undermine human rights as to uphold them. Similarly, the international arena is as much a source of inspiration and support as of much sorrow and grief. And the prospects for human rights in Africa remain firmly latched to the wobbly ox-wagon of development.

This essay seeks to explore the recent changes that have occurred in Africa's perennial struggle and search for human rights and development, the contexts that have framed the changes, the connections between human rights and development, and the roles of the state and society in promoting a developmentalist human rights agenda. It is divided into three parts. First, I discuss the changing contexts of human rights regimes focusing on four key factors—democratisation, globalisation, regionalisation, and militarisation—that have structured African political economies since the 1990s. Second, I examine the question of development in human rights discourse by revisiting some of the debates about the generations and hierarchy of rights, and exploring the articulation of the right to development and the challenges that face the implementation of that right in practice. Finally, I look into the role of the state in developing human rights norms and of the society in ensuring the pursuit of development and the protection of the right development as part of the broader repertoire of social, economic and cultural rights.

Changing Contexts of Human Rights Regimes

Contemporary African politics is marked by many complex and contradictory dynamics, four of which can be singled out for particular attention, namely, democratisation, globalisation, regionalisation, and militarisation, whose impact on human rights is equally complex and contradictory. Singly and collectively these factors have simultaneously facilitated and forestalled the growth and pursuit of human rights and development in Africa.

The Promises and Perils of Democratisation

For the purposes of this essay democratisation can be examined from three dimensions, the empirical, legal, and theoretical. There is ample evidence that since the turn of the 1990s the number of states following and abiding by features of democratic governance—principally elections and multi-party politics—has increased, notwithstanding reversals, blockages, and manipulations by Africa's wily dictators, many of whom have learned to manoeuver democratic politics to their advantage, and despite the fact that in many countries the new democracies amount to little more than the recycling of fractions of the same bankrupt political class, and elections are often marred by harassment and intimidation of the opposition, violence, vote rigging and human rights abuses, not to mention third term campaigns to allow incumbent presidents to stay beyond the constitutional limits of two terms.1 But even if the trunks of the old leviathan remain deeply rooted in Africa's rocky political soil, its branches have been tempered by the strong winds of social struggles for popular participation.[2]

From surveys on public opinion concerning the question of democracy, it is clear that there is overwhelming support for democracy across the continent. In one survey of twelve countries in Southern Africa and West Africa, support for democracy was sixty percent and above in all but two; in three it was over eighty percent; and only in one was it below fifty percent.[3] By democracy, most respondents saw it in terms of civil liberties and personal freedoms, followed by peace and unity, and socio-economic development. Large numbers perceived increases in freedoms and rights under multi-party politics, but were far less satisfied with government performance in addressing socio-economic development.[4]

The growth of democratically elected governments and governance has been accompanied by the expansion of legality as more domains of public life are governed by the rule of law established by democratic procedures. The tentacles of authoritarianism and arbitrariness have been withering as new rules are set establishing term limits for presidential office and stricter separation of powers between the various branches of government, and as demands for accountability are translated into public policies and popular opprobrium against corruption. To be sure, corruption remains endemic in many countries and the rule of law is still observed more in the breach than in compliance, but the political costs of doing so have risen.

More difficult to decipher and quite contentious in the literature is the impact of democratisation on human rights. Debate has centred on the relative roles of economic and political factors in human rights violations and measuring the correlations between democratisation and repression (personal or physical integrity rights). Before the current wave of democracy in Africa, the prevalence of authoritarian regimes was often attributed to the relatively low levels of economic development and the small size of the middle classes, a narrative that appealed to both racist western commentators dismissive of Africa's prospects and Africa's own dictators terrified of political pluralism and accountability. The association of levels of wealth and the disassociation of political and economic factors in the development of democracy and human rights is fraught with complications.[5]

In the 1990s African countries were not much richer, indeed some were a lot of poorer than in the 1980s—following a decade of unrelenting economic crises and structural maladjustment—yet there were becoming more democratic. If pauperisation rather than development drove Africa's democratisation, thereby demonstrating that poverty is not inimical to the quest for and the establishment of democracy and human rights, Africa's democracies and human rights improvements are ultimately untenable without development. As for political and economic factors there can be little doubt they have simultaneously compelled and conditioned the struggles for democracy and human rights. Underlying Africa's current search for a new political and socio-economic dispensation is the drive to establish sustainable democratic developmental states.

It is generally agreed that democracies are less repressive than autocracies. The positive correlation between democracy and respect for human rights is based on the assumption that democratic leaders are more accountable to their citizens and that coercive agents within democratic states not only wield less power than other competitive groups, but the availability of less coercive means of conflict regulation (such as elections) provides both a constraining factor and a preferable option.[6] But the effects of democratisation (the moment of transition from autocracy to democracy) on political repression are more complex. It has been demonstrated in many instances that repression may actually increase in new democracies because of lagging repressive tendencies from the past and the propensity for protest behaviour to increase at such times.[7] Some call this the 'more murder in the middle hypothesis'.[8]

Many of these analyses tend to focus on the state as the progenitor of human rights terror and repression. The role of civil society in engendering human rights violations is quite critical, and even more so during democratic transitions when centrifugal pressures can intensify as long suppressed group conflicts and identities find release in the newly opened political spaces where they sometimes proceed to produce and perform their chauvinism and antagonism, both real and imagined. Keen to shore up its power and authority the state often becomes embroiled in the volatile vortex of conflicting group claims and struggles, in the process of which repression can increase and may ultimately abort the democratisation process itself or threaten the very integrity of the nation-state. This is a particularly explosive mix in countries with traditions of political centralisation and authoritarianism, ethnic pluralism and polarisation, poverty and uneven development, rooted in colonial and post-colonial cultures and crises of underdevelopment, inequality, intolerance, exclusion, and violence.

Africa offers numerous examples of escalating conflicts and human rights violations since the recent wave of democratic transitions began in the 1990s.[9] Ethnicity has proven particularly salient as the most lethal social cleavage engendering conflict and repression. Since colonial times, ethnicity has embodied both moral and political imperatives; moral ethnicity constitutes a complex web of social obligations, loyalties and belonging, whereas political ethnicity is manifested in the mobilisation of ethnicity—the proverbial 'tribalism'—in intra-elite struggles for state power. In the formulations of Peter Ekeh and Mahmood Mamdani ethnicity is integral to Africa's bifurcated civil society; it serves as a primordial public for the masses estranged from the civic public of the elites, a sanctuary that extends its comforts and protective tentacles to the victims of political disenfranchisement, economic impoverishment, state terror and group rivalry.[10]

As the suffocating lid of state tyranny is lifted during moments of democratic transition the suppressed voices and expectations of civil society surge, but the stresses and strains arising from the competitive grind of democracy often find articulation in the entrenched identities, idioms, and institutions of ethnic solidarity. The case of Nigeria is quite illustrative in this regard. The democratic opening of 1999 has been accompanied by the resurgence of ethnic identities and the proliferation of regional and local struggles over the entitlements of citizenship expressed in the language of 'indigenes' and 'settlers'. These struggles have increasingly spilled into the formation of ethnic militias that have wrought havoc on Nigeria's civil society, unleashing periodic convulsions of inter-communal violence. Long a country with a militarised state, the militias are militarising society and helping to expand the culture of violence that is inimical to human rights and development. Religious conflicts have also periodically erupted into orgies of communal violence.

Spreading through contagion and demonstration as the beleaguered and newly installed democratic government failed to effectively contain the ethnic militias when they began to emerge, Nigeria's 'militant ethnicity', to use Michael Vickers's term, threatens the very survival of the country unless what Osita Agbu calls the three major institutional paradigms of ethnic conflict management— democratisation, devolution of power and power sharing—are pursued and implemented as a matter of urgency by Nigeria's political class. Notwithstanding their contradictions and unsavoury methods, the militias tap into popular desires to redress political and economic marginalisation, for more equitable distribution of resources, the decentralisation of power from the federal state, and better provision of security. In short, democratisation has brought the 'National Question' to the fore of the political agenda as never before as various regions and ethnic communities proclaim their right to determine their future in a renegotiated Nigerian political space.[11]

The challenge in Nigeria, as in other divided multicultural societies, is the need to balance group rights and individual rights. As Eghosa Osaghae has forcefully stated, the argument that the two kinds of rights are incompatible fails to see that these rights serve different purposes and that individual and group rights often shade into each other (as in the right to self-determination and minority rights) and their bases and justifications are basically the same.[12] But in so far as ethnic interests and cleavages are only one set among many other possible bases of political contestation—class, race, religion, region, and gender that often mediate and reinforce ethnic identities and antagonisms—there is the additional challenge of thinking about group rights beyond ethnicity.

The Sanctions and Seductions of Integration

Democratisation seems to have given a new lease on life for renewed regional integration, which has had largely positive effects on human rights in so far as the new institutions have incorporated principles and protocols to advance human rights. Also, many new human rights bodies have been established at the continental, regional and sub-regional level. No less critical are global forces and move-ments including those among the African diaspora that have emerged and are supportive of human rights struggles and agendas on the continent.

The African Union (AU), launched in July 2002, which supplanted the Orga-nisation of African Unity, is perhaps the most significant regional integration initiative in decades. The Constitutive Act of the AU clearly stipulates that one of the objectives of the Union shall be to 'promote and protect human and peoples' rights in accordance with the African Charter on Human and Peoples Rights and other relevant human rights instruments'. A series of principles related to human right are stated in Article 4 : 'promotion of gender equality; respect for democratic principles, human rights, the rule of law and good governance; pro-motion of social justice to ensure balanced economic development; respect for the sanctity of human life, condemnation and rejection of impunity and political assassinations, acts of terrorism and subversive acts'.[13]

Specifically the AU has created a number of organs that are critical for the human rights, principally the Pan-African Parliament, the African Court of Jus-tice (ACJ), the Economic, Social and Cultural Council (ECOSCC), and the Peace and Security Council. The ECOSOCC is an advisory organ composed of social and professional groups in order to facilitate civil society participation in the affairs of the Union. The ACJ is yet to be created, but the Pan-African Parliament was inaugurated in May 2004 with a woman, Gertrude Mongela from Tanzania, as its first president. In the initial period it will only enjoy consultative and advisory powers before assuming full legislative powers. Currently five parliamentarians are seconded from each national parliament, two of whom must be women. Another critical organ of the AU that is fundamental to its ambitions to promote development and human rights is the New Economic Partnership for Africa's Development (NEPAD) and its African Peer Review Mechanism (APRM).

Adopted in July 2001, NEPAD is an ambitious strategy and programme for Africa's renewal that grew out of a merger of two initiatives, the Millennium Programme developed by South Africa, Nigeria and Algeria and the Omega Plan developed by Senegal. These projects were rooted in a long history of development strategies going back to the Lagos Plan of Action of 1980. NEPAD focuses on four key objectives: democracy and good political governance; economic and corporate governance; socio-economic development; and the implementation of the African Peer Review Mechanism. Human rights are supposed to feature prominently in the pursuance of the first objective.[14] While few would quibble with NEPAD's objectives or many of its plans, some regard its expectations of massive international donor support as unrealistic. Critics have also accused it of pandering to and sanctifying the same neo-liberal prescriptions of the internatio-nal financial institutions that have done so much to wreck African economies. The lack of civil society involvement in the drafting of NEPAD has been another bone of contention for many scholars and activists.[15]

The APRM is intended to 'foster the adoption of policies, standards and practices that lead to political stability, high economic growth, sustainable development and accelerated sub-regional and continental economic integration through sharing of experiences and reinforcement of successful and best practices, including identifying deficiencies and assessing the needs for capacity building'.[16] The review criteria and processes are spelled out in admirable detail for each of the four objectives of NEPAD.[17] But the APRM's major flaw is that it is voluntary and it has no powers of sanction. The countries that need the reviews the most because of their record of human rights abuses and economic mismanagement are the least likely to volunteer. In fact, NEPAD and the APRM have been tarnished by their failure to censure Robert Mugabe's autocratic regime in Zimbabwe as it has descended into a tailspin of human rights violations and economic decline. The South African Finance Minister, Trevor Manuel, reportedly lamented in September 2004 that 'it was shameful that a year after the African peer-review mechanism was launched, less than half of Africa's countries had signed up to be independently reviewed... [He said] that if he had his way, signing up to a peer review would be a prerequisite for countries wanting to benefit from Nepad'.[18]

In addition to NEPAD and APRM there are numerous other human rights organisations that have emerged recently. The proliferation of African human rights instruments is a sign of the growing importance of human rights on the continent, but also a source of concern, contends Shadrack Gutto, in that many share the same mandate and 'the multiplicity of mechanisms leaves ordinary victims and survivors lost and sometimes without effective and appropriate remedy', which is itself a recognised form of human right abuse.[19] The African Commission on Human and Peoples' Rights (ACHPR), adopted in 1981 and entered into force in 1986, remains the continent's premier human rights body, whose work is in need of urgent reform and improvement.[20] Among the new bodies are the African Charter on Rights and Welfare of the Child and the African Court on Human and Peoples' Rights (its protocol was adopted in 1998 and entered into force in 2004), not to mention the truth and reconciliation commissions and special courts that have been established in some countries.

At the international level, there are the two international criminal tribunals for Rwanda and Sierra Leone prosecuting genocide, war crimes and crimes against humanity in the two countries. The establishment of the International Criminal Court in 2002, in the teeth of US resistance, has rightly been hailed as a milestone in international human rights law and enforcement.[21] The African diaspora, both the historic and contemporary, have also become increasingly vocal in protesting against human rights abuses in Africa. TransAfrica's campaign against Sani Abacha's dictatorship in Nigeria shows this clearly.[22] In recognition of the progressive role that people in the diaspora can play, diaspora representation and participation will be included in ECOSOCC.

But the international arena is as much as a source of inspiration and critical support as it is a source of much of Africa's development sorrows and human rights agonies. 'Africa's prospects for growth and development', bemoaned President Olusegun Obasanjo in 2002 in his address as Chairperson of NEPAD, 'are affected by trends prevailing in the global community. Due to the emergence of the global war on terrorism and the wars in Afghanistan, it can be argued that international issues have, to a large extent, displaced other priorities on the global agenda'.[23]

The Dreams and Discontents of Globalisation

Globalisation constitutes an important dynamic that has significantly transformed the discursive and material contexts in which human rights ideas, policies and instruments are articulated and implemented. There is little agreement in the literature on what globalisation actually means as a process, project and period in world history. To its advocates—the hyperglobalists—globalisation is seen as a new phenomenon involving a fundamental restructuring of the global system, whereas to its antagonists—the sceptics—there is really nothing new about globalisation. The ambivalents—the transformationalists—straddle the two positions arguing that the contemporary wave of globalisation surpasses that of earlier epochs in terms of the extensiveness of global networks, the intensity and impact of global interconnectedness, and the velocity of global flows.[24]

For me globalisation as a process refers to growing and deepening transnational flows among continents, countries and communities of materials, practices, peoples, ideas and symbols, from commodities to capital, images to information, labour to leisure, rights to reflexivities, viruses to visions. It has different dimensions, technological, economic, political, and cultural, each of which has its own internal particularities and propensities. As a project it is an ideological construct for global capitalism in general and neo-liberalism in particular designed to promote the liberalisation and integration of world markets. It is propagated most loudly by the international financial institutions including the World Bank, International Monetary Fund and the World Trade Organisation, and enacted in practice through structural adjustment programmes imposed with righteous zeal on governments worldwide, especially in the global South, and sanctioned by the enticements of direct foreign investment and the anxieties of being left behind and excluded. Most accounts of globalisation date it to the period after the end of the Cold War, so that the term becomes almost a synonym for the post-Cold War era.

But this era has been characterised by complex and contradictory developments in the world political economy that make a mockery of the fallacious claims made for globalisation by its loudest cheerleaders, who portray it as historically irreversible and inevitable, a force that is transcendental in being beyond anyone's control, beneficial to everyone, and good for the spread of democracy. This rhetoric seeks to depoliticise the discourses of globalisation and disarm its critics and paralyse its victims. The evidence is overwhelming that instead of the emergence of what former President Bush proclaimed as the 'new world order' and Francis Fukuyama as 'the end of history', both declared in the hasty triumphalism of the end of the Cold War, globalisation has reinforced inequalities, polarisations, chauvinism, and conflicts within and among nations.25

It has encouraged a widespread but uneven tendency toward the decomposition of civil society and traditional political formations as identities defined by religion, race, region, ethnicity, gender, or class are aggressively reaffirmed. The processes of chaos and fragmentation have been so pervasive and generic that some believe it is more apt to say we live in an age of fragmentation rather than globalisation. In reality, this has been an age of both globalisation and fragmentation, the two are sides of the same coin, for globalisation has not entailed the end of locality, but the production of localities on sites and scales that are increasingly globalised. In short, we live in a world of 'glocalisation' in which the local and global are mutually constituted and political and economic processes are rescaled both upward to the supranational or global scales and downwards to smaller units including communities and individuals.[26]

The relationship between globalisation and democracy is especially complicated. The number of 'democratic' states has increased as globalisation has spread, which would seem to suggest a conjunctural, if not causal, connection between the two. In fact, there are those who attribute the spread of democracy in Africa in the 1990s to the demonstration effects of communism's extinction in central and eastern Europe and to the examples of western democracies, transmitted to Africans through CNN and the BBC, and the conditionalities of the international financial institutions, leading some to even call them 'demonstration democracies' created to please international donors.[27]

Such characterisations betray ignorance of Africa's long histories of struggle against the tyrannies of slavery, colonialism and the post-colonial perversions of power. Nonetheless, it is true that many of these democracies, like the older and truncated democracies in other parts of the world, are minimalist, reducing democracy to periodic electoral contests, unencumbered by any developmentalist and distributive objectives. The rise of 'illiberal democracy', as Fareed Zakaria calls it, is often seen as peculiar to the global South and the former communist world.28 But the imposition of national security regimes in the western liberal democracies, especially the United States (whose botched 2000 elections ended with the selection of the president by the unelected branch of government, the Supreme Court) shows this is not the case. The misguided 'war on terror'—that has taken the mantle of communism's 'evil empire' and reinforced the West's anticipated civilisational clash with Islam as the new 'axis of evil'—threatens to further fortify America's 'choiceless democracy' of rising corporate control and electoral disenfranchisement.

In so far as globalisation represents an increase in the power of capital over other social classes, it contributes to the shrinkage of democracy. Repression of labour is seen as essential for attracting multinational corporations and direct foreign investment. As is quite evident in Africa, the austerities of structural adjustment programmes not only increase poverty, but also require authoritarian governance. In short, as capital and neo-liberal ideology have become more dominant, the sphere of private and unaccountable decision-making has expanded while that of public and accountable decision-making has diminished. The power of people to influence policy democratically at the national level is reduced by globalisation, yet at the global level there are no democratic institutions to enable people to effectively control or influence their destiny. The 'old geographies of democracy' have been shifting as the scales of political representation and economic organisation have become increasingly incongruous.[29] But far from making social movements and protests disappear they have re-emerged in new ways and on new scales as can be seen in anti-globalisation protests that have bedevilled the convocations of the international financial institutions and the Davos global elite.

In this context, the expansion of democratisation appears less a bequest of capitalist globalisation than its nemesis. Democratisation has emerged in the cracks of the mismatch between capital and labour, in the dialectic of new repertoires of power engendered by globalisation itself and its vulnerabilities that facilitate workers and other subaltern social classes to develop their own local and global networks of resistance and empowerment.[30] The point is that capitalist globalisation in its various historical phases has neither bestowed democracy on the world nor does it foreclose prospects for democratic struggles at local, national, and international levels. This is to suggest that analyses of globalisation must pursue a dual analytical agenda, mapping out the capital logic of globalisation and the logic of struggle by the powerless, disenfranchised, dislocated, and immiserated working peoples of globalisation. In other words, globalisation is not a mechanical and uncontested process of capitalist expansion. It involves and implicates labour and other social groups who challenge, mediate, and restructure the processes of globalisation at various spatial levels.

It is not a coincidence that since the late 1980s there have been unprecedented struggles against authoritarianism and for democracy, which have been inspired more by the ravages and recessions brought by globalisation to large masses of people, than by its successes and benefits. As a result of these changes, global human rights regimes, as is true in Africa, can only be described as exceedingly complex and contradictory. In some parts of the world the state of human rights is the same as it was before, in others there have been considerable improvements, and in several others the situation is far worse. The latter is particularly true in countries where domestic conflicts have increased, some of which have degenerated into bloody civil wars.

The democratic and human rights dividend of the end of the Cold War remains to be realised. A study by David Cingranelli and David Richards examining the extent to which respect for human rights had improved after the Cold War covering seventy-nine countries found that governments' respect for the four physical integrity rights—against torture, extrajudicial killings, disappearances, and political imprisonment—remained the same as before for the first three and only improved for the last one, most dramatically in Africa. In fact, there was more torture globally in 1996 than there had been throughout most of the Cold War. The data showed that states in intermediate levels of democracy, undergoing democratic transition, did not 'show significantly better respect for physical integrity rights than those with no democracy'.[31]

Improvements in the respect for the right against imprisonment might be explained by the fact that it is easier for governments to exercise direct control and be held accountable for political imprisonment than stopping the other violations, which requires the re-socialisation or replacement many of the gendarmes of state security. Following democratic transition members of the security forces are likely to continue committing human rights abuses if the state fails to transform its security services and convict human rights abusers. This is evident from several of Africa's newest democracies in Southern Africa where security forces continue to 'commit significant levels of human rights abuses, and hence undermine the state's attempts at democratic consolidation'.[32] Stemming such abuses requires concerted efforts by the state that requires strong political will to effectively deal with human rights violators and bringing them to account, human rights training within the security forces, and the existence of effective human rights monitoring institutions both state and non-state.

The policies of the major powers have not always helped in the promotion and protection of human rights in Africa. The European Union countries and the United States are the most critical players in this regard. Debate has centred on how to characterise these countries' policies towards the promotion of democracy and development, what drives them—donor interests or recipient needs—and the extent to which their policies changed in the period before and after the Cold War. In the 1990s the official rhetoric of western governments put a premium on the promotion of democracy as a necessary condition for development, and economic assistance was increasingly tied to political conditionalities for good governance and respect for human rights. In November 1991 the European Community, the EU's predecessor, adopted a resolution that sanctified the new democratic conditionalities for development aid, which was further elaborated in subsequent treaties and public statements by the EU and individual western European governments that collectively accounted for nearly fifty percent of global development assistance and a large share of total foreign aid to Africa.[33]

Notwithstanding these declarations, the argument seems compelling that the dissolution of the bipolar international system did not 'change the fundamental reasons or motivations of the OECD countries for giving aid'.[34] The conditionalities were imposed 'to ensure a continued minimum of popular support for aid, since development assistance had lost most of its political rationale with the ending of the Cold War'.[35] It could be added that conditionalities were also a means of currying favour and co-opting African pro-democracy movements that often called for the suspension of foreign aid to accelerate the collapse of the besieged dictatorial regimes. Undoubtedly EU support for democratisation proved critical in many countries from South Africa to Kenya, but the EU led by France, reportedly 'the most influential member state within the common European development system', dithered over Niger, a major supplier of uranium, and Algeria, a key supplier of migrants and oil, where military coups in 1996 and 1992, respectively, were tacitly endorsed. Indeed, to many EU governments the stability of dictatorships seems preferably to the instability of democratisation.

Clearly, after the end of the Cold War donor interests, based primarily on national security concerns and calculations continued as before to trump recipient needs. Even in the case of South Africa, the EU support of the regime was motivated by more than idealistic interest to promote democratisation and human rights in that beloved country benighted by apartheid; it was 'tied to the ambitions of the EU to become a world power, i.e. to strengthen the Common Foreign and Security Policy of Europe'.[36] It is tempting, therefore, to see western rhetoric about democracy and human rights as part of the discursive arsenal of neo-colonialism in the post Cold War era, invoking earlier discourses of 'civilisation' and 'modernisation' and wielded as weapons of mass deception for voting publics in the global North and the victimised peoples of the global South.[37]

The terrorist attacks on the United States on 11 September, 2001 removed the rhetorical gloves and exposed the primacy of the naked fist of national security. A dark cloud of public hysteria and hasty wars on terrorism hyped by states led by the world's lone and lonely superpower—the US—threatened to overshadow and stifle hard worn democratic freedoms and human rights across the world, including Africa.

The Wages and Wedges of War

The changing contexts of militarism have serious implications for democratisation and human rights in terms of the impact of military expenditures in general and its effects on people's security in particular. For contemporary Africa, militarism manifests itself primarily through internal conflicts and wars and the US-led war against terrorism, both of which are deleterious for building and consolidating cultures of democracy and respect for human rights.

Military expenditures have been expanding worldwide, all in the age-old names of national security and independence. Total global military expenditures grew by eighteen percent between 1994 and 2003, from $742 billion to $879 billion, 2.4 percent of the world's total gross domestic product. The largest increases occurred in the Middle East (48 percent and South Asia (41 percent). Africa's increase was twenty-four percent, the same as for North America, South America, and East Asia.[38] Although no African country was among the world's fifteen largest military spenders led by the United States, Japan, the United Kingdom, France and China,[39] in that order, four were among the twenty with the highest military burdens as a share of GDP, led by Eritrea 23.5 percent, Burundi 7.6 percent, Liberia 7.5 percent, and Ethiopia 5.2 percent. Not surprisingly, the expenditures on health and education were much lower in these countries.[40]

High military expenditures undermine economic well-being by diverting invaluable human, material, and financial resources. The trade off between defence and growth is well-established: 'It has been estimated that for every one percent of GNP devoted to military spending, overall economic growth is reduced by about 0.5 percent'.[41] Some attribute the economic decline of the United States relative to its major competitors, Japan and Germany, to its astronomical military expenditures that have produced massive budget deficits.[42] In short, there is overwhelming empirical and theoretical evidence that military spending depresses economic growth for it decreases investment in civilian sectors, it leads to lower employment and inefficient use of labour resources, and it diverts critical research and development funds and highly skilled personnel from the civilian economy. 'The result is a diversion', contends William Felice, 'of resources away from the collective human rights of education, health care and subsistence. The implementation of basic economic and social rights depends upon a shift in scare resources away from militarism and towards these areas of human need'.[43]

Building ever larger and stronger militaries has certainly not created a more peaceful world. Many of the world's wars are internal wars, which effectively turns many armed forces into instruments of internal repression. Warfare has a dreadful impact on people through direct and indirect deaths and injuries, sexual crimes and intimidation, population dislocations within and across national borders, the damage and distortions caused to societal networks and the fragile social capital of trust and interpersonal associations and intergroup interactions, not to mention the devastation of the ecosystem, agricultural lands and wildlife, the destruction of society's material and mechanical infrastructures, the outflow of resources including 'capital flight' and 'brain drain', the proliferation of pathological and self-destructive behaviours, and the deterioration in the aesthetic quality of life.

There has been no let up in armed conflicts and internal strife that create inauspicious conditions for democracy, development and human rights, although the cast of countries embroiled in major conflicts shifted from Bosnia to Rwanda to Sri Lanka and Colombia in the early 1990s to Chechnya, the Democratic Republic of the Congo, Afghanistan and Mexico in the late 1990s. In 2003, there were nineteen major armed conflicts in eighteen countries around the world, only two of which were interstate (the war over Iraq and the long-standing conflict between India and Pakistan over Kashmir). Four of these conflicts were in Africa (Algeria, Burundi, Liberia, and Sudan).[44]

Overall, the total number of conflicts have fallen since the early 1990s—from thirty-three in 1991 to twenty-four in 2001 (eleven and seven in Africa, respectively)—but they remain as devastating as ever for the countries and peoples involved. In addition, there are numerous other domestic conflicts involving various forms of civil violence. According to one study, the average level of domestic conflict increased 'from a mean score of 151 during the Cold War period to 235 during the post-Cold War period. Despite the fact that external sponsorship of civil wars has declined dramatically since the end of the Cold War, there has been an increase in civil conflicts around the world'.[45] Between 1998 and 2002, for example, ethnic and civil violence were reported in Nigeria with 5,000 deaths, Liberia with 1,000 deaths, Lesotho with 1,000 deaths, Congo-Brazzaville with 500 deaths and the Central African Republic with 600 deaths.[46]

These conflicts offer a compelling reason for rethinking the concept of 'security' tied to militarism, which at best creates the negative peace of deterrence, rather than the positive peace and security that can only arise from the elimination of the causes of war and violence and the protection of human rights and social justice within countries as well as between countries. At a minimum, 'inhibiting militarism while protecting personal security rights' would require 'curbing arms sales; initiating steps towards common security and basic deterrence; and launching institutions of war prevention and preventive diplomacy'.[47] Unfortunately, the post-September 11, 2001 environment does not seem propitious for the pursuit of such initiatives. With the US-led war against terrorism, the world, including Africa, has entered a particularly dangerous phase in the promotion and protection of human rights and development.

America's sanctimonious crusade against terrorism including its illegal invasion of Iraq on the false premises that the country possessed weapons of mass destruction has caused grievous damage to international law and human rights principles and standards in the United States itself and worldwide.[48] Many people around the world see the US administration, to use the words of the Council on Foreign Relations, 'as arrogant, hypocritical, self-absorbed, self-indulgent, and contemptuous of others'. The international support the country had garnered after the terrorist attacks in New York and Washington was quickly and recklessly squandered in its vengeful war in Afghanistan and 'pre-emptive' war in Iraq; to many the US was behaving as much of a rogue state as the states it condemned as the 'axis of evil'.[49]

The imposition of a stringent homeland security regime at home threatened the civil liberties of US citizens and the rights of immigrants in which Muslims and their institutions and people of 'Middle Eastern' appearance were targeted for racist attacks, while the scandals of the 'legal black hole' at Guantánamo Bay in Cuba where abducted suspects from around the world including children were subject to incommunicado interrogations and indefinite detentions without trial, and the pornographic images of torture, primal degradation, and gratuitous humiliation of Iraq prisoners at Abu Ghraib in Baghdad, unleashed a wave of dismay, contempt, and anger against the United States.[50]

These actions threatened to undermine the counter-terrorism measures by invoking the very instrumentalities of terrorism in their disregard for human rights, in ostensibly pursuing security at the expense of respect for human dignity. The backlash against human rights in the US-led war bred widespread resentment and even hatred that may have swelled the ranks of the insurgents fighting against the US in Afghanistan and Iraq and terrorists bent on attacking American interests elsewhere and fuelled divisions between the US and many of its allies in Europe and across the world.[51] They also provided alibis for governments including many in Africa, as well as international agencies, to violate or vitiate their human rights commitments and to tighten asylum laws and policies.[52] In the meantime, military transfers to countries with poor human rights records increased which portended ill for human rights.[53]

Many governments rushed to pass broadly, badly or cynically worded anti-terrorism laws and other draconian procedural measures, and set up special courts or allowed special rules of evidence that violate fair trial rights, which they used to limit civil rights and freedoms, and to harass, intimidate, and imprison and crackdown on political opponents.[54] This helped to strengthen or restore a culture of impunity among the security services in many countries. Amnesty International has issued reports critical of new draft anti-terrorism laws in several countries from Kenya to Tunisia that threaten to undermine international human rights standards.[55] African friends and foes of the United States have been basking in the new climate of intolerance and impudence. For example, Morocco, an archaic western friendly monarchy, used anti-terrorism laws to detain 5,000 people following the May 2003 bombings in the country. In Zimbabwe, a self-declared anti-imperialist enclave of declining radical credentials, there was a sharp escalation of state-sponsored intimidation, torture, arbitrary arrests and political killings, and orchestrated attacks on the independence of the media and judiciary.[56]

In addition to the restrictions on political and civil rights and the subordination of human rights concerns to anti-terrorism priorities, September 11 and the war on terror had other collateral damage for Africa. As the Human Rights Watch 2002 report noted, 'pre-existing political tensions between Muslim and Christian populations in a number of African countries threatened to become inflamed, and increasingly violent. Côte d'Ivoire, Ethiopia, Kenya, Nigeria, South Africa, and Tanzania all faced the possibility of worsening communal tensions. Bloody riots between Muslims and Christians in Kano, northern Nigeria, following demonstrations against the US bombing of Afghanistan, had already left a high death toll. A pro-Taliban demonstration was also reported in Kenya's predominantly Muslim coastal city, Mombasa'.[57] Western anti-travel advisories undermined the economies of countries dependent on tourism, while increased security and defence expenditures threatened to reduce humanitarian and development assistance.

Development in Human Rights Discourse and Practice

The contexts and conditions examined above make it quite difficult for the right to development to be implemented even were this right universally accepted, which is not the case. Where does the right to development fit in the array and hierarchy of human rights? How is it defined and articulated? What specific challenges does it face? The question of the right to development raises fundamental issues about the competing conceptions and composition of human rights as a whole. The tendency has been to dismiss it as auxiliary, more of a directive principle than a right that is justiciable in courts of law like civil and political rights (CPR), to see it as a rhetorical sop to the economic aspirations of developing countries without much philosophical of jurisprudential substance. I believe, however, that the right to development together with other economic, social, and cultural rights (ESCR) is indeed fundamental, that it is futile and unproductive to seal rights in strict confinements, to sequester them in dichotomies and polarities as is so often the case, for all forms of human rights are ultimately interrelated, interdependent, and indivisible.

As I have noted elsewhere, human rights discourses often suffer from four analytical traps. They tend to be idealistic, legalistic, dualistic, and ethnocentric; idealistic in that human rights are reduced to ideas abstracted from social history, so that they are seen as the outcome of concepts not conflicts, insights not instigations, philosophy not politics; legalistic in that their provenance is primarily located in the courts not culture, procedure not practice, rhetoric not reality, codes not contingency; dualistic in that they either polarise or prioritise civil and political rights against economic and social rights and vice-versa; and ethnocentric in that their source is usually located in the West by both the universalists and relativists.[58] The simple truth of the matter is that human rights have evolved out of concrete historical conditions and struggles, not simply textual or legal disputations, and they will continue to do so as human societies and needs change and new challenges and threats emerge, and there is no intrinsic reason that one set of rights—political and civil or economic and cultural rights—is inherently superior in promoting and protecting human dignity. In short, the internationalisation and universalisation of human rights is an ongoing process to which all world regions and cultures will continue to make contributions.[59]

Particularly unfruitful has been the debate between human rights universalism and relativism. The advocates and proponents of the two positions, whether framed in North-South oppositions or among radicals and conservatives within specific regions and countries, are essentially engaged in the production of ideological hegemony, each providing alibis for their respective governments and movements. It is well to remember that during the Cold War relativist interpretations of human rights suited western interests in dealings with Third World dictatorships. It was only after the end of the Cold War that the West became uncompromisingly universalist, now in pursuit of its global capitalist agenda, which it was prepared to defend at the cost of violating the same freedoms and democracy it purported to advocate. In the meantime, leaders in the South, boxed between western pressures and popular struggles for democratisation and human rights, reacted by espousing more and more relativist positions. Thus, different groups have supported the relativist and universalist perspectives at different times, rendering each one of them a potential tool of both oppression and liberation depending on the context.[60]

Contestations of human rights are not new even within specific regions, including in the so-called western world where different ideological and political traditions and perspectives, religious vs. secular, liberal vs. Marxist, nationalist vs. internationalist, philosophical vs. pragmatic, have battled for supremacy for a long time. Indeed, it is ultimately counterproductive to turn the idea of human rights into 'Western', 'Asian', 'African' or 'Islamic', for that would turn the language of human rights 'into a rhetorical weapon for intercultural competition... What is needed... is a critical defence of universal human rights in a way that gives room for different cultural and religious interpretations and, at the same time, avoids the pitfalls of cultural essentialism'.[61]

Certainly human rights are not organic to or a natural result of a fictive western tradition going back to ancient Greece, a teleological narrative of retrospective appropriation that is fundamentally ahistorical and intellectually flawed. An international human rights regime will only emerge out of what Heiner Bielefeldt calls 'a cross-cultural "overlapping consensus" on basic normative standards in our increasingly multicultural societies'.[62] The idea of 'human dignity'—ridiculed by some as characteristic of societies that have yet to develop a concept of 'human rights', is the only thread that connects the world's different religious, philosophical, and cultural traditions.[63] And human dignity for the human person with his/her multiple dimensions must surely encompass multiple rights.

The division and hierarchisation of rights has emerged out of international ideological struggles since the end of the Second World War, many of them played out in the confines of the United Nations (UN). In the early years of the UN, the US and its allies were dominant and they succeeded in splitting the proposed human rights covenant into two, one for CPR, which they championed, and the other for ESCR, which found loud support in the Soviet Union and among its allies and the emerging Third World, despite a resolution by the UN General Assembly that the two groups of rights were 'interconnected and interdependent'.[64] In the 1960s many of the organs of the UN, including those involved in the institutionalisation of human rights norms such as the UN Commission for Human Rights (UNCHR), were increasingly dominated by Third World countries organised around the Non-Aligned Movement. The early 1970s were the heydays of Third World militancy and demands were made for the restructuring of the international system—the calls for a New International Economic Order and a New World Information and Communication Order. It was in this context that in 1972 a Senegalese jurist, Kéba Mbaye, proclaimed the right to development (RTD), which was adopted seven years later by the UNCHR. Soon other rights, for example to peace and a protected environment, were added to the repertoire of what came to be known as solidarity rights (SR).

This gave rise to the notion that there were three generations of rights, a loose analytical construction proposed by scholars that soon acquired a rigid ideological life of its own that has been unproductive for human rights discourse.[65] According to this schema, CPR are first generation rights apparently rooted in eighteenth century bourgeois revolutions in France and the United States (never mind that in the US many CPR rights like the right to vote only came in 1920 for white women and in 1965 for racial minorities); ESCR then constitute second generation rights and their paternity was awarded to the socialist revolutions of the early twentieth century (forget the strong commitment to these rights by the Roosevelts that was overtaken by anti-communist paranoia in the US in the 1950s); and development rights are supposedly part of third generation solidarity rights that emerged from anticolonial revolutions after the Second World War (how about earlier nationalist struggles in nineteenth century Latin America and elsewhere also motivated by the desire for national independence and development?).

It is often said the first generation rights are negative rights (requiring states to protect individual autonomy and freedom), while the second and third are positive rights (requiring states to promote collective well-being). These distinctions are not entirely false. Certainly western countries have been the chief proselytisers of CPR, while ESCR found particular favour among socialist countries, and RTD is deeply cherished by many in the global South including Africa. Their implementation also entails different things, in the case of CPR limiting state intrusions while in the case of ESCR and RTD expanding state interventions. Broadly stated the former are freedom claims, the latter resource claims. But there is really no Chinese wall that separates these claims in terms of their spatial provenance, let alone in their import for human dignity and security.

The search for hierarchy among rights is not only driven by ideological contestations, but also by the fact that, as Theodore Meron has argued, 'national legal systems are characterized by a well-established hierarchy of norms.

Constitutional provisions prevail over ordinary statutes, the latter prevail over secondary legislation or administrative regulations, and so on. It is therefore only natural that international lawyers, trained in national legal systems, should seek hierarchical principles in the international legal system as well. But in its present stage of development, the international community has no single and supreme legislature whose decrees would prevail over those of subordinate lawmaking bodies. Moreover, such an institution is not likely to be established in the foreseeable future'.[66] It is extremely difficult to create widely accepted criteria or standards to choose between what some see as fundamental human rights and other rights and select the fundamental human rights.

More often than not, the characterisations of fundamental rights pander to subjective preferences based on national traditions and aspirations. This is one more reason for jettisoning regional ethnocentricities and developing bases and processes of norm setting that involve as much of the international community as possible. This is what is sometimes called an interpretive approach that valorises cross-cultural dialogue as the most viable means of constructing an international human rights regime.[67] Some believe that the proliferation of human rights instruments makes it necessary to establish a list of non-derogable rights and ranking such rights ahead of derogable rights. But Abdullahi An-Na'im argues forcefully that 'to affirm the full human rights quality of ESCR, it is necessary to abandon any classification of human rights, and approach the implementation of each specific right on its own terms, instead of limiting it to what is deemed appropriate for one purported class of rights or another'.[68]

The incorporation of the right to development in international human rights discourse and instruments has been gradual. Although the notion that political and civil rights and economic and social rights are interrelated, interdependent, and indivisible was recognised at the time when the Universal Declaration of Human Rights was adopted in 1948, the right to development received an important boost with the promulgation of the International Covenant on Economic, Social, and Cultural Rights in 1966, the creation of the African Charter on Human and Peoples' Rights in the 1980s, the adoption of the of Declaration on the Right to Development by the UN General Assembly in 1986, and the 1993 Vienna Declaration and Programme of Action. The right to development entails everyone's right to participate in, contribute to, and enjoy economic, social, cultural, and political development and it enjoins states to promote principles of substantive equality, social justice and non-discrimination in ensuring the realisation of that right and equality of opportunities for all to access basic resources, food, housing, employment and the fair distribution of income, and to pursue appropriate national and international development policies and processes.[69]

The challenge, as with most human rights instruments, is one of implementing the right to development in practice, turning rhetorical commitment into concrete action. Three challenges can be identified, one is globalisation, the unequal international economic system that reinforces the gap between the rich and poor among and within countries, and which Africa has largely experienced through the disastrous programmes of structural adjustment. The second is militarism, examined earlier, whose devastation of resources, lives, and livelihoods erodes the possibilities of sustaining and strengthening human rights. The third concerns the justiciability of social and economic rights. For the right to development to be effectively implemented at the international level it is essential that the UN Declaration on the Right to Development be transformed into an international treaty with effective monitoring structures. At the national level, countries should entrench the right to development and economic and social rights in their cons-titutions that should also contain effective enforcement mechanisms. Developing jurisprudence on the enforceability of the right to development has proven quite vexatious.

African countries differ in their views on the justiciability of ESCR. In Ghana and Nigeria, for example, these rights are cast as Directive Principles of State Policies (DPSP), while in South Africa they are constitutional obligations—the state is expected to 'respect, protect, and fulfil' the right to housing, health, and other elements of ESCR. The South African Constitutional Court has done much to clarify and mainstream the justiciability of these rights.[70] As noted above, An-Na'im is adamant that ESCR should be as justiciable as CPR. He believes it is 'critical to challenge the assumption that the implementation of ESCR should be confined to the realm of social policy and administrative processes of governments because these rights do not fit the model of judicial enforcement developed for specific civil and political rights... to leave the matter to the unfettered discretion of governments, however democratic they may be, without any possibility of judicial guidance and supervision, defeats the whole purpose of recognizing ESCR as international human rights'.[71]

Others caution against excessive reliance on justiciability as the primary means to realise the progressive implementation of social and economic rights (many of whose concepts lack precision they believe), arguing that such rights can best be mainstreamed principally through political pressure on the elected executive and legislative branches of government. To quote Jill Cottrell and Yash Tandon: 'People should be lobbying parliaments and governments, not courts... Justiciability is not enough. The classical role of justiciability is that of last resort—one goes to court when all else fails. But the problem with ESCR has been that in far too many countries all else has not been tried'.[72]

Prospects for economic development and the realisation of social and economic rights are often frustrated by officially sanctioned corruption. Many human rights activists therefore insist that corruption is a human rights viola-tion, a violation of people's social and economic rights.[73] The empirical and theoretical evidence is compelling that political and bureaucratic corruption lowers both investment and economic growth and can endanger the very viability of democracy by reinforcing the processes that undermine human rights and prevent human needs from being met. Bribery constitutes an additional tax on investment, and in an unpredictable legal environment lacking secure property rights and bedevilled by bureaucratic red tape and mismanagement investors cannot plan effectively and are often discouraged. Government expenditure also becomes skewed, as highly corrupt governments tend to under-invest in human capital, especially education and health. The poor are disproportionately affected because they spend relatively more of their incomes on bribes, their access to public services is severely curtailed, and they are denied development.[74]

Several African countries rank highly in the global corruption league. In Transparency International's Global Corruption Report 2004, three ranked among the ten most corrupt countries in the world, led by Nigeria in second place, Cameroon in eighth, and Angola in tenth.[75] The lost development opportunities are staggering. Despite earning $200 billion from oil between 1970 and 1990, by 1990 Nigeria had become the seventh poorest country in the world.[76] Corruption in African is rooted in the colonial and post-colonial structures of underdevelopment and uneven development and the accumulation propensities of the aspiring national bourgeoisies, and has been perpetrated by the activities and policies of local governments and private business, as well as by transnational corporations, foreign governments, and the international financial institutions. The culprits are many indeed.

Democratisation has fuelled anti-corruption drives, as manifested in the enactment of national anti-corruption laws, the establishment of anti-corruption commissions, and the adoption of anti-corruption protocols by regional organisations such as the Southern African Development Community (SADC) (in August 2001) and by the Economic Community of West African States (ECOWAS) (in December 2001). At the continental level, the Africa Union's Convention on Preventing and Combating Corruption and Related Offences was adopted in July 2003 and must be ratified by fifteen member states to come into force. It concentrates on prevention, punishment, cooperation and education as strategies to combat corruption. Its major problem is that the convention's board lacks powers of investigation, it depends on submissions from national anti-corruption authorities whose independence is not guaranteed, and signatories can opt out of some or all provisions.[77]

Indeed, many of the anti-corruption drives are proclaimed with great fanfare only to wither in inactivity. More drastic institutional reforms are required by adopting the so-called root and branch approach: strengthening the autonomy of the judiciary, increasing fair access to information and the independence of the media, enhancing legislation on political funding and disclosure and conflict of interest, and raising public transparency and participation in the budget process.[78] These problems are by no means confined to African anti-corruption agencies as examples from other parts of the world clearly demonstrate. For example, in December 1997 the OECD adopted the Anti-Bribery Convention, which came into force in February 1999, but the new laws have yet to be enforced by most national governments. In 1996 the UN General Assembly adopted the Declaration against Corruption and Bribery in International Commercial Transactions and the UN Convention against Corruption was signed in December 2003 as the first global anti-corruption instrument, but its impact has been minimal so far. More effective have been national instruments, such as the US's Millennium Challenge Account that has included corruption in the selection of eligible aid recipients under its auspices. Several African countries have been denied aid because of their high corruption indices.[79]

The Roles of the State and Society

The state has a responsibility to ensure the promotion and protection of human rights principles, norms, and instruments. Civil society also has a role to play through its struggles and participation in building a human rights culture. In examining the nexus between the state and human rights we can look at the articulation of human rights in terms of recognition and enforcement, the levels at which the norms are articulated from domestic to the regional to the continental and the global, and the coordination between the forms and levels of articulation.

There is a high level of human rights norm recognition in African constitutions including a distinctive emphasis on duties and social economic rights. According to Christof Heyns and Frans Viljoen, 'most African states have ratified many of the six most important United Nations human rights treaties', with rates of between 21 and 29 percent of global ratification totals.[80] As for regional instruments, Africa together with Europe and the Americas are the only regions with regional human rights protection systems. The African regional system is anchored on the African Charter on Human and Peoples' Rights, which recognises both civil and political rights and social and economic rights as well as rights and duties.

But enforcement is relatively weak. The enforcement mechanism through the Commission on Human and Peoples' rights, for example, remains problematic. Charged with promoting and protecting the rights in the Charter, the Commission has been particularly slow in implementing its protective mandate, partly because of its rather low funding and staffing levels, and the difficulties of guaranteeing effective regional diversity and independence of the Commissioners. Above all, the Charter itself needs to be revised to reflect new circumstances and improve its enforceability. Also, the development of sub-regional institutions and an indigenous African human rights jurisprudence and enforcement system is crucial.

The domestic level is the most important in the protection of human rights, followed by the regional and global systems. The domestic level has the benefit of direct enforcement and the regional has the advantage of peer pressure that the global often lacks. The sub-regional economic associations such as ECOWAS, SADC, the Maghreb Union, and the Common Market of Southern and Eastern African States (COMESA) tend to be quite weak in their human rights norm recognition and enforcement. As we noted earlier, the AU is trying to strengthen its human rights promotion and protection mechanisms through the creation of various instruments. The effectiveness of these mechanisms and their capacity to facilitate the coordination of human rights norm recognition and enforcement among its member states have yet to be proven.

The interface between civil society and human rights raises many complex issues about the nature of African civil societies, the role of non-governmental organisations (NGOs) as the most developed forms of civil society engagement in human rights discourses and practice, and the question of popular participation as mediated by the social inscriptions and hierarchies of gender, class, religion, and language. We noted earlier Eke's and Mamdani's conceptualisations of African civil societies as bifurcated. Even if one does not agree with their characterisations, the fact remains that whatever measures are used African civil societies have expanded; the ties that bind the multicultural societies of African nations together and the tensions that tear them apart are extraordinarily complex requiring deft strategies of community and conflict management in which respect for human rights must rank high indeed as a powerful adhesive of common citizenship and a dissolvent of communal conflicts.

In the last two decades human rights NGOs have emerged as powerful instruments in Africa's drive for the promotion of human rights and development. The proliferation of NGOs is one of the truly remarkable stories of African social and political transformation. The NGO movement is both a progenitor and product of Africa's democratisation. But the euphoria that once greeted NGOs has been replaced by more sober assessment of the challenges they face. Makau Mutua is particularly critical of human rights NGOs. He charges that many of them are replicas of their northern counterparts in their organisation, objectives, tactics and strategies. Indeed, they are largely dependent on Northern resources and support.[81]

While the international human rights NGOs have made positive contributions to, and some have worked in partnership with, African NGOs, Mutua believes that the relationship has been characterised mostly by paternalism and dependency which limits the capacity of African NGOs to undertake independent initiatives, address the human rights needs of their societies in an integrated manner by going beyond the obsession with their civil and political rights and incorporating violations and promoting economic, social and cultural rights, developing more fruitful South-South cooperation and networking, and cultivating local sources and structures of support, without which their long term future is doomed.

Claude Welch is more sanguine about the nature of North-South NGO relations. He thinks there is a growing solidarity of purpose between indigenous and
international NGOs and between some NGOs and members of society. He shows,
for example, that the International Commission of Jurists—once headed by
Senegalese Adama Deng—played a critical role in the preparation and ratification of the African Charter on Human and People's Rights. Similarly, Amnesty
International—also once headed by Senegalese Pierre Sané—and the Africa Division of Human Rights Watch have moved increasingly toward cooperation
with indigenous NGOs in their investigations and reporting. On the whole, he
stresses, human rights NGOs have made significant accomplishments in Africa,
although he concedes that they tend to be small in size, limited in budget, cluster
in urban areas, concentrate on civil and political rights, and are dependent on
external sources.[82]

The two positions find echoes in many other studies of human rights NGOs.
For example, the notion that NGOs are brokers and defenders for human rights
is strongly challenged by Monica Juma, who argues that the image of good NGOs
and bad states is flawed because the two have often worked together to undermine
the rights of refugees and internally displaced populations (IDPs) in East Africa.
In the 1990s both Kenya and Uganda saw dramatic rises in refugees and IDPs,
which occurred at the same time as the governments became less generous and
adopted the containment model of refugee and displaced populations. National
legislation and practices became more restrictive or ruthless: asylum was
determined in terms of groups rather than individuals; camps that were virtually
beyond the rule of law became the mainstay of refugee protection; and forced
repatriation assumed prominence over local integration and third country
resettlement.[83]

The situation was even worse for IDPs, often regarded by states as a security
or political threat, and access to whom is tightly controlled. NGOs responded to
the situation in ways that tended to restrict, rather than expand, the rights of
refugees and IDPs, by avoiding confrontation with the state, downplaying the
scope and scale of displacement, focusing on band-aid type interventions, de-
emphasising government responsibility, and engaging in programmes that support government interests. The situation will only improve if, Juma suggests, a
comprehensive human rights response structure is instituted, one that pursues
an integrated approach incorporating both state and non-state actors, tackles all
the issues pertaining to the causes, course and consequences of displacement,
realises the indivisibility of rights, institutes democracy, transparency and
accountability within the NGOs sector itself, and returns agency to the victims
of displacement by curtailing the excessive paternalism of the refugee and IDP
business.

If Juma leans towards Mutua's position, Jotham Momba writing on the complex
role that NGOs played in Zambia's democratic transition echoes Welch. The

NGO movement participated in the creation of the Movement for Multi-party Democracy (MMD), a loose coalition of several civil society organisations, including the labour movement, professional associations, churches and women's groups, that went on to defeat the party that had run the one-party state since independence. Despite the positive political changes, Momba notes, problems concerning the rule of law and human rights persisted, and the new MMD government soon fell out with many of its civil society partners, who continued monitoring and publicising human rights abuses.[84]

Although a minority out of the more than 400 NGOs that emerged, the human rights NGOs pursued their advocacy campaigns through education workshops for the public and training workshops for activists. Awareness raising campaigns were also undertaken against abuses of political power. Several NGOs conducted election monitoring and civic workshops in subsequent elections and succeeded in raising the level of public awareness about civil and political rights, and sensitised the international community to hold the government accountable for its human rights record, which did not endear the NGOs to the state. But the civil society organisations suffer from internal weaknesses, including ideological divisions, leadership infighting and over-reliance on external resources, which undermines their advocacy work.

Clearly, the missions and roles of NGOs change with new circumstances. This is no better illustrated than in South Africa where, as Vincent Saldhana has shown, NGOs played a crucial role in the country's tumultuous transition from apartheid to democracy. During the 1980s, when their numbers expanded, NGOs were not merely non-governmental, but anti-government, and were an integral part of the mass democratic movement. With the demise of apartheid in the 1990s, the NGOs found themselves in uncharted waters: donor support dwindled, some of their leaders joined the state bureaucracy, the new constitution adopted extensive human rights provisions, including a Bill of Rights, and the government established human rights monitoring and enforcement agencies, including a Human Rights Commission. South African NGOs had to redefine their role.[85]

The NGO movement now saw itself as an independent monitor and champion of the marginalised and began to focus primarily on issues such as poverty eradication, the national debt, and macro-economic issues. While jealous of their independence, the NGOs felt the need, Saldhana tells us, to work with the state in drafting and implementing new laws and socio-economic initiatives as part of their human rights agenda. He advises NGOs to maintain their political independence, commitment to democratic and human rights values, to promote programmes for sustainable poverty alleviation, show vigilance against corruption, nepotism and patronage, build their capacity for research, analysis and intellectual understanding of the content of social and economic rights, and strengthen their regional and international networking relationships.

The question of popular participation goes beyond formal associations such as NGOs of course. The mediations of gender, class and religion and other similar social registers are quite important. Given the limitations of space, it would not be possible to discuss fully the ways that class, gender, religion, age and generation have affected and been affected by struggles for democratisation, human rights and development in contemporary Africa, except to underscore that they are essential for a comprehensive understanding. It might be pointed out, for example, that the growth of the women's movement has been critical to struggles for human rights in many African countries, but as the women's movement has expanded it has become more differentiated in its composition, objectives and tendencies, incorporating within its ranks associations of presidents' wives, middle class professionals, women traders, peasant women, working class women, income generating activities and cultural organisations.[86]

Similarly, African class formations have been drastically altered by the recessions and reforms of the last two decades that have implications for human rights struggles. Public sector employees have witnessed retrenchment and pauperisation, while new entrepreneurial classes have emerged tied to new sectors from information and communication services to private education and health provision. Ordinary workers in particular have faced considerable difficulties as their real wages have fallen or stagnated, but African labour movements have remained at the forefront of the struggles for democracy and progressive social change. With democratisation, the conditions for labour organisation have improved in law as the corporatist chains of state control have loosened, but become more difficult in practice as employment security has declined thanks to liberalisation.[87]

Religious movements have also been a crucial part of Africa's changing cultural and political economies. As noted earlier, the fallout of America's war on terror has affected Christian-Muslim relations in several countries. No less important, religious groups, both Christian and Muslim, were critical to struggles against state tyranny in the 1980s and 1990s, as they were often the last public spaces to be directly confronted by the state, even if they might harbour their own intolerant visions of reordering society.88 And the youth—the majority of the African population—have embodied in their restlessness, rebelliousness, apparent delinquency and cosmopolitan affectations the failures and reconfigurations of the post-colonial project, suggesting in their behaviours, actions and pleasures new expressions of political action both violent and non-violent, formal and informal, and desperate desires to escape the bankrupt political and moral discourses, the increasingly sterile obligations of state and gerontocratic power that has robbed them of the long-jaded promises of independence, and to fashion new patterns of socialisation and sociability, associational and political commitments, and new aesthetics and idioms of empowerment, living, belonging and citizenship.[89]

At the heart of the drive for human rights in Africa is a linguistic conundrum, the continued supremacy of European languages and the relative marginality of local languages in official human rights discourses. Two issues are at stake, the language of law, that is, the language of politics, the courts, and human rights instruments and documents, and the question of linguistic rights—the rights of languages and to languages—that are crucial for the exercise of freedom of speech and the import of that freedom. Alamin Mazrui has deplored the fact that the entire discourse on human rights is trapped in a European linguistic idiom, which has grave consequences for African human rights culture and consciousness. The imperial languages were introduced to Africa as media of command, not of rights, and after they had shed that role they remained languages of a middle class minority patronised by the West and well attuned to its liberal or neo-liberal doctrines.[90]

Barred from this middle class linguistic enclosure, the ordinary masses, proficient in their own languages that are not languages of the law, government and business, are prevented from influencing the reconceptualisation of the dominant human rights discourse. Indeed, they are excluded from full participation in public affairs, whether parliaments or the courts, and African languages are denied the opportunity to develop a robust legislative and human rights register. Linguistic alienation from the law, Mazrui concludes, may be a major cause of the failure of democracy and human rights culture to take deep roots on the continent.

Often, the preference for the colonial languages is based on the contention that Africa is a Tower of Babel, with hundreds if not thousands of languages. Kwesi Prah ripostes: 'To this, the Dutch anthropologist Simon Simonse once, in conversation, remarked that, if the sort of criteria used to count African languages is applied to Holland, there will be more than twenty languages in that case. The work done by the Centre for Advanced Studies of African Society on the Classification of African Languages on the Basis of Mutual Intelligibility has so far demonstrated that, as first and second language speakers, over 80 percent of Africans speak no more than twelve key languages (clusters which enjoy 85 percent mutual intelligibility... The central problem hindering the unification of mutually intelligible speech forms, is again the lack of political will of the ruling elites in Africa'.[91]

Conclusion

The challenges of expanding and deepening human rights cultures in Africa are as multifaceted as the contexts that shape them. In this paper it has been argued and demonstrated that while considerable improvements have been made in many parts of the continent in terms of democratisation, which has improved the prospects for human rights in general, the constraints against development and the realisation of the right to development and social, economic and cultural rights more generally remain daunting.

Notes

1. For a detailed report on the human rights implications of recent political developments in Africa as a whole and in specific countries, see Human Rights Watch, Human Rights Watch World Report 2002 (New York, *Human Rights Watch,* 2002).

2. For a recent and detailed account of changes in political and human rights regimes in Africa, see Paul Tiyambe Zeleza and Philip J. McConnaughay, eds., *Human Rights, the Rule of Law and Development in Africa,* Philadelphia,University of Pennsylvania Press, 2004.

3. The percentages were as follows: Tanzania 84, Botswana 83, Nigeria 81, Ghana 77, Zambia 74, Mozambique 74, Zimbabwe 71, Malawi 66, Mali 60, South Africa 60, Namibia 57, and Lesotho 39. See, João C.G. Pereira and Yul Derek Davids, 'Political Reforms in Mozambique: Attitudes to Democracy among Ordinary People', in Yul Dereke Davids, et al., *Measuring Democracy and Human Rights in Southern Africa,* (Uppsala, Nordiska Afrikainstitutet, 2002), p.11. Data from Namibia indicates that supporters of democracy 'are more likely to live in urban areas, be better educated and have higher incomes than non-democrats. Both clusters are present in all thirteen regions and in all language groups... Overall, Namibia does not have sufficient young Democrats to make the consolidation of democracy a foregone conclusion. There is a large segment of the Namibian youth (the less educated, rural poor) for whom democracy is not yet "the only game in town"'. See Christiaan Keulder and Dirk Spilker, 'In Search of Democrats in Namibia: Attitudes Among the Youth', in Yul Dereke Davids, et al., *Measuring Democracy and Human Rights in Southern Africa,* p.28.

4. For example, while more than 60 percent of those polled (and sometimes as high as over 80 or 90 percent) in Botswana, Zimbabwe, Zambia, Malawi, Mozambique, Lesotho, Namibia and South Africa agreed that 'people can join any organisation', 'each person can freely choose who to vote for', and with slightly lower percentages that 'anyone can freely say what he or she thinks', in six countries less than 50 percent (and as low as 12 percent in Mozambique) said 'people have an adequate standard of living' (the exceptions were Namibia with 57 percent and strangely Malawi with 51 percent). Governments were generally rated higher in addressing educational needs (from 71 percent in Botswana to 46 percent in Mozambique) than keeping prices low (ranging from 41 percent in Botswana to 8 percent in Malawi) and creating jobs (ranging from 52 percent in Botswana to 10 percent in South Africa). See tables 9 and 11, which show considerable national variations, João C.G. Pereira and Yul Derek Davids, 'Political Reforms in Mozambique...' in Yul Dereke Davids, et al., *Measuring Democracy and Human Rights in Southern Africa,* pp.15, 17.

5. Some scholars have tried to measure the relationships between economic and political conditions and human rights violations. Examining the incidences of

imprisonment and torture, two researchers conclude that the economic hypothesis that wealthier countries tend to enjoy better human rights records than poorer ones seems better supported than the political explanations concerning political culture (for example, nature and length of colonial experience) and regime types (the bizarre authoritarian-totalitarian regime typology or the liberal-communitarian typology). See Neil J. Mitchell and James M. McCormick, 'Economic and Political Explanations of Human Rights Violations', *World Politics*, 40, 4 (1988): 476-498. The first typology was advanced by Jeanne Kirkpatrick, 'Dictatorships and Double Standards', Commentary, 68 (November 1979): 34-45, and the second by Rhoda Howard and Jack Donnelly, 'Human Dignity, Human Rights, and Political Regimes', *American Political Science Review*, 80 (1986): 801-818.

6. For a sample of this literature see Eduard Ziegenhagen, The Regulation of Political Conflict, New York, Praeger, 1986; Conway Henderson, 'Conditions Affecting the Use of Political Repression', *Journal of Conflict Resolution*, 35 (1991) 120-142; Steve Poe and C. Neale Tate, 'Repression of Personal Integrity in the 1980s: A Global Analysis', *American Political Science Review*, 88, 4 (1994): 853-872; Christian Davenport, 'Multi-dimensional Threat Perception and State Repression: An Inquiry Into Why States Apply Negative Sanctions', *American Journal of Political Science*, 39 (1995): 683-713; Ron Francisco, 'Coercion and Protest: An Empirical Test in Two Democratic States', *American Journal of Political Science*, 40 (1996):179-204; and Rudolph J. Rummel, *Power Kills: Democracy as a Method of Nonviolence*, New Brunswick, NJ, Transaction, 1997.

7. See Christian Davenport, 'The Weight of the Past: Exploring Lagged Determinants of Political Repression', *Political Research Quarterly*, 49 (1996): 377-403, and 'Human Rights and the Democratic Proposition', *Journal of Conflict Resolution*, 43, 1 (1999): 92-116—this article is based on a large data set from 137 countries for the period 1950-1982. Also see Juan Linz and Alfred Stepan, *Problems of Democratic Transition and Consolidation: Southern Europe, South America, and Post-Communist Europe*, Baltimore: Johns Hopkins University Press, 1996; and Mathew Krain and Marissa Myers, 'Democracy and Civil War: A Note on the Democratic Peace Proposition', *International Interactions*, 41 (1997): 109-118.

8. See Helen Fein, 'More Murder in the Middle: Life-Integrity Violations and Democracy in the World', *Human Rights Quarterly*, 17 (1995), pp. 170-191.

9. The literature on current conflicts in Africa is vast and not all of it is related to democratisation. For discussions of democratisation and the escalation of ethnic and other group conflicts see some of the contributions in Eshetu Chole and Jibrin Ibrahim, eds., *Democratisation Processes in Africa*, Dakar, Codesria, 1995; Adebayo Olukoshi and Liisa Laasko, eds., *Challenges of the Nation State in Africa*, Uppsala, Nordiska Afrikainstitutet, 1996; Kidane Mengisteab and Cyril Daddieh, eds., *State Building and Democratisation in Africa: Faith, Hope, and Realities*, Westport, Conn., Praeger, 1999; Jibrin Ibrahim, ed., *Expanding Democratic Space in West Africa*,

Dakar, CODESRIA, 1997; Julius O. Ihonvbere and John M. Mbaku, eds., *Political Liberalization and Democratisation in Africa: Lessons From Country Experiences*, Westport, Conn., Praeger, 2003; and John M. Mbaku and Julius O. Ihonvbere, eds., *The Transition to Democratic Governance in Africa: The Continuing Struggle*, Westport, Conn., Praeger, 2003. Also see the studies by Okwudiba Nnoli, *Ethnicity and Development in Africa*, Aldershot, Ashgate, 1995; Seyoum Hameso, *Ethnicity in Africa: Towards a Positive Approach,* London, TSC Publications, 1997; E. Conteh-Morgan, *Democratisation in Africa: The Theory and Dynamics of Political Transitions,* Westport, Conn., Praeger, 1997; David Wippman, International Law and Ethnic Conflict, Ithaca, Cornell University Press, 1998; Claude Ake, *The Feasibility of Democracy in Africa,* Dakar, CODESRIA, 2000; Richard Sandbrook, *Closing the Circle: Democratisation and Development in Africa,* Toronto, Between the Lines, 2000; and Mohammed A. Salih, *African Democracies and African Conflicts*, London, Pluto Press, 2001.

10. Peter P. Ekeh, 'Colonialism and the Two Publics in Africa: A Theoretical Statement', *Comparative Studies in Society and History,* 17, 1 (1975): 91-112; and Mahmood Mamdani, Citizen and Subject: Contemporary Africa and the Legacy of Late Colonialism, Princeton, New Jersey, University of Princeton Press, 1996.

11. Michael Vickers, *Ethnicity and Sub-Nationalism in Nigeria: Movement for a Mid-West State,* Oxford, Worldview Publishers, 2000; Osita Agbu, *Ethnic Militias and the Threat to Democracy in Post-Transition Nigeria,* Uppsala, Nordiska Afrikainstitutet, 2004.

12. Eghosa E. Osaghae, 'Human Rights and Ethnic Conflict Management: The Case of Nigeria', *Journal of Peace Research,* 33, 2 (1996): 171-188.

13. The African Union, The Constitutive Act at http://www.Africa-union.org/

14. For the organisation's history, see, NEPAD, *NEPAD Annual Report 2002: Towards Claiming the Twenty-First Century,* Johannesburg, NEPAD, 2002. For a detailed list of its action plans see *NEPAD, A Summary of NEPAD Action Plans,* Johannesburg, NEPAD.

15. See for example, Jikang Kim, 'Africa's Sustainable Development and the Establishment of NEPAD', AISA Electronic Monograph, 5 December 2003. http://www.ai.org.za/electronic_monograph.asp?ID=15 and Siphamandla Zondi, NEPAD: Taking the Commodity to the Consumers, AISA Electronic Monograph July 30, 2003. http://www.ai.org.za/electronic_monograph.asp?ID=6

16. 'NEPAD, Objectives, Standards, Criteria and Indicators for the African Peer Review Mechanism' (NEPAD/HSGIC-03-2003/APRM/Guideline/OSCI 9 March 2003).

17. See NEPAD, 'Guidelines for Countries to Prepare for and to Participate in the African Peer Review Mechanism' (NEPAD/APRM/Panel2/guidelines/11-2003/Doc8).

18. Economics Editor, 'Manuel Slams Peer-Review Dodgers', *Business Day* (15 September 2004).

19. Shadrack Gutto, 'The African Commission on Human and Peoples' Rights in the new institutional landscape: TRCs, Special Courts, the ICTR, New Constitutions, the AU, NEPAD, the African Court on Human and Peoples' Rights, CSSDA, APRM', Paper presented at International Conference on The African Commission on Human and Peoples' Rights and the Current Challenges of Promoting and Protecting Human Rights, organised by the African Commission on Human and Peoples' Rights, Nordiska Afrikainstitutet, the Council for the Development of Social Science Research in Africa, and the Swedish NGO Foundation for Human Rights, Uppsala, Sweden, 9-10 June 2004.

20. See Frans Viljoen, 'Strengthening the African Commission on Human and Peoples' Rights: Procedures, Mechanisms, Partnerships and Implementation', Paper presented at International Conference on The African Commission on Human and Peoples' Rights and the Current Challenges of Promoting and Protecting Human Rights, organised by the African Commission on Human and Peoples' Rights, Nordiska Afrikainstitutet, the Council for the Development of Social Science Research in Africa, and the Swedish NGO Foundation for Human Rights, Uppsala, Sweden, 9-10 June 2004.

21. Africa has added its voice on universal jurisdiction for international crimes with the Cairo-Arusha Principles, named after resolutions that were passed at two meetings organised by Legal Aid, an NGO, in Cairo, Egypt in July 2001 and in Arusha, Tanzania in October 2002, see *AFLA Quarterly* (October–December 2002) 'Special Issue of The Cairo-Arusha Principles on Universal Jurisdiction in Respect of Gross Human Rights Offences: An African Perspective'.

22. See accounts in the autobiography of the founder and long-term former president of TransAfrica, Randall Robinson, *Defending the Spirit: A Black Life in America,* New York, Dutton, 1998.

23. NEPAD, NEPAD *Annual Report 2002,* pp.8-9.

24. For a summary of the vast and still growing literature on globalisation see Paul Tiyambe Zeleza, *Rethinking Africa's Globalisation,* Chapter 1. For conceptions of globalisation in different world regions see the succinct papers in Manfred B. Steger, ed., *Rethinking Globalism,* New York, Rowman and Littlefield, 2004.

25. This thesis was first presented in an article that was later expanded into a book, Francis Fukuyama, 'The End of History?', *The National Interest,* (Summer, 1989), and *The End of History and the Last Man,* London, Hamish Hamilton, 1992.

26. See some of the following studies by T. W. Luke, 'New World Order or Neo-world Orders', in M. Featherstone, S. Lash, and R. Robertson, eds., *Global Culture: Nationalism, Globalisation and Modernity,* London: Sage, 1995; E. Swyngedouw, 'Neither Global nor Local: «Glocalization» and the Politics of Scale', in K. R. Cox, ed., *Spaces of Globalisation: Reasserting the Power of the Local,* New York, The Guilford Press: 137-166, 1997; Robert W. Cox, 'A Perspective on Globalisation', in James H. Mittelman, ed., *Globalisation: Critical Reflections,* Boulder, Colorado, Lynne Rienner:

21-30, 1997; Ian Clark, *Globalisation and Fragmentation: International Relations in the Twentieth Century,* New York, Oxford University Press, 1997; and James N. Roseneau, 'The Challenges and Tensions of a Globalised World', *American Studies International,* 38, 2 (2000): 8-22.

27. Terms coined by Edward S. Hermann and Frank Broadhead, *Demonstration Elections,* Boston, MA, South End Press, 1984. For a summary of these debates see Michael Bratton and Nicolas van de Walle, *Democratic Experiments in Africa: Regime Transitions in Comparative Perspective,* Cambridge, Cambridge University Press, 1997, and Paul Tiyambe Zeleza, 'Democracy in Africa', in Maryanne Horowitz, ed., *The History of the Dictionary of Ideas,* New York, Scribners, forthcoming.

28. Fareed Zakaria, 'The Rise of Illiberal Democracy', in Patrick O'Meara, Howard D. Mehlinger, and Mathew Krain, eds., *Globalisation and the Challenges of a New Century,* Bloomington and Indianapolis, Indiana University Press, 2000: 181-195.

29. Murray Law, 'Representation Unbound: Globalisation and Democracy', in K. R. Cox, ed., Spaces of Globalisation: Reasserting the Power of the Local, New York, The Guildford Press, 1997: 240-280. For a succinct discussion of globalisation and democracy see Kidane Mengisteab, 'Globalisation and Narrowing the Scope of Democracy in Africa', in Paul Tiyambe Zeleza and Philip J. McConnaughay, eds., *Human Rights, the Rule of Law and Development in Africa,* pp. 94-105.

30. See the fascinating analyses on globalisation and workers' repertoires of resistance by Frances F. Piven and Richard A. Cloward, 'Eras of Power', *Monthly Review,* 49 (January, 1998): 11-23, and 'Power Repertoires and Globalisation', Politics & Society, 28, 3 (2000), pp. 413-430.

31. David L. Cingranelli and David L. Richards, 'Respect for Human Rights after the End of the Cold War', *Journal of Peace Research,* 36, 5 (1999), p. 521.

32. Guy Lamb, 'Debasing Democracy: Security Forces and Human Rights Abuses in Post-Liberation Namibia and South Africa', in Yul Dereke Davids, et al., *Measuring Democracy and Human Rights in Southern Africa,* p.30.

33. On the growing use and limits of political conditionalities of bilateral and multilateral foreign assistance to Africa and the global South in general, see G. Sorensen, ed., *Political Conditionality,* London, Frank Cass, 1993; P. Uvin, 'Do as I Say, Not as I Do: The Limits of Political Conditionality', *The European Journal of Development Research,* 5, 1 (1993); O. Stokke, ed., *Aid and Political Conditionality,* London, Frank Cass, 1995. For the United States, see Steven C. Poe, 'Human Rights and the Allocation of U.S. Military Assistance', *Journal of Peace Research,* 28 (1991), pp.205-216; Mark Peceny, 'Two Paths to the Promotion of Democracy During US Military Interventions', *International Studies Quarterly,* 39 (1995), 371-401; James Meernik, Eric L. Krueger and Steven C. Poe, 'Testing Models of US Foreign Policy: Foreign Aid During and after the Cold War', *Journal of Politics,* 60 (1998), 63-85; and by Shannon Lindsey Blanton, 'Promoting Human Rights and Democracy in the Developing World: US Rhetoric versus US Arms Exports',

American Journal of Political Science, 44, 1 (2000), pp. 123-131, who makes the rather unconvincing argument that the US tends to export its arms to countries that are democratic and respect human rights rather than non-democracies.

34. Gorm Rye Olsen, 'Europe and the Promotion of Democracy in Post Cold War Africa: How Serious is Europe and For What Reason?', *African Affairs,* 97 (1998), p. 346.

35. Olsen, 'Europe and the Promotion of Democracy in Post Cold War Africa...', 346. The same argument has been made by K. Griffin, 'Foreign Aid After the Cold War', *Development and Change,* 22 (1992): 645-685.

36. Olsen, 'Europe and the Promotion of Democracy in Post Cold War Africa...', p.353. For more on the debate between the relative roles on recipient needs and donor interests in EU aid see, P. Bowles, 'Recipient Needs and Donor Interests in the Allocation of EEC Aid to Developing Countries', *Canadian Journal of Development Studies,* 10, 1 (1989); E. R. Grilli, *The European Community and the Developing Countries,* Cambridge, Cambridge University Press, 1993; A. Noël and J-P. Thérien, 'From Domestic to International Justice: The Welfare State and Foreign Aid', International Organisation, 49, 3 (1995): 523-553; M. Breuning, 'Words and Deeds: Foreign Assistance Rhetoric and Policy Behavior in the Netherlands, Belgium and the United Kingdom', *International Studies Quarterly,* 39 (1995): 235-254; and M. Lister, The European Community and the South. Relations With Developing Countries, London, Routledge, 1997: 161-165. For updated annual overviews of the role of key international players including the EU, France and Britain on the African human rights scene see the annual reports of Human Rights Watch.

37. There are considerable differences among the western countries of course when it comes to the consistency and level of support for African development in general and the rule of law and human rights in particular. For an interesting study on Swedish assistance, see Per Sevastik, ed., *Legal Assistance to Developing Countries,* Stockholm, Kluwer, 1997.

38. The increase was 35 percent for North Africa and 15 percent for sub-Saharan Africa. Europe registered a decline (-2 percent in which -8 percent was for Central and Eastern Europe and -2 percent for Western Europe), so did Central America (-2 percent). See the (Stockholm International Peace Research Institute) *SIPRI Yearbook* 2004, appendix table 10A.1 and table 10A.3.

39. The United States spent 47 percent of the world total, and together the top five countries accounted for 64 percent and the top fifteen for 82 percent.

40. For example, Eritrea spent 2.8 percent and 4.8 percent on health and education, respectively.

41. William F. Felice, 'Militarism and Human Rights', *International Affairs,* 74, 1 (1998), p.28.

42. The USA spends about 5 percent of GDP on the military compared to one percent for Japan and three percent for Germany. It has been argued that the

economic prosperity enjoyed by the United States during the Second World War, which ended the Great Depression, left a deep impression about the positive effects of military expenditure that has not been questioned by any administration since then. See, Felice, *Militarism and Human Rights*, p.27.

43. Felice, *Militarism and Human Rights*, p.31.

44. Three were in the Americas (including the USA war in Afghanistan), 8 in Asia, and 3 in the Middle East), see *SIPRI Yearbook* 2004 'Press Release', New York, Oxford University Press, p.10. For a comprehensive overview of a data set on interstate conflicts from the early nineteenth century to the 1990s see, Daniel M. Jones, Stuart A. Bremer, and J. David Singer, 'Militarized Interstate Conflicts, 1816-1992: Rationale, Coding Rules, and Empirical Patterns', *Conflict Management and Peace Science,* 15, 2 (1996), pp.163-215.

45. Cingranelli and Richards, 'Respect for Human Rights after the End of the Cold War', p. 521.

46. Monty G. Marshall, 'Major Episodes of Political Violence 1946-2002', Center for Systematic Peace, http://members.aol.com/CSPmgm/warlist.htm

47. Felice, 'Militarism and Human Rights', p.36.

48. The UN Secretary General, Kofi Annan, finally declared the war illegal in September 2004, a view already widely held around the world. See, Ewen MacAskill and Julian Borger, 'Iraq war was illegal and breached UN charter, says Annan', *The Guardian,* 16 September 2004.

49. Council on Foreign Relations, Public Diplomacy: A Strategy for Reform, A Report of an Independent Taskforce on Public Diplomacy sponsored by the Council on Foreign Relations, 30 July 2002), as quoted in Amnesty International, United States of America. Undermining security: violations of human dignity, the rule of law and the National Security Strategy in 'war on terror' detentions (AI Index: AMR 51/061/2004), p.10, which primarily looks at conditions in Guantánamo Bay. For another critical report on Guantánamo Bay and the detention of suspects from the Gulf and the Arabian Peninsula and the overall impact of the so-called war on terror on human rights in the sharp deterioration of human rights in the region in which local governments and the US work in collusion see, Amnesty International, The Gulf and the Arabia Peninsula: Human rights fall victim to the 'War on terror' (AI Index: MDE 04/002/2004).

50. For the treatment of prisoners in Iraq including at Abu Ghraib, see the Report by International Committee of the Red Cross (ICRC) on the Treatment by the Coalition Forces of Prisoners of War and Other Protected Persons by Geneva Conventions in Iraq During Arrest, Internment and Interrogation (February 2004). Also see the critical report against Coalition Provisional Authority by Amnesty International, Memorandum of concerns relating to law and order (AI Index: MDE 14/157/2003).

51 One of the most scathing attacks against the war on terror is offered by an anonymous writer currently serving as a US intelligence officer who argues that groups like al-Qaeda are motivated by opposition to specific US policies in the Muslim world rather than the imaginary and self-serving litany offered by the Bush administration and its academic friends—hatred of democracy, the American way of life, or modernity. See Anonymous, *Imperial Hubris: Why the West Is Losing the War on Terror,* Washington, D.C., Brassey's, 2004. For an insightful critique from an Africanist perspective, see Mahmood Mamdani, *Good Muslim, Bad Muslim: America, the Cold War and Roots of Terror,* New York, Pantheon, 2004.

52. For example, Human Rights Watch has accused the United Nations' Security Council of disregarding human rights in the work of its Counter-Terrorism Committee and the Counter-Terrorism Executive Directorate established by resolutions passed after September 11, 2001, both of which have to date shown reluctance to address the human rights implications of anti-terrorism laws and strategies of member states. See 'Human Rights Watch, Hear No Evil, See No Evil: The U.N. security Council's Approach to Human Rights Violations in the Global Counter-Terrorism Effort', *Human Rights Watch Briefing Paper,* August 10, 2004.

53. Amnesty International, The backlash-human rights at risk throughout the world, AI Index No. ACT 30/027/2001, p.5.

54. See for example the following Amnesty International reports, United Kingdom: Creating a shadow criminal justice system in the name of fighting international terrorism, AI Index: EUR 45/019/200; and United States of America: Memorandum to the U.S. Attorney General—Amnesty International's concerns relating to the post 11 September investigations, AI Index: AMR 51/170/2001.

55. Amnesty International, Tunisia: New draft 'anti-terrorism' law will further undermine human rights, AI Index: MDE 30?021/2003; and Kenya: Draft anti-terrorism legislation may undermine Kenyan constitution and international law, AI Index: AFR 32/004/2004. Also see Amnesty International's detailed critique of the convention adopted by the League of Arab States, 'The Arab Convention for the Suppression of Terrorism a serious threat to human rights', http://web.amnesty.org/library/print/ENGIORS510012002, which Amnesty believes presents a serious threat to human rights in Arab countries, many of which are of course in Africa.

56. Amnesty International, 2002, UN Commission on Human Rights: Rights at Risk, AI Index: IOR 41/025/2001, pp.28-34.

57. Human Rights Watch, *Human Rights Watch World Report* 2002, p.3.

58. Paul Tiyambe Zeleza, 'Introduction: The Struggle for Human Rights in Africa', in Paul Tiyambe Zeleza and Philip J. McConnaughay, eds., *Human Rights, the Rule of Law and Development in Africa,* pp.6-7.

59. According to Susan Koshy, internationalisation 'involves the agreement, in political-legal principle and in rhetoric, that individual human rights are of international concern at the level of diplomacy, international relations, and international law', while universalisation 'refers to the acceptance, in principle and rhetoric, of the idea of human rights by all societies and governments, and it is reflected in their incorporation into national constitutions and law'. Susan Koshy, 'From Cold War to Trade War: Neocolonialism and Human Rights', *Social Text*, 58 (Spring, 1999), pp.3-4.

60. For an informative discussion of human rights in the post-Cold War era characterised by new Western-Asian splits, realignments, and Europe-US splits, and the growing importance of trade imperatives see Koshy, 'From Cold War to Trade War...', pp.10-27. Since September 2001, security imperatives have reasserted themselves.

61. Heiner Bielefeldt, '"Western" versus "Islamic" Human Rights Conceptions?: A Critique of Cultural Essentialism in the Discussion of Human Rights', *Political Theory*, 28, 1 (2000), pp.90-121. He offers an equally nuanced discussion of varieties of conceptions of human rights in the Islamic tradition, especially among contemporary Islamic scholars.

62. Bielefeldt, '"Western" versus "Islamic" Human Rights Conceptions?', p.114.

63. Tibi Bassam asserts that the two, 'human rights' and 'human dignity', should not be confused with each other, while Rhoda Howard states quite categorically that the African concept of human rights is actually a concept of human dignity; the latter can be protected in a society that is not based on rights. See, Tibi Bassam, 'The European Conception of Human Rights and the Culture of Islam', in A. A. An-Naim and Francis Deng, eds., *Human Rights in Africa. Cross Cultural Perspectives*, Washington D.C., The Brookings Institution, 1990, pp.104-132; Rhoda Howard, 'Is There an African Concept of Human Rights?', in R.J. Vincent, ed., *Human Rights in Foreign Policy: Issues and Responses*, Cambridge, Cambridge University Press, 1984, and 'Evaluating Human Rights in Africa: Some Problems of Implicit Comparisons', *Human Rights Quarterly*, 6 (1984): 160-179. For a vigorous critique of this position and the sterile universalist-relativist debate, see Bonny Ihbawoh, 'Restraining Universalism: Africanist Perspectives on Cultural Relativism in Human Rights Discourse', in Paul Tiyambe Zeleza and Philip J. McConnaughay, eds., *Human Rights, the Rule of Law and Development in Africa*, pp. pp.21-39.

64. Koshy, 'From Cold War to Trade War...', provides a succinct account of US machinations to split human rights and prioritise CPR. For longer analyses see Tony Evans, *US Hegemony and the Project of Universal Human Rights*, New York, St. Martin's Press, 1996; and Belden A. Fields, *Rethinking Human Rights for the New Millennium*, New York, Palgrave Macmillan, 2003.

65. According to Koshy, 'From Cold War to Trade War...', p.8, this tri-generational schema of rights was first proposed by Kavel Vasak, 'Inaugural Lecture to the

Tenth Study Session of the International Institute of Human Rights', 2-7 July 1979.

66. Theodore Meron, 'On a Hierarchy of International Human Rights', The *American Journal of International Law*, 80, 1 (1986): 1-23.

67. Daniel A. Bell, 'Which Rights Are Universal?', *Political Theory*, 27, 6 (1999), pp.849-856.

68. Abdullahi A. An-Na'im, 'To Affirm the Full Human Rights Standing of Economic, Social and Cultural Rights', in Yash Ghai and Jill Cottrell, eds., *Economic, Social and Cultural Rights in Practice: The Role of Judges in Implementing Economic, Social and Cultural Rights*, London, Interights, 2004, p.7.

69. For a brief but insightful analysis of the right to development see Pansy Tlakula, 'Human Rights and Development', in Paul Tiyambe Zeleza and Philip J. McConnaughay, eds., *Human Rights, the Rule of Law and Development in Africa*, pp.109-119.

70. See how it has dealt with the right to housing for example in Geoff Budlender, 'Justiciability of Socio-Economic Rights: Some South African Experiences', in Yash Ghai and Jill Cottrell, eds., *Economic, Social and Cultural Rights in Practice*, pp.33-41. For examples from other non-African countries see Claire L'Heureux-Dubé, 'A Canadian Perspective on Economic and Social Rights'; S. Muralindar, 'Economic, Social and Cultural Rights: An Indian Response to the Justiciability Debate'; and Adras Sajo, 'Implementing Welfare in Esatern Europe after Communism', all in Yash Ghai and Jill Cottrell, eds., *Economic, Social and Cultural Rights in Practice*. In Canada where ESCR provisions are not incorporated in the Canadian Charter, the courts and human rights tribunals have nonetheless played an active role in protecting ESCR. In India an activist judiciary has creatively interpreted the constitutionally entrenched 'right to life' to adjudicate and enforce some ESCR provisions. In the former communist countries of Eastern Europe where ESCR were entrenched in previous constitutions concerns have centred on the practical enforceability of ESCR, whose effect has been to narrow the conception of welfare entitlements and protect the already better-off.

71. An-Na'im, 'To Affirm the Full Human Rights Standing of Economic, Social and Cultural Rights', p.7.

72. Jill Cottrell and Yash Tandon, 'The Role of the Courts in the Protection of Economic, Social and Cultural Rights', in Yash Ghai and Jill Cottrell, eds., *Economic, Social and Cultural Rights in Practice*, p.88.

73. Corruption is defined in the social science literature in several ways, first, in terms of unacceptable behaviour in the performance of the duties of public office (engaging in bribery, nepotism, misappropriation); second, in relation to the distortions of market operations by the imposition of high levels of government regulations which civil servants spend time assisting entrepreneurs to evade in exchange for bribes to augment their incomes; and finally, as institutional

opportunism designed to generate benefits for individuals or groups at the expense of the public interest. The literature on corruption has grown in quantity and quality over the last decade. See, K.A. Elliot, ed., *Corruption and the Global Economy,* Washington, D.C., Institute for Economics, 1997; K. Frimping and G. Jacques, eds., *Corruption, Democracy and Good Governance in Africa: Essay on Accountability and Ethical Behaviour,* Gaborone, Lentswe La Lesedi Publishers, 1999; B. Rider, ed., *Corruption: The Enemy From Within,* London, Kluwer Law International, 1999; K. R. Hope and B.C. Chikulo, eds., *Corruption and Development in Africa: Lessons From Country Case Studies,* London, Macmillan Press, 2000 and John M. Mbaku, *Bureaucratic and Political Corruption Africa: The Public Choice Perspective,* Malabar, FL, Krieger, 2000.

74. See Transparency International, *Global Corruption Report 2004*, London and Sterling, VA, Pluto Press, 2004, especially Part Three: 'Corruption Research'. Despite variations in attitudes towards corruption around the world, which do not always correlate with corruption levels, a survey of 40,838 people in 47 countries showed the vast majority regarded political parties as the most corrupt institution, followed in distant second place by the courts and the police. The private sector was near the bottom at 3.1 percent.

75. *Transparency International, Development in Africa: Lessons From Country Case Studies,* pp.284-6.

76. See Yemi Osinbajo, 'Human Rights, Economic Development, and the Corruption Factor', in Paul Tiyambe Zeleza and Philip J. McConnaughay, eds., *Human Rights, the Rule of Law and Development in Africa,* pp. 120128. He shows the corrosive impact of corruption in Nigeria where successive military governments, sold to the public as corrective regimes to ineffectual and corrupt civilian governments, justify their assault on human rights, beginning with civil and political rights, whose suppression creates an auspicious environment for the pillaging of public resources, using cultural relativist arguments. Before long, grand corruption sets in. Billions of dollars have been looted and wasted in a massive privatisation of public resources, a kleptocratic swindle that reached its apogee under the regime of the late Sani Abacha who reportedly embezzled $2-5 billion.

77. See Akere Muna, 'The African Union Convention against Corruption', in Transparency International, *Global Corruption Report* 2004, pp.116-21.

78. See Adewale Banjo, Africa: Still on the Anti-Graft Crusade, Africa Institute of South Africa Electronic Monograph, http://www.ai.org.za/; also see Joel Friedman, 'Budget Transparency: Assessments by civil society in Africa', in Transparency International, *Global Corruption Report 2004*, pp.330-32.

79. See Fritz Heinmann, 'Will the OECD convention stop foreign bribery?', pp.128-35 and Steve Radelet, 'Governance, corruption and the Millennium Challenge Account', pp.135-42, both in *Transparency International, Global Corruption Report* 2004.

80. The six conventions are: the Convention on the Elimination of All Forms of Racial Discrimination (28 percent of global ratifications), the International

Covenant on Economic, Social and Cultural Rights (29 percent), the International Covenant on Civil and Political Rights (29 percent), the Convention on the Elimination of All Forms of Discrimination Against Women (28 percent), the Covenant Against Torture (21 percent) and the Convention on the Rights of the Child (27 percent). See Christof Heyns and Frans Viljoen, 'The Regional Protection of Human Rights in Africa: An Overview and Evaluation', in Paul Tiyambe Zeleza and Philip J. McConnaughay, eds., *Human Rights, the Rule of Law and Development in Africa*, p.133.

81. Makau Mutua, 'African Human Rights Organisations: Questions of Context and Legitimacy', in Paul Tiyambe Zeleza and Philip J. McConnaughay, eds., *Human Rights, the Rule of Law and Development in Africa*, pp.192-197; and *Human Rights: A Political and Cultural Critique*, Philadelphia, University of Pennsylvania Press, 2002.

82. Claude Welch, 'Human Rights and Development in Africa: NGOs', Paul Tiyambe Zeleza and Philip J. McConnaughay, eds., *Human Rights, the Rule of Law and Development in Africa*, pp.199-208; and *Human Rights and NGOs: Promises and Performance*, Philadelphia, University of Pennsylvania Press, 2001.

83. Monica Kathina Juma, 'The Compromised Brokers: NGOs and Displaced Persons in east Africa', in Paul Tiyambe Zeleza and Philip J. McConnaughay, eds., *Human Rights, the Rule of Law and Development in Africa*, pp.235-55; and Monica K. Juma and Astri Suhrke, eds., *Eroding Local Capacity: International Humanitarian Action in Africa*, Uppsala, Nordiska Afrikainstitutet, 2000.

84. Jotham C. Momba, 'Civil Society and Struggles for Human Rights and Democracy in Zambia', in Paul Tiyambe Zeleza and Philip J. McConnaughay, eds., *Human Rights, the Rule of Law and Development in Africa*, pp.216-34.

85. Vincent Saldhana, 'NGOs and the Promotion of Human Rights in South Africa', in Paul Tiyambe Zeleza and Philip J. McConnaughay, eds., *Human Rights, the Rule of Law and Development in Africa*, pp.209-215.

86. See, for example, the following studies, Judith Tucker, ed., *Arab Women: New Boundaries, New Frontiers,* Indianapolis, Indiana University Press, 1993; S. Wieringa, ed., *Subversive Women: Women's Movements in Africa, Asia, Latin America and the Caribbean,* London, Zed Books, 1995; S. Rai, ed., *International Perspectives on Gender and Democratisation*, Basingstoke, Macmillan, 2000; Aili M. Tripp, 'Women's Movements and Challenges to Neopatrimonial Rule: Preliminary Observations from Africa', *Development and Change*, 32 (2001): 33-54. For one of the best collections on African gender studies, see Oyeronke Oyewumi, ed., *African Gender Studies: Theoretical Questions and Conceptual Issues*, New York, Palgrave McMillan, 2004, and for an exemplary study on the cultural and economic politics of middle class women, see Philomina E. Okeke-Ihejirika, *Negotiating Power and Privilege: Igbo Career Women in Contemporary Nigeria,* Athens, OH, Ohio University, 2004.

87. See Paul Tiyambe Zeleza, 'The Devaluation of Africa's Labour', in *Manufacturing African Studies and Crises,* Dakar, CODESRIA, 1997, pp.328-69; and Mahmood

Mamdani and Ernest Wamba-dia-Wamba, eds., *African Studies in Social Movements and Democracy,* Dakar, CODESRIA, 1995.

88. See Paul Tiyambe Zeleza, 'Imagining and Inventing the Postcolonial State in Africa', *Contours: A Journal of the African Diaspora*, 1, 1 (2003): 101-123.

89. See the brilliant short essay on African youth by Mamadou Diouf, 'Youth', in Paul Tiyambe Zeleza and Dickson Eyoh, eds., *Encyclopedia of Twentieth Century African History,* London and New York, Routledge, 2004, pp.613-19.

90. Alamin Mazrui, 'Globalism and Some Linguistic Dimensions of Human Rights in Africa', in Paul Tiyambe Zeleza and Philip J. McConnaughay, eds., *Human Rights, the Rule of Law and Development in Africa*, pp.52-70.

91. Kwesi K. Prah, 'The Idea of an African Renaissance, the Languages of the Renaissance and the Challenges of the 21st Century', in Kurimoto Eisei, ed., *Rewriting Africa: Toward Renaissance or Collapse,* Osaka, Japan, Center for Area Studies, 2001, p.189.

Chapter 6

Expanding the Human Rights Regime in Africa: Citizens, Indigenes and Exclusion in Nigeria

Jibrin Ibrahim

Introduction

There is a universal consensus developing that human rights must be continuously promoted and defended around the world. Since the adoption of international human rights instruments following the Second World War, states have made commitments to promote and defend the freedoms, rights and dignity of all human beings. The commitment of states to the protection of human rights did not develop overnight. Indeed, it has been argued that:

> Many of the states that contributed to the drafting of the Universal Declaration saw no apparent contradiction between endorsing international norms abroad and continuing oppression at home. They thought that the Universal Declaration would remain a pious set of clichés more protected in the breach than in the observance (Ignatieff 2001:6).

Once they have been articulated and adopted however, the language and norms of rights offered a new lease of life to civil rights struggles both in the colonial world and in the developed countries. Oppressed people everywhere now had an ideological and an international legal framework that encouraged and justified their struggles. Even authoritarian states were forced to make rhetorical commitments to human rights. Of course the emergence of the Cold War led to a decline in public state support to human rights norms and language but with the end of the Cold War in 1989, the trend set in motion following the Second World War regained its vigour.

This is particularly true in Africa where struggles for human rights were systematically repressed by corrupt and authoritarian regimes that for decades had no public commitment to the protection of rights. In the process, human rights and the rule of law have suffered considerably. So serious was the destruction of state institutions and basic human decency that many Africans started questioning the utility of the state for their existence and well-being. Indeed, the state became a personalised instrument for the selfish interests of those who controlled its apparatuses and in the process became a burden and even a threat to most Africans who were subjected to the use of its arbitrary powers.

The institutional kaleidoscope of human rights in Africa has improved considerably over the last few years. In addition to the African Commission on Human and Peoples' Rights and the African Charter on the Rights and Welfare of the Child, the transition from the Organisation of African Unity to the African Union has led to the decision to establish the Pan-African Parliament, the African Court of Justice, the Maputo Protocol on the Rights of African Women, the Economic, Social and Cultural Council, the African Peer Review Mechanism and the Peace and Security Council. These developments signal the acceptance by a majority of African leaders that greater opportunities for the promotion and protection of rights need to be created. As the institutional mechanisms for the promotion and protection of rights broaden, it is important that energies are focussed on making these opportunities effective in concretely improving the regime of rights of the African people.

Indeed, the multiplication of these institutions might lead to a decline in the regime of rights Africans enjoy if the question of efficacy is not addressed. For example, as these mechanisms emerge and multiply, the basic rights of Africans are being eroded in the context of growing armed conflicts that are leading to mass massacres, mass rape, massive displacement of people and a growing refugee problem. At the same time, the growing HIV/AIDS pandemic is seriously compromising the rights of Africans to health, and indeed to life. In addition, the citizenship rights of a growing number of Africans are being denied on the grounds that they are settlers rather than indigenes of the communities in which they live. This Chapter will briefly address this problem of the erosion of citizenship rights.

Resolving the Dilemma of Citizenship and Rights

The African Commission has constituted a working group on indigenous populations and communities but it is not clear what the work of the group entails in the African context. The language of indigenous communities makes sense in many parts of the world such as the Americas and Australia where the said communities have suffered greatly from the ravaging actions of settler communities. In many African countries however, the language of indigenous communities, defined as autochthons, has been used to deprive other indigenous Africans of their citizenship rights. The Banyamulenge problem in the Democratic Republic of Congo, the Ivoirité politics in Côte d'Ivoire, the Berber problem in North Africa, the crisis of non-Arabs in the Sudan, the problems associated with 'makwerekwere' (foreigners) in South Africa and the settler/indigene problem in Nigeria all pose serious problems concerning the erosion of citizenship rights in Africa which the emerging institutions seem to disregard as serious problems of rights and freedoms.

Our argument is that in essence, the growth of formal democracy and citizenship rights is being checkmated by complex identity conflicts in which rights and entitlements of some groups are being whittled down by other groups who are able to use the ideology of difference and xenophobic tools to reduce the citizenship rights of the other so that their own can be enhanced. There are developing in large sections of Africa rapid processes through which social and political actors at the national and transnational levels are constructing hierarchies of citizenship that reduce the rights of other Africans. The result is a growing gap between sets of citizens with full rights and others with subaltern rights. We shall illustrate this argument with the Nigerian example.

The Nigerian Case

Nigeria is a multi-ethnic and multi-religious country inhabited by about 470 ethnic groups. These groups are not only distinguished by language, customs and myths of origin, but they also vary in size, power and influence, making Nigeria a classic example of a country with unequal ethnic relations. The country is also marked by cultural, geographical and religious heterogeneity, and above all, by a long history of migrations which makes settlers of virtually all Nigerians. It is in recognition of this fact that the architects of modern Nigeria, especially the early nationalists, settled for a federal system of government as a mechanism for coping with problems associated with the deep ethnic and religious divisions that exist.

Over the years, as part of the efforts to cope with the problems of a multi-ethnic society and to accommodate differences in the true spirit of 'unity in diversity', policy makers have adopted a number of measures. Some of these include the creation of new states and local governments and the entrenchment of certain provisions in the constitution to guarantee fairness and equity such as the 'federal character' principle enshrined in the 1979 Constitution of the Federal Republic of Nigeria. Consociational measures of this type which involve some elements of power sharing and a deliberate attempt to regulate competition and access to resources, as a means of protecting groups considered to be relatively disadvantaged, are not alien to federal systems.

However, in the Nigerian context this has had a boomerang effect in the sense that the problems which they are meant to solve are instead reinforced. Consociational measures or related policies that emphasise 'ethnic arithmetic' are meant to moderate the divisive nature of ethnic and regional competition for power and opportunities. Unfortunately, in the Nigerian situation, especially due to the manner in which they have been implemented, the result is the heightening of ethnic tension and ill feelings. A good example of such measures which has created more problems than it was intended to solve is the provision in the Constitution regarding the implementation of the federal character principle which limits existing opportunities to those defined as 'indigenes'. The consequence is that millions of Nigerians who find themselves residents in places other than where they can claim 'indigeneity' or where they are accepted as 'indigenes' are labelled as 'strangers' and 'settlers'. Nigerians so defined are subjected to all kinds of exclusions and deprivations, which differentiate them from the 'natives', and members of the 'host communities'. What this does immediately is to place obstacles in the path of Nigerians who are so labelled to the enjoyment of their full citizenship rights, which are formally guaranteed in the elaborate provisions in the Constitution regarding the fundamental rights of citizens. This outcome completely blocks possibilities of deepening civil and political rights of individuals and groups in the country as those people stigmatised as settlers are perpetually denied their civil and human rights.

The Mamdani Principles: The Indigene/Settler Antipodes

Professor Mahmoud Mamdani is one of the leading African intellectuals who has closely examined the concepts of indigene/settler and put forward a number of principles that are germane to the Nigerian case. There are three main principles that can be derived from his numerous publications on the subject:

(i) The two categories—indigenes/settlers—are interdependent as the one defines the other. Settlers exist because some people have succeeded in defining themselves as indigenes in order to exclude others who they have defined as settlers.

(ii) Settlers are not defined by immigration, as virtually all African groups and peoples have migrated over time. The concept of settler is a political definition attributed on the basis of conquest, state power and law—customary and modern.

(iii) The settler can never become an indigene because the basis of the differentiation is the denial of civic citizenship through a political imposition of a permanent and exclusionary tribal or religious label.

This means that the historical methods of gaining citizenship through migration and immersion in the language, culture and norms of the new community through time are excluded. The implication of these principles is that as long as we continue with the affirmation of the indigene/settler divide, our dreams of deepening democratic governance will remain elusive. When we look at the most spectacular cases of indigene/settler conflicts in Nigeria in recent times, the negative effects of this politics of permanent exclusion become obvious. The longstanding fratricidal war between the Hausa and the Kataf (Atyab) in Zango-Kataf in southern Kaduna, the protracted Jukun/Tiv conflict in Wukari, and the Chamba and Kuteb conflict in Taraba as well as the deadly confrontation in Nasarawa between the Bassa and Ebira are all cases of this political decision to permanently deny citizenship to the other, defined as a settler.

This is true even in situations where anthropological evidence suggests that the two groups are of the same ethnic origin, as the examples of the Ife/Modakeke crisis in which both groups are Yoruba, and the Umuleri/Aguleri conflict in which both groups are Igbo, have clearly shown. The sheer weight of human tragedy that has accompanied these conflicts in terms of the death of thousands of people, the destruction of property and the displacement of population draw attention not only to the security threat they pose to the state, but the potential danger they pose to the country's nascent democracy. Although the basis of the crisis of citizenship is in Nigeria's colonial and post-colonial history, and the conflicts arising from it had been there before the recent return to democratic rule, the general expectation is that democracy should provide the most congenial environment for finding lasting and enduring solutions to the problem. Surprisingly, this has not been the case as has been clearly borne out by the numerous examples of communal violence and ethno-religious conflicts that have appeared to exert enormous stress on the new democratic experiment in the country.

There has been a steady rise in communal tensions and conflicts since the introduction of the indigeneity clause into Nigerian public law through the 1979 Constitution. Since then, numerous cabals of local political elites have devoted considerable resources and time to defining themselves as indigenes, natives and autochthons, while defining others in their communities as settlers, migrants and strangers. With the return of democratic rule in 1999, there has been an explosion rather than a reduction of political and religious conflicts. As the number of conflicts and the death toll and destruction of property increases, the strains on democratic governance and indeed political stability have been enormous.

On 19 May 2004, the Nigerian Senate and House of Representatives voted massively to give validity to a state of emergency that had been declared by President Olusegun Obasanjo in Plateau State. The President had suspended the State Governor, Deputy Governor and House of Assembly for six months, citing the rights conferred on him to do so by section 305 of the Constitution. For the declaration to enter into force, the President needed the support of at least two-thirds of the National Assembly, and he got it.

The reason the President gave for taking such a drastic action was the breakdown of law and order in Plateau state and its ripple effects with more violence or the threat of violence growing in neighbouring states such as Bauchi,

Nassarawa, Taraba, Kano, Gombe, Kaduna and Benue. The President also cited the state governor's lack of 'Interest, desire, commitment, credibility and capacity to promote reconciliation, rehabilitation, forgiveness, peace, harmony and stability' (President Obasanjo's Address to the Nation, 18 May 2004).

The Plateau state governor, Joshua Dariye, had indeed been making incendiary remarks questioning the citizenship of the Hausa-Fulani Muslim population in Plateau state, whom he refers to as settlers, as the following quotations indicate:

> Jos, capital of Plateau state is owned by the natives. Simple. Every Hausa man in Jos is a settler whether he likes it or not.

> Even if I spend 150 years in Bukuru, I cannot become an indigene of Du.

> It is an Al-qaeda agenda to bring down Plateau state... The ulama were chased out of Kaduna during the Babangida regime. If they were so good why were they sent out of Kaduna? And they came to form their headquarters in Jos. ('What Dariye Did Say', *Weekly Trust*, 15 May, 2004).

With this type of encouragement from their state Governor, the 'indigenes/natives' of Plateau state, previously known as a haven of peace, have since 2001 been engaged in a series of bloody clashes with the Muslim Hausa-Fulani minority population, thousands of whom have been killed. While some of the Hausa-Fulani are relatively recent settlers with memories of their homeland, many have been in the region for hundreds of years and have no memory of a home other than the Plateau.

The 1999 Constitution, Citizenship and Rights

The provisions on Citizenship and Fundamental Rights in the 1999 Constitution of the Federal Republic of Nigeria are contained in chapters Three and Four respectively. The most salient provisions are as follows. Chapter Three, which focuses on citizenship, contains provisions relating to citizenship by birth, registration and naturalisation in addition to provisions relating to dual citizenship, renunciation and deprivation of citizenship. Chapter Four provides a detailed checklist of the fundamental rights, which are the entitlements of Nigerian citizens. These include the right to life, the right to the dignity of the human person, the right to personal liberty as well as the right to fair hearing and the right to family and private life. Others are: the right to freedom of thought, conscience and religion, the right to freedom of expression and the press, the right to freedom from discrimination, the right to freedom of movement and the right to acquire and own immovable property.

As can be seen from the above, there is nothing to suggest that the enjoyment of these rights may entail any discriminatory application. A reading of other relevant provisions of the Constitution lends credence to the point that the promotion of the political objectives of national integration and cohesion are of central constitutional concern. For instance, Chapter Two, Section 14 (3) provides as follows:

> The composition of the Government of the Federation or any of its agencies and the conduct of its affairs shall be carried out in such a manner as to reflect the Federal Character of Nigeria and the need to promote national unity, and also to command national loyalty, thereby ensuring that there shall be no predominance of persons from a few states or from a few ethnic or other sectional groups in that government or any of its agencies.

Section 14 (4) calls on the states and local governments in the country to implement the federal character principle. Furthermore, Section 15 (3) of the same chapter states that: 'For the purpose of promoting national integration, it shall be the duty of the state to (a) provide adequate facilities for and encourage free mobility of people, goods and services throughout the Federation; (b) secure full residence rights for every citizen in all parts of the Federation'. It is also instructive to note that the Constitution allows anyone to contest elections anywhere he or she wishes, as indigeneity is not a requirement for election to such bodies as the Senate, the Federal House of Representatives, or the State Houses of Assembly. The 1999 Constitution goes further to encourage 'inter-marriage among persons from different places of origin, or of different religious, ethnic or linguistic associations or ties' in Section 15 (3c).

What seem problematic however are the constitutional provisions regarding the implementation of the federal character principle. The issues of federal character and the quota system have their origins in the recommendations of the Constitution Drafting Committee (CDC) in 1976, which had reasoned that there was a need to give every ethnic group in the country a sense of belonging. At the risk of repetition, Section 14 (3) of the 1979 Constitution which captures the reasoning of the CDC defined the objective of federal character as ensuring that the

> Composition of the Government of the Federation or any of its agencies, and the conduct of its affairs, shall be carried out in such a manner as to reflect the federal character of Nigeria, and the need to promote national unity, and also to command loyalty, thereby ensuring that there shall be no predominance of persons from a few states or form a few ethnic groups or other sectional groups in that government or any of its agencies.

However, this provision has made it more convenient for the aspiring politicians and ambitious elite to hang on to birth and descent as criteria to determine citizenship.

In this sense the most problematic aspect of the issue of citizenship derives from the way in which the 'indigeneity' clause in the 1979 constitution has tended to legitimise discriminatory practices against Nigerians who reside within a state which is 'not their own'. According to the Constitution, 'indigeneship' of a state is conferred on a person whose parents or grandparents were members of a community indigenous to a particular state. We shall return to the specific ways in which the issue of 'indigenes' and 'natives' has provided practical obstacles to the implementation of the rights conferred on Nigerians by their citizenship of the Nigerian state.

The 1999 Constitution, apparently in recognition of the controversy generated by the 'indigeneity' clause in the 1979 Constitution, has no definitional clause. However, the Constitution still requires the implementation of the federal character principle. The interpretation of Section 147 regarding the appointment of Ministers shows clearly that the notion of 'indigeneity' has not been expunged from the Constitution. It states: 'Provided that in giving effect to the provisions aforesaid the President shall appoint at least one Minister from each state, who shall be an indigene of such state.' What this means in effect is that Nigerians who cannot prove that they are indigenes of a state cannot be appointed to such positions no matter the length of their residence.

The implication is that a tension exists between the formal provisions in the Constitution regarding citizenship and fundamental rights on the one hand, and the practical application of these rights because of the reality of difference introduced by the politically generated dichotomy between elites seeking to increase their power by defining themselves as 'indigenes' and 'natives' through the definition of others as 'settlers' and strangers. These categories have tended to undermine the very essence of Nigerian citizenship in the sense that one is not really a citizen of Nigeria, but only a citizen of the place in which one is 'indigenous'. The result is that it has created a multi-layered system of citizenship as follows:

(i) Those most privileged are those who belong to the indigenous communities of the state in which they reside.

(ii) Those citizens who are indigenes of other states are less favoured.

(iii) The least favoured are those citizens who are unable to prove that they belong to a community indigenous to any state in Nigeria.

(iv) Women who are married to men from states other their own are in a dilemma, as they can neither be accepted in their 'states of origin' nor in those of their husbands.

In addition to these problems, it is particularly difficult for migrants in rural locations to have access to farmlands because indigeneity implies membership of the local ethnic community. The system gives undue power to the traditional authorities and power brokers in regulating access to land understood as the collective, natural possession of the ethnic group. We shall further analyse the specific ways in which the categories 'indigenes' and 'settlers' are at conflict with the idea and practice of national citizenship in Nigeria and how the political crisis which has arisen from the issue play into Nigeria's population dynamics.

The categories of 'indigenes', 'settlers' and 'natives' are social and political constructions of the Nigerian power elite in their search for legitimacy within the local community/state and their quest for access to power and resources. In the ordinary meaning of the words, 'indigenes' and 'natives' simply refer to a region or country of birth—aborigines and autochthones. In countries such as the United States of America and Australia with a unique history of conquest of indigenous populations such as the native Indians (United States) and Aborigines (Australia), it may be more or less straightforward to use these categories to delineate between the natives and conquerors or settlers. Such a usage does not make sense in Nigeria given the country's peculiar history of state formation, constant migration of people and population shifts in the period prior to and after colonisation.

Indeed, a major study of our region, *West African Long Term Perspective Study* (1994) undertaken by the African Development Bank and the Club du Sahel, revealed that West Africa had become a region of migrants and settlers with two profound modes of migration that had completely transformed the population dynamics of the region. The first was movement from the Sahel to the middle belt and forest zones, which produced extremely cosmopolitan towns and cities. The second was movement from rural to urban areas, which turned the region into an urban majority zone. By 1990, almost fifty percent of the people in Nigeria had moved from rural to urban settlements in the post-independence period. When we factor in the pre-colonial migration patterns with the current trends, it becomes clear that the great majority of Nigerians, and indeed West Africans, are settlers, not indigenes, of the places in which they live and work.

In spite of this fact, self-declared indigenes and natives are pitched against settlers in deadly confrontations over access to local power, resources and questions of identity. These labels have become potent instruments for the negative mobilisation of peoples' sentiments and feelings in ways that undermine the national political objectives of integration and the evolution of a harmonious political community. Given the peculiar history of Nigeria just alluded to, every group resorts to history in order to prove its claim to the indigeneity of some specific local political space. It is this issue which is the major source of communal violence and ethno-religious conflicts in both urban and rural Nigeria.

Citizenship is applicable to a person endowed with full political and civil rights in a state. It defines the political, civil and social rights attributable to the individual as a member of a state. In the modern state, the acquisition of citizenship can be through birth (the law of blood), law of place, and through naturalisation. The notion of citizenship was developed in the context of the bourgeois revolution and the ascendancy of liberalism. The idea evolved with the collapse of feudalism and the medieval state, which limited the rights, and freedom of the individual. The rights and freedom which were won and secured with the birth of the modern state therefore transformed the individual from subject to citizen. Citizenship is thus defined in terms of the special status granted by the state to its members and expresses at the formal level the equality of all before the state.

In the contemporary Nigerian context, the discourse on citizenship and the application of citizens' rights often generates political tension and violence because it is intricately tied into the issue of ethnic identity, ethnicity and religion. This is the case in so far as indigeneity is tied to membership of a particular local ethnic community.

There are three reasons why ethnicity is problematic in relation to the discourse on identity and citizenship. Ethnic identity is not a fixed form of identity. Although it may appear as a natural community distinguished by a common language, ancestry and myth of origin as well as a common consciousness of being one in relation to others, it is not a static category. It is subject to frequent reconstitution and redefinition. It is interesting to note for example that from what the British colonialist identified as ninety ethnic groups in the early part of the last century, the number of ethnic groups in Nigeria has expanded to over 470. Ethnic identity has had a constant history of redefinition, re-composition and reconstitution.

Second, Nigeria is characterised by a state of unequal ethnic relations reflecting an intensely unequal competition for state resources. The most important resource is state power itself, particularly its coercive and resource allocating elements. Finally, there have been historical processes of integration and migration of various communal groups that were in place before the intrusion of colonialism. This often makes it difficult to establish which group can claim the 'native' or 'indigenous' status of a place at the expense of others.

What all this means is that the ethnic category on which the definition of citizenship hinges is a very fluid one. It partly explains why the political disputations arising from contradictory notions of citizenship often lead to conflict and violence. In some instances, the groups in conflict over such claims are not necessarily from different ethnic groups. The contesting groups may thus be sub-ethnic communities of the same ethnic group, as is the case of the recurrent Ife/Modakeke conflict.

What needs to be emphasised is the fact that after several decades of colonial capitalist development, and the tremendous expansion of infrastructure across the country as well as increasing cultural diffusion, Nigeria cannot simply be reduced to a mere geographical expression. These conflicts relate to the crisis of citizenship in the sense in which groups in conflict deploy or even twist history in the contestation of identity by using it to establish 'indigeneity' over a particular political space—which could be a state or a local government area. In most of the recorded cases located within semi-urban and rural locations, attempts are often made to establish 'indigeneity' over a local government or any other local political and economic space. A few illustrations will shed some light.

The use of the history of migration, early patterns of settlement or local history about patterns of power and domination among the different ethnic groups in establishing 'indigenous' claims are evident in virtually all the cases. On the Mambilla Plateau, the series of attacks in the early 1980s on the Banso and Kamba by the Mambilla hinged on this conception of citizenship. The Mambilla who laid indigenous claim over the entire Mambilla Plateau do so precisely on the historical claim that their settlement predated the arrival of other ethnic groups such as the Fulani, Banso and Kamba. For the Banso and the Kamba whose presence on the Plateau is more or less recent, the bulk of them having arrived in the post-Second World War period, it is a lot easier to attract the label of 'alien'. It is in this context that one understands the basis of exclusion to which the so-called indigenous group seeks to subject the 'stranger' elements.

The situation in Zango-Kataf is fairly unique and more complex as centuries of interaction between the Hausa on the one hand, and communal groups such as Bajju and Kataf (Atyab) on the other, have failed to produce the basis of a more enduring harmonious community life. In this respect the situation differs from other cases where the adoption of the Islamic religion and intermarriage have attenuated the level of social and cultural distance between 'immigrant' Hausa population and the 'host' communities. What one finds in the Zango-Kataf area of southern Kaduna is the tendency for ethnic boundaries to remain impervious to social and cultural exchanges such as marriages across ethnic and religious boundaries.

The representation made to the Cudjoe Commission by the Kataf following the violence of February 1992 largely hinged on the claim that the land belonged to the Kataf who accommodated Hausa immigrants on generous terms. By the traditional system of land holding, the Kataf claim, such land in principle should revert to the original owners. However, this historical claim to indigeneity is contradicted by the position of the Hausa community who claimed centuries of effective residency.

Similar claims by 'indigenous' groups aimed at excluding 'strangers' appear to be central in the communal conflicts between the Kuteb and Chamba in the Takum Local Government Area of Taraba state and the unending circle of communal clashes in Nasarawa involving the Ebira, Bassa and Gbagyi. These cases illustrate the enormous difficulty of resorting to history to resolve the contest over identity. The difficulty arises from the fact that there can be no such a thing as eternal historical facts. There is the tendency for facts to be either carefully selected or for the same set of facts to be subjected to conflicting interpretations.

Take the Kuteb/Chamba conflict for example. Although a number of ethnic groups such as Hausa, Jukun, Kuteb and Chamba are found in the Takum area, the major contest has been between the Kuteb and Chamba. From the available historical evidence, both Kuteb and Chamba had taken effective residency of the area around Takum prior to the colonial intervention. However, in the present context of contestation over the 'ownership' of Takum, each of the two communal groups has resorted to different accounts of the past to bolster its claim.

The Chamba account, which is strongly challenged by the Kuteb, appeared to have been the version initially accepted by the colonial authorities. It puts forward the Chamba as a warrior group, who conquered and displaced the more numerous Kuteb around 1830. The Kuteb on the other hand, who make a strong historical claim over the area in addition to being the most populous, deny the claim by the Chamba to have conquered them at any point in history, and even cite colonial records in support of their position. Instead it is argued that the Chamba whom they claim migrated from Cameroon were given a place to settle by the Kuteb.

The rule of the Kuteb in Takum was later codified by the government of the Northern region in 1963. The situation was, however, reversed in 1975 when the Chamba, apparently using their influence in the military government that followed the collapse of the First Republic, managed to persuade the then Benue Plateau state government to amend the 1963 law. The amendment ensured the eligibility of two Chamba families to contest and ascend to the Ukwe throne, increased the representation of the Chamba and Jukun on the King's Selection Committee to three, while reducing that of the Kuteb to two—thus ensuring advantage for the Chamba.

In 1976, a riot broke out between the Chamba and Kuteb in Takum. The cause of the riot was the alleged manipulation of electoral wards by the Secretary of Takum local government, a Chamba, in order to give electoral advantage to Chamba contestants. The victory of a Chamba candidate where the Kuteb constitute the majority was not acceptable to the latter. Some of the allegations were later confirmed by a government panel, which had been set up to investigate the communal disturbances. However, renewed violence between the two communal groups has its roots in the process of democratising the local government, which commenced in 1987. The numerical strength of the Kuteb had conferred on them electoral advantage in the elections that had been organised since then until the outbreak of violence in 1997. Although it would appear on the surface as tension between democratisation and multi-ethnic existence, it has a deeper basis in contestation over identity and for control of local power and resources.

The crisis in Ife/Modakeke is fuelled by the same dynamics despite the fact that it pitches one sub-Yoruba group against another. The Modakeke, who are believed to be refugees from the Yoruba wars that followed the breakdown of the Old Oyo Empire, are thought to have come from Oyo. Political tension and conflicts leading to the death of thousands of people has characterised the relationship between the two communal groups over the last two decades. The reasons for the conflict between the two communities seem to have been generated by disagreements over the creation of new local government areas. It goes to show that the question of access to local power is at the core of the unending conflict between the two communities.

In putting forward proposals for ensuring harmony and a just balance between constitutional provisions on citizenship and rights and their practical applications, three pertinent observations are necessary.

First, there is a clear dilemma between individual and group rights in Nigeria's constitutional history. The basic foundation of a liberal democratic order is the rights and freedom attached to the individual as a legal entity. Citizens' rights are primarily conceived as individual rights. At the same time, given the existence of deep divisions in the society along ethnic, religious and regional lines, giving rise to 'minority' and 'majority' identities, there is also the need to provide constitutional guarantees for disadvantaged groups—as the 'federal character' and 'quota' provisions have sought to do. But there appears to be a greater obsession with group rights to the detriment of individual rights in the Nigerian debate.

Second, the notion of 'indigeneity' entrenched in the 1979 Constitution is at variance with Nigerian public law tradition. It has seriously compromised the definition of citizenship in the Independence Constitution which conferred citizenship on all those persons whose communities had been in the Nigerian territory on 1 October 1960. The indigeneity struggle is now leading to the questioning of the citizenship of groups who have been in the Nigerian area even before the colonisation of the country in 1900.

Third, the result of these phenomena is that a significant number of Nigerians are being excluded from access to certain rights and privileges conferred by public institutions. They include employment in the public service, government contracts, admission in schools, access to privileges such as scholarships, training opportunities, health facilities and even access to vital resources such as land and water (for farming, grazing and fishing). It is vital for the political health of the country that the constitutional provisions that have been used to buttress discrimination against other Nigerians be addressed with urgency.

Citizenship and Constitutional Reform Issues

The concept of 'indigene' should be completely deleted from the Nigerian Constitution because it produces a majority of losers rather than of winners. Since the majority of Nigerians are settlers, there is a need to address the issue of residency rights for Nigerian citizens in the places where they live and work. There should be a constitutional provision which provides that a Nigerian citizen who has resided continuously for a period of five years in any state of the federation and performs his/her civic duties, including paying taxes, shall be entitled to all the rights and privileges of the state. This will be in accord with the practice in most federations, and will strengthen efforts at national integration. Should this provision be accepted, it would mean that anybody who had spent five years in a state could be eligible for any political appointment and enjoy access to all the rights and privileges currently restricted to indigenes.

Given the numerous problems suffered by women who have married outside their states of origin, there is also a need for the specific protection of the citizenship rights of women. The Constitution should state in express terms that a woman married to any man from a state other than her own should have the right to choose which of the states to claim as her own. Similarly, there is a need to amend Section 26 (2) (a) such as to give foreign men married to Nigerians the opportunity to acquire citizenship, a right foreign women married to Nigerian men already enjoy.

At a more general level, it would be useful to devise means for the promotion of social citizenship in the country. The provisions on social and economic rights, which are not justiciable, should be made so. This is important because poverty and the lack of access of most Nigerians to the basic means of livelihood are the primary cause of much if not most of communal strife currently prevalent in Nigeria. Of course the Nigerian state does not currently have the capacity to provide all the needs of the population. What is being proposed is a constitutional device similar to the one in the South African Constitution that would compel the government to provide for social needs to the extent of its capacity. The South African constitutional provision also involves the entrenchment of independent commissions to monitor the implementation of these social and economic rights.

References

African Development Bank/Club du Sahel, 1994, *West African Long-Term Perspective Study: Population,* Land and Development, Paris.

Centre for Law Enforcement Education, 2000, *Law Enforcement Review,* July-September.

Citizen's Forum for Constitutional Reform, 2002, 'Memorandum Submitted to the Presidential Committee on Provisions and Practice of Citizenship and Rights in Nigeria'.

Citizen's Forum for Constitutional Reform, 2002, 'Memorandum Submitted to the Presidential Committee on National Security in Nigeria'.

Citizen's Forum for Constitutional Reform, 2001, 'The Position of the Citizen's Forum for Constitutional Reform on the Review of the 1999 Constitution of the Federal Republic of Nigeria', Lagos.

Ibrahim, Jibrin, 2001, 'Civil Society, Religion and Democracy in Contemporary Africa', in B. Beckman et al., *Civil Society and Authoritarianism in the Third World*, Stockholm, PODSU, Department of Political Science, University of Stockholm.

Ibrahim, Jibrin, ed., 1997, *Expanding Democratic Space in Nigeria*, Dakar, CODESRIA.

Ignatieff, Michael, 2001, *Human Rights as Politics and Idolatory,* Princeton, Princeton University Press.

Lindbolm, T., 1999, 'Article 1', in Alfredsson, G and Eide, A., eds., *The Universal Declaration of Human Rights: A Common Standard of Achievement,* The Hague, Martinus Nighoff Publishers.

Mamdani, Mahmood, 1998, 'When Does a Settler Become a Native: Reflections of the Colonial Roots of Citizenship in Equatorial and South Africa', Inaugural Lecture, University of Cape Town.

Okoth-Ogendo, H.W.O., 1996, 'Constitutionalism without Constitutions: The Challenge of Reconstruction of the State in Africa', in Zoethout et al., eds., *Constitutionalism in Africa: A Quest for Autochthonous Principles,* Rotterdam, Sanders Institute.

Okoye, Festus, ed., 2000, *Victims: Impact of Religious and Ethnic Conflicts on Women and Children in Northern Nigeria,* Kaduna, Human Rights Monitor.

Preus, U.K., 1994, 'Constitutional Power-making for the New Polity', in Rosenfeld, M., ed., *Constitutionalism, Identity, Difference and Legitimacy: Theoretical Perspectives,* Durham, Duke University Press.

Rosenfeld, Michael, ed., 1994, *Constitutionalism, Identity, Difference and Legitimacy: Theoretical Perspectives,* Durham, Duke University Press.

Shyllon, F. and Obasanjo, O., 1980, *The Demise of the Rule of Law in Nigeria Under Military Rule: Two Points of View,* Ibadan, Institute of African Studies.

Snrech, Serge, 1994, *Pour préparer l'avenir de l'Afrique de l'Ouest: une vision a l'horizon 2020,* Paris, OCDE/BAD.

Chapter 7

Strengthening the African Commission on Human and Peoples' Rights: Procedures, Mechanisms, Partnerships and Implementation[1]

Frans Viljoen

Introduction

The African Charter on Human and Peoples' Rights ('African Charter'), adopted in 1981, entered into force on 21 October 1986. Today, all the members of the African Union are party to the African Charter. The African Charter provides for rights and duties, and establishes a supervisory mechanism, the African Commission on Human and Peoples' Rights ('African Commission'). As the African Commission started operating in 1987, it has now been in existence for seventeen years. The Commission's activities therefore provide a wealth of experience that justifies retrospection. In 1998, the OAU Assembly of Heads of State and Government (OAU Assembly) adopted the Protocol to the African Charter, establishing an African Court of Human and Peoples' Rights (Protocol). On 25 January 2004, the Protocol entered into force, when fifteen ratifications had been acquired.[2] Reform of the Commission's work therefore has to be informed by the likelihood of a Court supplementing its protective mandate in the future.

As the African Commission exists in a broad political context, much of its functioning depends on its relationship and interaction with state parties and the African Union. While acknowledging the importance of these macro-level determinants, this paper focuses on the functioning of the Commission and its Secretariat as such, that is, at the micro level. As will become clear, it is my view that the activities and mandate of the Commission may be strengthened significantly by addressing concerns arising at this level.

Procedures

Communications

Problematic aspects and suggestions to strengthen the Commission

(a) Small number of communications submitted

The number of individual communications submitted against state parties, broken down per year, is as follows:

Year	Number submitted
1988	9[3]
1989	5
1990	8
1991	12
1992	22
1993	24[4]
1994	16
1995	3
1996	14
1997	14[5]
1998	15
1999	10[6]
2000	2
2001	8
2002	12[7]

This is a total of 174 communications over 15 years, or an average of 11.6 communications per year. According to the numbering system adopted by the Secretariat, each new communication is assigned a number. Towards the end of 2002, this numbered 252/2002. The apparent discrepancy between the two totals (252 and 174) can be explained by the fact that communications against non-state parties (23 communications) are excluded. Also, in two particular instances, numerous communications that are closely linked in time and substance have been taken together as one communication. The two major instances are:

Communications 109/93 to 126/93 (18 communications), one complaint submitted against a number of countries, found to be inadmissible; and Communications 164/97 to 196/97 (32 communications), the Mauritanian Widows' case.

All AU member states have been state parties to the Charter since January 1999. Although not entirely accurate, in that some parties only ratified the Charter some time after 1986, these figures represent an average total of three cases submitted per country, over 15 years. Given the kinds of human rights violations that had been taking place in Africa over this period, the question must be asked why so few applications have been made to the Commission.

The reason may lie in some of the issues discussed below, such as delay in finalisation, the ineffectiveness of remedies ordered by the Commission, and the lack of adequate publicity.

Suggestions:

- In a very real sense, the Commission is its own biggest potential promotional tool—once its effectiveness is illustrated through its work and given wide visibility, more communications are bound to follow.

- The non-submission of communications indicates a lack of awareness of the *African Charter* and Commission. The general visibility of the Commission should therefore be increased. The two major formal promotional tools of the Commission are the publications, the *Review of the Commission* and the *Bulletin*. Both of these appear irregularly—the last issue of the Review was dated 2000, and the last issue of the Bulletin covered the period July to December 2000. Their distribution is also very limited. The timely diffusion of all such material on the web-site should be encouraged.

- The Commission's web-site should be given more prominence in the Secretariat's work, and should be kept updated, with communications in an accessible and user-friendly format.

- The most important time to focus attention on the work of the Commission is during its sessions, and when the *Annual Activity Report* is adopted. While the Secretariat has been quite successful in focussing attention on the work of the Commission where sessions take place, the opportunity to focus on the much richer information contained in Annual Activity Reports has been lost. Accessible press release should be made contemporaneous to the release of the Annual Activity Report.

(b) Unnecessary delays in finalising communications

Many commentators have pointed to delays in the finalisation of communications as a factor seriously inhibiting the work of the Commission. The extent of the rate of finalisation can be brought home best by stating that of the 174 communications submitted so far, only 102 have been finalised. One of the worst examples of delay is that in Communication 73/92, Diakité v Gabon. This communication is dated 10 April 1992, and was disposed of finally on 11 May 2000—more than eight years later. One of the main reasons for this lengthy period of delay is an attempt at amicable settlement, which can hardly be ascribed to any party alone.

The number of communications finalised per year, either resulting in a finding of inadmissibility or a final decision on the merits, is as follows:

Year	No. finalised
1988	1
1989	2
1990	2
1991	0
1992	1
1993	8
1994	14
1995	14
1996	5
1997	4
1998	3
1999	10
2000	17
2001	5
2002,	31st sess. 3
2002,	32nd sess. 0
2003,	33rd sess. 10
2003,	34th sess. At least 3

Given that two sessions had taken place per year, these figures translate to an average of about three communications being finalised per session (or six per year). It is noticeable that although the Commission finalised far less than this average during its sessions in 2001 and in 2002, this disconcerting trend seems to be reversed in 2003.

Delay is caused by a myriad of factors, and may be attributed to the Commission, its Secretariat, the respondent states and the complainants or their lawyers. It seems that most of the delaying factors are attributable to the Commission: the distinction between seizure and admissibility; the injudicious joiner of communications; lack of prioritising the consideration of communications during sessions; the failure to adopt a report subsequent to its mission in respect of Nigeria.

The distinction between the 'seizure' and 'admissibility' phases leads to an inevitable delay of about six months. It is not clear what purpose seizure has. In fact, the Commission has in all the 102 cases finalised so far decided to be seized of the matter. In one instance, the decision indicates disagreement about whether the Commission should be seized, without providing any more details.[8] This distinction has been explained as a formal 'acknowledgement of receipt'. Such a practice is not required though, as this is already done by the Secretariat. Seizure may have made sense when the Commission started dealing with communications and many were submitted against non-state parties. However, the Rules of Procedure now provide that no such communication should be placed before the Commission (meaning that these complaints are not considered to be 'communications' for the purpose of the African Charter).[9] The Secretariat should ensure that everything placed before the Commission meets the threshold of being a 'communication', containing the particulars set out in the Rules of Procedure.[10]

Another cause for delay is the joinder of communications that are submitted at different times, one after the other. A case against Zaire provides an example.[11] The Commission received a communication in 1989, related to torture and indefinite detention near Kisuka, on 19 January 1989. This was followed by communications received in October 1990, in the 'summer of 1991' and in April 1993. The complaints had in common that they all alleged serious violations of human rights against the government of Zaire. The final decision in this matter came in March 1996. Although there must be room for the joinder of related communications against a state party,[12] it is clear that such a step should be taken with caution. In this particular case, the delay in respect of the initial communication was seven years and two months. The same happened in respect of a series of communications against Rwanda, submitted between 1989 and 1993.[13] The case was only finalised in October 1996, just under seven years after the first case has been submitted.

On numerous occasions, consideration of communications has been postponed due to lack of time.[14] This is a reflection of the lack of priority accorded to the most pertinent function of the Commission. Although the session is organised by the Secretariat, the Commission has to take full responsibility for the final agenda and the time allocated to consideration of communications.

The Commission's inability to finalise its report pursuant to the mission undertaken to Nigeria (7–17 March 1997) caused delay in the finalisation of communications against Nigeria. For example: Communication 102/93, Constitutional Rights Project and another v Nigeria, was received on 29 July 1993, and was finally decided on 31 October 1998—a delay of five years and three months. This communication was first postponed awaiting the result of the mission to Nigeria, but thereafter pending the discussion (and adoption) of the mission report. This report was in fact never adopted, and the eventual decision on the merits does not make any reference whatsoever to the mission.

Delays are further enhanced by the Secretariat. When the Commission cannot decide the issue of admissibility on the material before it, the complainant or state party may within three months supply additional information.[15] Similarly, once the Commission has admitted a case, the respondent state is allowed three months to respond, or to remedy the situation.[16] In applying these Rules, the Secretariat has not always been consistent and has allowed states too much leeway.[17]

Delay is sometimes due to the conduct of states. In the already-mentioned communication against Zaire, the Commission decided to send a mission 'in order to create a dialogue'.[18] Such visits require the prior consent of the state, which was not forthcoming. Part of the delay in this case was occasioned by the lack of co-operation of the state. According to the decision against Rwanda mentioned above, the Commission attempted unsuccessfully to send a mission to Rwanda between 1990 and 1995. Even in respect of countries to which missions have successfully been undertaken, such as Nigeria, the state contributed significantly to delays by creating obstacles to and uncertainties about the mission.

In some instances, at least part of the delay may be attributed to the complainants or their lawyers. Apart from the fact that the mission report was awaited in respect of Communication 102/93, mentioned above, on one occasion, the case was postponed 'pending the submission of scholarly articles and court case (sic) by the complainant'.[19]

One of the most recent cases decided by the Commission illustrates the problem of delay and the confluence of factors causing delay. In Communication 155/96, The Social and Economic Rights Centre and another v Nigeria (SERAC case), the delay between the receipt of the communication and the finalisation thereof was five years and seven months (March 1996 to October 2001). The delay may to a very limited extent be attributed to the state party, through its obstruction to the mission to Nigeria. The complainant contributed to some part to delay, as one postponement was made 'pending the receipt of written submissions from the Complainants'.[20] The delays mostly emanate from the Commission itself—the discussion of the Nigeria mission report and 'lack of time' are cited as reasons why the case was postponed on two occasions.[21] More disconcerting, and more difficult to interpret, are the numerous unexplained postponements, which only make reference to a decision to 'postpone' or 'defer' the final consideration.[22]

Suggestions:

- Electronic submissions of communications should be encouraged. The Secretariat should request electronic versions of communications even when hard copies have been submitted. Electronic correspondence will speed up the process of communication with parties to the case, it will make it more difficult (if not impossible) for states to allege that they had not received correspondence, and it will ease considerably the process of providing Commissioners with texts to enable them to prepare cases before sessions.

- The seizure and admissibility phases should be fused. In no recorded case has the Commission ever declined to be seized with a communication. This will lead to an automatic reduction of at least six months.

- The Secretariat should apply the Rules of Procedure, especially the requirement that states should respond on the question of admissibility within three months of being notified of the communication.[23]

- The Commission should prioritise communications that are urgent and have been delayed for some time.

- The Commission should revive its Working Group on Communications. This group could meet during the inter-session, or one day prior to the official opening of the Commission's session, to act as a 'filtering' mechanism, for example to deal with admissibility of all new cases, or to discuss substantive issues arising from decisions on the merits. The working group will then be able to make recommendations to the full commission during its private sessions on communications.

- Better communication with the state party should be ensured. It is not sufficient to send a letter to for example the Ministry of Foreign Affairs. States should establish a bureau or officials within a particular government department who is designated to liaise and keep contact with the Commission.

- More time at sessions should be devoted to finalising communications. The agenda should be organised around the communications. In other words, the number of days required for communications should be set aside, with an indication of dates on which particular cases are likely to be considered.

(c) Insufficient remedies ordered

As far as the sufficiency of remedies recommended by the Commission is concerned, three categories may be distinguished: no remedy, a very open-ended remedy, and a specific and detailed remedy. Examples of the latter are found in the SERAC case, as well as the Mauritanian Widows' case. Our concern is with the other two categories, of which there are numerous examples.

Examples of relatively recent instances where the Commission found violations of the Charter, but left the issue of an appropriate remedy totally open are Communication 225/98, Huri-Laws v Nigeria, and Communication 223/98, Forum of Conscience v Sierra Leone.

Open-ended remedies do not make it clear to states what they are required to do. This lack of clarity will impede any follow-up or implementation, as the form and nature of the remedy is bound to be contested. Examples of these are the following: In Communication 224/98, Media Rights Agenda v Nigeria, the respondent state was urged 'to bring its laws in conformity with the provisions of the African Charter'. In a number of other communications, the Commission merely stated that the state should 'draw all the legal consequences from the decision'. Such remedies are unhelpful to both the state and the complainant, since the state does not know exactly what it is required to do, and the complainant does not know what he or she may be entitled to.

Suggestions:

- The legal officer preparing a case should spell out the remedy required in the draft decision.

- If legal counsel appears for the complainants, the Commission should engage them on the issue of an appropriate remedy. The same applies to counsel representing the government.

- Ultimately, it remains the responsibility of the Commission to ensure that all its decisions address this aspect adequately.

(d) Inadequate publicity of and access to decisions

It follows from the description above that the decisions are not accessible enough and are not widely disseminated. There is no systematic publication of the Commission's decisions.

Suggestions:

- The full texts of decisions should be placed on the Commission's web site as soon as the AU Assembly has adopted the Annual Activity Report in which these decisions are contained.

- Whenever the Annual Activity Reports are published, they should contain the decisions on communications.[24] The Commission's publication, Review of the African Commission on Human and Peoples' Rights, should appear regularly, at least annually, should contain the Annual Activity Reports and should be widely disseminated.

- An official law report series of the Commission's decisions should be published, with a user-friendly index, and sold at a reasonable price. If needs be, the Commission should enter into a partnership with an NGO or academic institution to ensure that such a publication becomes a reality.

- The Publicity officer should draft a press release providing a background and historical context to each case. This should be done immediately after an Annual Activity Report has been made public. The widest possible publicity should also be given to interim measures issued under Rule 111 of the Rules of Procedure, as for example in the Ken Saro-Wiwa case.[25]

(e) Lack of clarity in procedures before the Commission

The Commission follows an ad hoc, un-codified procedure during hearings. Uncertainty about issues, mostly arising in respect of fact-finding remains, such as the following:

- Do complainants have the rights to testify, and to call witnesses?

- Does the respondent state have a similar right?

- What is the procedure with witnesses—are they sworn in, may they be cross-examined, is there an opportunity for re-examination, what is the role of the Commission?

- What is the burden of proof and the applicable rules of evidence?

- Are the two phases—violation and remedies—treated as one, or are the issues separated?

Suggestions:

- The Commission should discuss and clarify the procedure it adopts during oral hearings, particular on the issue of fact-finding. This is all the more important in the light of the impending establishment of an African Court of Human and Peoples' Rights. The future co-existence of the African Commission and the African Court is likely to require that the Commission develop its ability and capacity to undertake fact-finding and to resolve factual disputes.

- The Secretariat should propose an amendment to the Rules of Procedure to stipulate clearly what procedure is followed during oral hearings.

(f) Decisions on communications lack rigour

Over the last few years, the quality of the Commission's decisions has improved markedly.[26] The reasoning is more rigorous, and there is a broader reliance on sources. However, this practice is not yet consistent.

All the decisions adopted so far have been by consensus. No doubt, there are sound reasons for the lack of any minority opinion or view. Unanimity is indeed the general approach of the Commission; it may be argued that the Commission's findings have greater legitimacy if they rely on the backing of the full Commission; and the nature of most cases on the merits before the Commission has been such as to reveal clear instances of human rights violation.

Suggestion:

Members of the Commission should consider adopting and expressing a minority view in appropriate cases. Such a step would illustrate the rigour of the debates at the Commission, could reduce time-consuming and deferral of decisions due to a lack of consensus, would illustrate the maturity in the Commission's development, would enrich the jurisprudence of the Commission, and would be in line with the practice of for example the UN Human Rights Committee, where minority views are expressed quite frequently. Although the Commission's Rules of Procedure do not explicitly allow for minority views, such a possibility is compatible with the Rules. Under the Rules, voting should be resorted to if efforts to reach consensus fail.[27] Any proposal or motion may be put to the vote at the request of a member,[28] and members have the right to explain their votes.[29]

(g) Inability to deal with emergency situations

One of the gravest failures of the Commission has been to deal with emergency situations (see also section on protective missions). The Commission has for example been urged at the last session to take interim measures in respect of a communication that relates to the situation in the Darfur region of Sudan. It was also revealed that the Commission has not reacted to calls for such measures requested by the complainants.

Suggestion:

The Commission should publicise its internal procedure for dealing with emergency situations. A more streamlined and effective way of dealing with interim measures during the inter-session should be devised. A seminar or workshop should be held on this topic.

State Reporting

Reports Examined

The examination of state reports started at the 9th session, held in Banjul in October 1991. The following state reports have since then been examined:

1991—9th session: Libya, Rwanda, Tunisia. 10th session: None.

1992—11th session: Egypt, Tanzania. 12th session: Gambia, Senegal I and II,30 Zimbabwe.

1993—13th session: Nigeria, Togo. 14th session: Ghana.

1994—15th session: None. 16th session: Benin, Cape Verde, Gambia II.

1995—17th session: None. 18th session: Tunisia II.

1996—19th session: Algeria, Mozambique. 20th session: Mauritius.

1997—21st session: Sudan, Zimbabwe II.31 22nd session: None.

1998—23rd session: Guinea, Namibia. 24th session: Angola.

1999—25th session: Burkina Faso, Chad, South Africa. 26th session: Mali.

2000—27th session: Burundi, Libya II, Rwanda, Swaziland, Uganda. 28th session: Benin II, Egypt II.

2001—29th session: Algeria II, Congo, Ghana II, Namibia II. 30th session: none.

2002—31st session: Cameroon, Togo II, Lesotho, Mauritania. 32nd session: none.

2003—33rd session: Saharawi Arab Democratic Republic. 34th session: DRC, Senegal III.

2004—35th session: Burkina Faso II, Niger, Sudan II.

This list shows the reports examined by the Commission, rather than all those submitted by state parties. Reports from at least one country have been submitted, but have not yet been examined. This state is the Seychelles, whose report had already been submitted in 1994. The Seychelles report has as yet not been examined due to the absence, at numerous sessions, of a government representative to engage in a dialogue with the Commission.

These data show that 19 of the 53 member states have never submitted a report. They are: Botswana, CAR, Comoros, Côte d'Ivoire, Djibouti, Equatorial Guinea, Ethiopia, Eritrea, Gabon, Guinea-Bissau, Kenya, Liberia, Madagascar, Malawi, São Tomé e Principe, Sierra Leone, Somalia and Zambia. More than half of these 19 states have eight reports overdue. The data also underlines that very few states (a total of 13 states) have submitted more than one (initial) report.

Since November 1995, almost all reports have combined countries' overdue reports.

Problematic Aspects and Recommendations

Although there are still some problematic aspects relating to the process of state reporting, some aspects have improved recently. After numerous and continuous complaints by Commissioners that state reports are not translated, it appears that most reports have been available in at least English and French at the 35th session.

(a) Compliance with the Reporting Guidelines is difficult

The Guidelines, adopted in 1989 are too lengthy and complicated to comply with. They are also not readily accessible. The 'Umozurike[32] amendment' is only two pages long. It highlights certain important issues, but is too brief and its provisions are too vague to stand alone as guidelines. The relationship between these two sets of guidelines is never spelt out and remains uncertain. The status of the 'Dankwa[33] document' is uncertain.

During the examination of state reports, some questions are routinely asked. At most examinations, questions are posed about the participation of civil society in the preparation of the state report; the process of drafting the report; the domestic legal status of international law and, in particular, the African Charter; the number, capacity and occupancy of prisons; conditions of detention; awareness and adherence to the Commission's Declaration on Freedom of Expression; the presence and special treatment of indigenous communities; compliance with recommendations arising from communications submitted against that state; the situation of handicapped persons, the ratification of the Protocol establishing the African Court, the African Charter on the Rights and Welfare of the Child and the Protocol on the Rights of Women in Africa.

Suggestion:

- The Commission should adopt updated, unified and simplified Guidelines for State Reporting. This process should be guided by the initial Guidelines, the 'Umozurike amendment' and the 'Dankwa document'.

- The contents should be adapted to incorporate the subsequent experience of the Commission. The questions raised consistently relate in essence to the work of the Special Rapporteur on Prisons, on Women, the Focal Point or Working Groups on Indigenous Communities, and Freedom of Expression. New developments such as the Protocol on the African Court, the Protocol on the Rights of Women, and the threat posed by HIV/AIDS, should also be incorporated. The new guidelines should also take note of questions posed consistently by the Commissioners during examination of state reports over the years mentioned above.

(b) Non-submission or late submission of reports

One of the biggest problems faced by the Commission is the non-submission or late submission of reports. Of these, non-submission is the gravest problem. By failing to submit reports, states evade the supervisory role of the Commission. It should be recalled that 19 states have not submitted a single report to the Commission.

Suggestions:

- The Commission should provide more publicity, revealing the names of the states that have not yet reported at each session in press releases and on its web-site. In this regard, the Commission must interface with the AU's political mechanisms.

The role of the AU, at the macro level, is also of importance in ensuring compliance with the obligation to report. In this regard, the AU has (as had its predecessor, the OAU) adopted resolutions calling on states to submit reports. The political pressure at this level has, however, not gone much beyond the formality of adopting resolutions.

- The Commission should also reiterate that states report every second year, notwithstanding the concession to submit consolidated reports of a number of overdue reports. The Commission should clarify that the submission of consolidated reports remains a measure of last resort, and should not be regarded as the recommended procedure.

- The Commission should schedule the examination of the human rights record of states in the absence of a report. The UN CERD[34] Committee has adopted this as a long-standing practice, and the Human Rights Committee has also more recently embarked on this road. There is no doubt that such a course is not ideal, as the treaty body has to rely on sources other than that of the official state records, and will be deprived of party with whom it could enter into a 'dialogue'. However, the advantages in my view outweigh these disadvantages. Even in the absence of a report, the treaty body would be able to subject the situation in that country to international scrutiny in an impartial setting, and would be in a position to make recommendations that may initiate reforms.[35] The UN experience also shows that in many instances notice about the intention to take such drastic action has galvanised states into action, either to submit reports, or at least to be present at the examination. In any event, one of the possible consequences is that the state may be encouraged to submit its subsequent reports as required.

(c) Non-attendance by state representative

On relatively rare occasions, the state representative did not attend the session at which the examination of the state report was scheduled. This is particularly true of the Seychelles, whose report has not been considered, and also happened when the delegations of Ghana and Namibia were not present at the Commission's 28th session. The DRC report was scheduled for examination in October 2002, at the Commission's 32nd session, as wells as its 33rd session. Due to the absence of government representatives on both these occasions, the report has not yet been considered.

Suggestion:

The Commission should, in the absence of an acceptable explanation for non-attendance and after one 'warning', continue with the consideration of the report in the absence of a state representative. Although this is not conducive to a constructive dialogue, this will alert states to the importance of being present and will ensure that the process is not indefinitely delayed or stalled through the non-attendance by representatives, as in the case of Seychelles.

(d) Lack of credibility of exercise

The examination often lacks rigour. Although it is accepted that the examination should take the form of a dialogue between the Commission and a particular state, the questioning is often too facile and not sufficiently critical of the state. Government representatives usually do not answer all of the questions posed, often totally ignoring uncomfortable questions or promising to answer them later. There has never been an effort to correlate the answers provided with the questions asked, and thus to take up unanswered issues with the government.

Credibility relies on a fair and efficient procedure. Time management during examination of state reports is of great importance. Departing from the assumption that Commissioners have access to and have studied the report, government delegations should be restricted to only a few minutes when introducing their reports. Questioning by Commissioners should be focussed on those issues that are of pertinent concern, so as not to flood the delegation with questions that could not possibly answer in the allotted time. The time allocated to answer should at least be equal to that allowed for questioning. Placing severe restrictions on the time allowed to delegates to answer invites them to deal with issues in a superficial way, and to omit answers on issues that are particularly problematic. At the most recent session of the Commission, for example, the questions by Commissioners took up approximately one and a half hours, while the delegation was told to conclude thirty minutes into its reply. In the event, the government completed its reply in fifty minutes. Time allocation in respect of the Sudanese report was no different. After allowing the delegate to introduce the report for about half an hour, and questions by Commissioners lasting two hours fifteen minutes, the government was pressured to complete its response in seventy minutes.

Suggestions:

- The Commission should put system in place whereby a list is made of all of the questions asked, by numbering them, and of then noting the government's reply, thus ascertaining which issues are left unanswered. This proposal is linked to the practice of the suggestion of sending questions to states in advance, of more focus in the questions by Commissioners, clearer concluding observations, and an improved system of follow-up, mentioned elsewhere.

- Questions by the Commissioner who acts as rapporteur in respect of a particular report should be communicated to the state party at least a month before the scheduled date of the examination.

- In allocating time, it should be made clear to delegations that they have a very brief period to introduce the report, and to Commissioners that they should focus on the areas of major concern. The delegation should be provided with ample opportunity to respond to the questions.

(e) Lack in precision and of dissemination of concluding observations

The adoption of concluding observations after the examination of state reports is a relatively recent phenomenon. When they are adopted, there is a lack of exposure and dissemination of concluding observations. In those cases where concluding observations were adopted, they were not given sufficient publicity, and never became part of the Commission's official record in the form of either the session reports or Annual Activity Reports.

As far as they have been accessible, the formulation of the concluding observations in some respects reveal a lack of precision, leaving the state unsure about what changes the state is required to effect. The following examples may be provided. In respect of the Algerian report, for example, the Commission recommended that 'questions relating to women's rights are paid more attention by the authorities'. The government of Congo was urged to 'grant special attention to the rights of women and vulnerable groups such as ethnic minorities'.

Suggestions:

- The Commission should, as a matter of consistent practice, adopt concluding observations after the examination of state reports.

- The concluding observations should be adopted during the session at which the report was examined.

- The recommendations contained in the concluding observations should be drafted in as precise terms as possible, so as to enable the government to know what is expected of it, and to avoid subsequent dispute about the implications of concluding observations, for example when the next periodic report is examined.

- These concluding observations should be treated as public documents. They should be made public through press releases and at the press conference following the session. They should also be posted on the Commission's web-site as soon as possible after the session. The concluding observations should be contained in the session report, and in the subsequent Annual Activity Report. Publication of the concluding observations, at least in the Annual Activity Reports, will be in line with the current procedure of the UN Human Rights Committee.

- The concluding observations should obviously also be transmitted to the state concerned. However, the government should not be required to send draft observations for its comments. Not only will such a procedure delay the impact of these observations, but experience has also shown that states often do not respond in such circumstances.

(f) Lack of continuous dialogue

More and more states are now starting to present second or even third (periodic) reports. In most instances, the examination shows total disregard for the fact that the states had reported previously. Questions about the basic structure of state institutions, in principle covered in the initial report, are sometimes posed. There is no link to issues that have been raised at a previous examination, to questions that were left unanswered, to subsequent responses by the government, or lack thereof, or even to concluding observations, if they had been adopted. All this creates the impression of a formalistic once-off exercise, without taking into account the institutional memory or the fact that a second examination forms part of a dialogue with the state.

Suggestion:

Many of the concerns addressed above will be accommodated if the Commission consistently adopts and publicises concluding observations at the end of examining state reports. Such observations should form the basis of the subsequent examination.

(g) Inadequate accessibility to and publication of reports

State reports are mostly submitted in hard copy. This requires photocopying, and delays distribution of the report. The examinations of the reports, and the reports themselves, have been published systematically, covering the 9th to the 14th sessions.[36] Since then, no publication of the proceedings related to reporting has appeared.

Suggestions:

- The Commission should encourage (or require) states to submit state reports electronically (via e-mail or on disk). This will enable the Secretariat to send copies of reports to Commissioners much more speedily, and will facilitate distribution of the report to other role players (such as translators and NGOs).

- The examination of state reports should be followed up by the systematic publication of the reports, the oral proceedings during the examination, and any other relevant written documentation.

Missions

Procedure followed by the Secretariat and Commission

The legal basis of the Commission's mandate to undertake missions to state parties is found in article 46 of the Charter, which provides for 'any appropriate method of investigation' to be used by the Commission. In its initial practice and procedure, the Commission has drawn a principled conceptual distinction between protective and promotional missions. Protective missions are undertaken on the basis of communications formally submitted to the Commission under the Charter. Promotional missions are all other missions undertaken within the broad mandate of promotion. For this purpose, the countries party to the Charter are distributed among the Commissioners. In both instances, the missions take place in co-operation with and with the consent of the government.

Protective Missions: Its practice of undertaking missions started with protective missions. Five missions with a clear protective mandate have taken place. These have been to:

- Togo (March 1995).

- Senegal (1–7 June 1996), undertaken by Commissioners Duarte and Nguema.

- Mauritania (19–27 June 1996), undertaken by Commissioners Nguema, Rezag-Bara and Ondziel.

- Sudan (1–7 December 1996), undertaken by Commissioners Dankwa, Kisanga and Rezag-Bara.

- Nigeria (7–14 March 1997), undertaken by Commissioners Atsu Koffi Amega and Dankwa.

One of the major difficulties experienced with these missions had been the lack of co-operation by states. The mission to Nigeria, for example, was postponed on numerous occasions due to difficulties raised by the government before it took place. In a number of other instances, the Commission tried in vain to obtain the permission of states.

Missions (earmarked 'High Level Missions' or 'fact-finding visits') to Côte d'Ivoire and Zimbabwe have taken place. These mandates were not clearly defined as 'protective'. By the start of the 35th session, these reports had not been adopted or made public. At the same time, attempts to organise a mission to Darfur have failed.

Promotional Missions: These missions have taken off over the last two years.[37]

Problematic Aspects and Suggestions

(a) Reports of Missions

In respect of protective missions: Three of the five missions culminated in a mission report, adopted by the Commission, made part of the Annual Activity Report, and published as booklets in the name of the Commission. When the Togo mission took place, this procedure had not been well developed. The lack of a report after this visit may to some extent be ascribed to the novelty of the procedure. However, there seems to be very little justification for the lack of a final, public report following the visit to Nigeria.[38]

In respect of promotional missions: A very unequal practice exists. Commissioners report orally at public sessions of the Commission. Sometimes they have written reports that are handed to the Secretariat. In some instances these reports are photocopied and distributed at the sessions. Sometimes no written report exists. Translated versions of reports have only been available in exceptional cases. These reports do not give rise to debates among Commissioners, or to the adoption of recommendations. The reports have not been adopted officially, and are not made part of the official record of the Commission. These reports are therefore never appropriated by the Commission, and are not integrated into the collective memory of the Commission. These circumstances suggest that the Commission itself attaches very little stature and importance to an activity that takes up a significant amount of its members' (and legal officers') time and energy. There are some indications that these concerns are being addressed.

Suggestions:

A report should be drafted after every visit. The report should provide an overview of the visit, and should deal specifically with issues such as:

- The submission of state reports;

- The implementation of concluding observations and individual communications finalised by the Commission in respect of that state; and

- The ratification of the African Charter on the Rights and Welfare of the Child, the African Court of Human and Peoples' Rights and the Statute of the International Criminal Court.

The report should contain recommendations to the state. At the session immediately following the visit, the Commission should discuss the report. To this end, the reports should be translated, and copies should be provided to other Commissioners and the public attending the session. The Commission should formally adopt the report, or at least the recommendations contained therein, at that session. The adopted report should be contained in the Annual Activity Report.

(b) Conflation of protective and promotional missions

The dividing line between the two kinds of missions has increasingly become blurred. Missions with a distinctive protective element have been earmarked as 'promotional', such as the mission to Côte d'Ivoire undertaken on the basis of a resolution adopted in October 2000.[39] This mission should rather have been characterised as a protective mission, as it was aimed at fact-finding about the political situation, and its impact on the protection of human rights after the coup d'état. The reason for the conflation of the two types of missions lies in the difficulties associated with a distinctly 'protective' mission. The main difficulty with 'protective' missions was obtaining the consent of the state.

Suggestion:

The Commission's Rules of Procedure should be amended to include particulars about missions, including the way in which a distinction is to be drawn between promotional and protective missions.

(c) Lack of clear guidelines for missions

There are no clearly formulated guidelines or policy on missions. Guidelines for promotional and protective missions should be distinct. Protective missions should be directed at the investigation of human rights violations.

Mechanisms

Special Rapporteurs

Special Rapporteur on Extra-Judicial, Summary and Arbitrary Executions in Africa

(a) Establishment and appointment

The first Special Rapporteur appointed by the African Commission was the Special Rapporteur on Extra-Judicial, Summary and Arbitrary Executions in Africa. Commissioner Ben Salem was assigned to this position at the Commission's 16th ordinary session (October 1994). This followed in the wake of the genocide in Rwanda (which took place predominantly between early April and July 1994). NGOs, in particular Amnesty International (AI), provided the pivotal energy for its establishment. No framework for this appointment was in place: no mandate (Terms of Reference) existed; there were no measures for administrative support in place and no budget had been allocated. Commissioner Ben Salem resigned from the position between the 28th and 29th sessions. By the 35th session (May 2004) the position remained vacant.

(b) Mandate

The mandate of the Special Rapporteur was approved only at the 18th session (October 1995). The mandate is threefold: finding information about relevant cases and keeping a register thereof (investigation); studying ways in which executions could be prevented (intervention); and setting up a monetary scheme to provide for victims (compensation). The Special Rapporteur reported that he had received information about executions in Burundi, Chad, DR Congo, Comoros, Djibouti, Nigeria and Rwanda. The investigation part of the mandate never went beyond reports about names that still required verification.[40] Little is known about the intervention part of the mandate apart from some indications, through oral reports, that the Rapporteur effected such interventions. No written record or report about this aspect exists. The compensation fund was never set up, nor even discussed.

(c) Secretarial support

The Special Rapporteur complained continuously about the difficulties he faced. These complaints include the lack of secretarial support, the lack of funds, difficulties related to travel insurance, and administrative difficulties (faxing and making telephone calls).

(d) Financing/budget

No part of the Commission's budget was specifically allocated to the work of the Special Rapporteur. In fact, the position was created without any clear idea about the financial implications involved. The Rapporteur submitted a budget that was approved at the Commission's 19th session (March 1996).

(e) Visits

The Special Rapporteur had not undertaken any visits in this capacity. He ascribed this fact to the unwillingness of states to allow him to undertake visits.

(f) Collaboration with partners

Financial support was obtained for an initial portion of the mandate, from North-South Centre of the Council of Europe and the Swiss Directorate of Co-operation for Development and Humanitarian Aid. No sustained collaboration agreement was established with any NGO, despite offers from the Institute for Human Rights and Development in Africa, Interights,[41] HURIDOCS[42] and other NGOs. AI did not sustain its initial interest in the work of the Special Rapporteur.

(g) Reports

The Special Rapporteur submitted oral reports to the Commission, during public sessions, and one written report.

(h) Consideration or adoption of reports

These reports were discussed, and on one occasion adopted.

(i) Publication of and accessibility to reports

The Special Rapporteur's report was contained in the Annual Activity Report on one occasion.[43]

Special Rapporteur on Prisons and Conditions of Detention in Africa

(a) Establishment and appointment

NGOs, in particular Penal Reform International (PRI), were pivotal in the establishment of this Special Rapporteur. The position of Special Rapporteur on Prisons and Conditions of Detention in Africa was established at the Commission's 20th session. Commissioner Dankwa was appointed as the first Special Rapporteur, and served until he resigned in November 2000. Commissioner Chirwa was appointed Special Rapporteur in November 2000, at the Commission's 28th session.

(b) Mandate

At the time of the Special Rapporteur's appointment, the mandate of had already been finalised, with the assistance of PRI and other NGOs, in particular the now defunct Observatoire International des Prisons (OIP). Its mandate is much more elaborate than that of the first Special Rapporteur. The mandate is directed primarily at the examination of and reporting on prison conditions in Africa (investigation). The mandate further includes the possibility of proposing urgent action and of making recommendations to prevent 'disasters and epidemics' (intervention).

(c) Secretarial support

Secretarial support has, from the start, been provided mainly by PRI, and to a very limited extent by the Secretariat. The role of the Secretariat has been enhanced more recently. PRI was mostly responsible for providing an interpreter if required, and for making travel and logistical arrangements. An executive assistant to the Special Rapporteur on Prisons has been appointed, who supports her work from an office in Malawi. She is assisted by a dedicated legal officer at the Secretariat (Mr Robert Eno).

(d) Funding/budget

The activities have mainly been sponsored by Norwegian Development Agency (NORAD).

(e) Visits

Commissioner Dankwa undertook the following eight visits, at an average of two per year: Zimbabwe (23 Feb–3 March 1997); Mali (20–30 Aug 1997, and again 27 Nov–8 Dec 1998); Mozambique (14–24 Dec 1997); Madagascar (10–21 Feb 1998); Gambia (21–26 June 1999); Benin (23–31 Aug 1999); and Central African Republic (19–29 June 2000). He was on each occasion accompanied by a representative from either PRI or from the Secretariat, or both.

Commissioner Chirwa has undertaken the following visits, with three in the first year: Mozambique (4–14 April 2001); Malawi (17–26 June 2001); Namibia

(17–28 Sept 2001); Uganda (11–23 March 2002); Cameroon (5–12 Sept 2002); Benin, second visit (2003) and Ethiopia (15–29 March 2004). She was also accompanied by a member of PRI or the Secretariat, or both. However, she has also been assisted by Dr Oumar Sankarella Diallo, the Chief Physician of the Guinean Prison Services on all visits except the last one to Ethiopia.

(f) Collaboration with partners

From the start, this Rapporteur has been functioning in close collaboration with PRI.[44] Over the last two years, more and more responsibility has shifted to the Secretariat, thus reducing the role of PRI.

(g) Reports

Reports of the visits are published, with the technical assistance of PRI and the financial assistance of NORAD. Nine such reports have appeared, all in English and French, and on occasion also in Portuguese and Arabic. These reports deal with the visits to Zimbabwe, Mali, Mozambique, the Gambia, Benin, Central African Republic and Malawi, as well as the follow-up visits to Mali and Mozambique (Mali Revisited and Mozambique Revisited). The first seven reports show progress in the way in which issues are addressed. However, they all remain overly descriptive and do not engage in an in-depth analysis of prison conditions and other conditions of detention, its causes and solutions. The last three reports are more analytical, and use fixed headings and have a clear structure.

(h) Consideration and adoption of reports

These reports never seemed to have been discussed and were never officially adopted by the Commission. Reference is always made to these reports, as part of the general overview and report to the Commission.

(i) Publication of and accessibility to reports

So far, reports of all the visits undertaken by Commissioner Dankwa, except the one to Madagascar, has been finalised and published. These reports are not included in the Annual Activity Reports, but are published in a separate series. The report of the first two visits undertaken by Commissioner Chirwa has been published, but the others are pending.

Special Rapporteur on the Rights of Women in Africa

(a) Establishment and appointment

NGOs, such as Women in Law and Development in Africa (WILDAF) have for a number of years advocated the creation of a Special Rapporteur dealing with the rights of women. The position was established at the 23rd session, and Commissioner Ondziel-Gnelenga was appointed to the position. At its 30th session, the Commission elected Commissioner Melo as Special Rapporteur to replace

Commissioner Ondziel, who was not re-elected as commissioner by the OAU Assembly (in July 2001).

(b) Mandate

The mandate was not so much directed at visits, resulting in reports, but rather at general studies and collaboration with NGOs and governments. The mandate specifically calls for the elaboration of guidelines to assist states to report better about the situation of women, and for the finalisation of the Draft Protocol on the Rights of Women. One of the major accomplishments of this Special Rapporteur has indeed been the progress towards the adoption of the Draft Protocol to the African Charter on the Rights of Women in Africa. The latest version thereof was adopted in Addis Ababa in November 2001, by a meeting of experts.

(c) Secretarial support

According to the Rapporteur, she received no support from the Secretariat. Commissioner Ondziel was assisted by Mme Ndayisaba, an assistant, funded by Rights and Democracy.[45]

(d) Funding/budget

No specific planning was undertaken, and no budgetary allocation seemed to have been made at the Commission.

(e) Visits

Commissioner Ondziel-Gnelenga undertook the following visits as part of this mandate: Liberia (26–31 May 1999); Chad (12–20 September 2000); Côte d'Ivoire (5-8 February 2001); Nigeria (20 February–2 March 2001). Commissioner Melo has undertaken many visits to, amongst others, Djibouti, the DRC, Sudan, and São Tome e Principe.

(f) Collaboration with partners

The Special Rapporteur received a computer and printer from a Canadian NGO, Rights and Democracy.

(g) Reports

The Special Rapporteur presented 'activity reports' at sessions. Commissioner Ondziel also mentioned, in her oral reports to the Commission, a study on 'Poverty amongst women in Francophone West and Central Africa and Violence against Women'. The first of these has apparently been completed.[46]

(h) Consideration of and adoption of reports

These reports were discussed but never adopted as reports.

(i) Publication of and access to reports

The reports were never made part of any Annual Activity Report and, strictly speaking, therefore remain unofficial.

Problematic aspects and suggestions

The Commission placed a moratorium on the creation of new special procedures pending a report on Special Rapporteurs, which was entrusted to Commissioner Butegwa. After Commissioner Butegwa's term expired at the end of 2001, this task was entrusted to Commissioner Pityana. Although his report has not been tabled with the Commission, it is clear that the Commission has acknowledged that the mechanism of the Special Rapporteur is in need of review. The three Special Rapporteurs are now dealt with separately, before some overlapping suggestions are given.

(a) Special Rapporteur on Extra-Judicial, Summary or Arbitrary Executions in Africa

This position should be filled. So far, little tangible work has been done or accomplished. Commissioner Ben Salem was not personally equipped to realise the mandate. He was not an expert in the area concerned, and struggled to work with states and NGOs. There was insufficient support by the Secretariat for his activities. No budget was allocated. He did not start off with a clear written mandate. With one exception, no public record of the Special Rapporteur's work was given.

(b) Special Rapporteur on Prisons and Conditions of Detention in Africa

A number of reports, for example on Madagascar and Cameroon, still need to be published. Reports have to follow as soon as possible after a visit.

(c) Special Rapporteur on the Rights of Women in Africa

The mission report in respect of the visit to Nigeria is a good example of problematic aspects associated with this position. The mission was, rightly in our view, preoccupied with the application of Sharia law. In her report, the Special Rapporteur investigated aspects of its application, and the effect on human rights. She then made recommendations, directed at both the federal government of Nigeria and the Commission. The Commission has never adopted this very valuable report, with its potentially useful recommendations. It is only to be found in an un-translated version (in French) at the Secretariat. The report has not become part of the institutional memory of the Commission. This turn of events may be explained partially by the Commissioner's illness, or the fact that she was not re-elected. But it also illustrates the lack of integration of the work of Special Rapporteurs into the Commission, the total lack of any action on the basis of reports. The distinct impression is that the reports are presented as a formal obligation, just to dispose of the agenda point.

One gets the impression that all things are bundled together—more attention is given to prepare an activity report than the substantive reports. The activity reports of Commissioners could certainly be given orally. Of greater importance are the reports undertaken in respect of particular mandates, and the recommendations that may arise from these.

General suggestions:

- It is disconcerting to note that the Commission does not seem to have learnt its lessons of the appointment of the first two Special Rapporteurs, when it appointed a third. The Commission should hesitate to establish any more positions of Special Rapporteurs under its auspices, without first clarifying the exact nature and feasibility of the proposed mandate; ensuring the personal competence, expertise and suitability of the individual to be appointed; and analysing the material and financial requirements for establishing that position, and the resources available to meet those requirements, as in fact the Rules of Procedure require.[47]

- Where appropriate, a collaborative agreement with a partner, spelling out the contributions of the different parties to that agreement, should be reached. Experience has shown that Special Rapporteurs function more effectively when they have the material and secretarial support of a partner institution.

- When filling the position of an existing Special Rapporteur, or any such future position, the Commission should consider the appointment of 'outside' experts. When the first position of Special Rapporteur was considered, this possibility was raised. It was mentioned that Commissioners often do not have the time required for visits and studies. To this may be added the lack of experience or expertise. Counter-arguments were that it was thought to be outside the competence of the Commission to appoint a non-commissioner in such a capacity. It was thought expensive to appoint outside 'consultants' and that outsiders could not be trusted and controlled. Such appointments would create the impression that the Commission is not sufficiently competent to perform these functions. No attempt will be made here to provide a final answer to this debate—rather, the Commission is urged to consider this question before it makes any further appointments. The Commission's great benefit from a highly motivated, competent, African non-Commissioner to perform this function should be investigated as a possibility. As for the legal objections—'any appropriate means of investigation', in article 46 of the Charter—seems to be broad enough to allow for such appointments.

- The nature and extent of the secretarial and administrative assistance provided by the Secretariat should be clarified. This assistance should include a personal assistant close to the Rapporteur, as well as an office with basic equipment. This has been provided to the Special Rapporteur on Prisons. All Special Rapporteurs should be given equal support.

- The budget available to each Special Rapporteur should be clear. This amount should include an allowance for costs in respect of communications and correspondence. The Special Rapporteurs should also be an agenda post on the budget submitted to the AU.

- Agreements with NGOs should be encouraged, and should be channelled through the Secretariat.

- The reports of the Special Rapporteurs, elaborated after specific visits within its mandate, such as the visits of the Special Rapporteur on Prisons, should be made part of the Annual Activity Reports.

- Continuity between successive holders of the position of Special Rapporteur should be ensured.

Working Groups and Focal Points

Other participants have dealt with this important new development. This development is another illustration of the Commission interpreting its mandate in an expansive manner, and of the role of NGOs in furthering the aims of the Commission. However, uncertainty about the coexistence of these mechanisms with Special Rapporteurships, concern about the proliferation of mechanisms that do not all function effectively or consistently, and lack of clarity about the nature of their mandates, make the adoption of guidelines for the functioning of thematic mechanisms (Special Rapporteurs, Working Groups, Focal Points and other 'committees') all the more pressing.

Partnerships

NGOs

NGOs have played an important role in the work and progress of the Commission. There are at least three main reasons for the prominence of NGOs in the African system. First, by emphasising the role of promotion, the African Charter opens the door for the contribution of civil society to realise continent-wide promotion. Second, NGO participation grew as a counter-weight to the relative weakness of the system, which from the outset struggled against a lack of resources, uncertainty about the Commission's mandate, administrative and secretarial limitations, and non-cooperative states. Third, with increasing state participation, the sessions of the Commission provide a unique forum where NGOs have the opportunity to raise issues and confront governments in an impartial African setting.

NGOs are granted observer status with the Commission.[48] At the moment more than 300 NGOs enjoy such observer status. Workshops of NGOs preceding sessions have been an important feature of the African regional human rights system. These workshops have been initiated by the International Commission of Jurists (ICJ). More recently, the African Centre for Democracy and Human Rights Studies took over responsibility for the organisation of these workshops.

The main obligation of the NGOs with observer status is to submit reports about their activities. Most NGOs do not comply with these requirements. This is partially due to the fact that these reports seem to serve very little purpose. It would therefore seem that the energy and attention spent on keeping this information updated could be better spent. An alternative to the current system of random ill-defined reports is the following: The Commission (Secretariat) could prepare and send out a NGO circular, formalising their relationship. In this, the Commission could for example keep NGOs informed about upcoming sessions, and stipulate on what reporting should be done.

Some of the most important contributions and suggestions about how their role may be enhanced are now discussed.

(a) Elaboration of human rights treaties

From the outset, NGOs have been instrumental in the drafting of important human rights instruments in Africa. This statement applies even to the African Charter itself, but much more so to the African Charter on the Rights and Welfare of the Child, the Protocol on the Rights of Women in Africa, and the Protocol on the Establishment of the African Court on Human and Peoples' Rights.

(b) Adherence to treaties

NGOs have also played an important role in ensuring the ratification of these treaties. A recent example is the formation of the Coalition for the African Court, which directs itself at the early ratification of the African Court on Human and Peoples' Rights.

(c) Promotion of the Charter

The Charter stipulates that it 'shall be the function of the Commission to... organise seminars, symposia and conferences'.[49] It soon became clear that the Commission neither has the resources nor the expertise to fulfil this function by itself. It therefore entered, and continues to enter, into partnerships with NGOs to organise seminars and conferences about aspects of the African Charter. The Commission mostly plays a largely symbolic role in the fund-raising and organisation. The Charter also requires of the Commission to disseminate information. Awareness-raising cannot be undertaken all over the continent by the Commission alone. In this respect, the contribution of NGOs is indispensable. Many NGOs have published and distributed promotional material on the Charter. They have also been involved in organising numerous conferences and seminars on human rights in Africa, mostly in collaboration with the Commission. Some (such as the Institute for Human Rights and Development and HURISA50) have organised training workshops for activists and practitioners on submitting communications to the Commission. Promotional visits to state parties may play some role in the process of creating awareness of the African Charter, especially if such visits enjoy extensive media coverage. Creating an understanding of and providing information about the Charter can evidently not be the task of the Commission alone. In fact, many NGOs have undertaken training and awareness-raising. The important role that NGOs have played in raising awareness about the Charter and of empowering people to submit communications should be focussed on lawyers, through Bar Associations continued training.

(d) Further elaboration and precision of standards

A number of the seminars and conferences eventuated in the adoption of substantive guidelines in the form of 'declarations', which provide greater clarity on the relatively vague provisions of the Charter.

(e) Influencing the Commission's agenda

Realising the importance of the role of NGOs, the ICJ started to organise NGO Forums for a few days preceding the African Commission's sessions. When the ICJ redirected its priorities, the Centre took over this role. Although the full potential of these Forums still remain to be realised, they have served as a space where NGO concerns and especially pressing human rights problems can be raised. One of the main outcomes of the Forum is the adoption of resolutions, which are then tabled at the subsequent session. In a number of instances, the Commission has taken up and adopted the resolutions.

(f) Support to the protective mandate

Given the lack of awareness of the African human rights system among the general population in African states, and lawyers in particular, it is unrealistic to depend on either individuals or practising lawyers to submit communications to the Commission. This was particularly true of the early years. In most cases before the Commission NGOs play an important role, either by instituting the case in its own name (when the complainant is unable or unwilling to do so), or on behalf of the complainant acting as legal advisor in preparing the communication and arguing it before the Commission. As no legal aid is available to bring cases to the Commission, NGOs have also been providing financial assistance to complainants and witnesses, enabling them to attend oral hearings. Compared to the UN human rights treaty bodies, a remarkable feature of the complaints procedure before the African system is that the Commission allows for oral hearings. This was not the case from the outset, and developed through the efforts of NGOs. Written and oral arguments by lawyers from NGOs contributed to the professionalisation of the procedure before the Commission, as well as the quality of the Commission's findings. Some NGOs have also started highlighting the importance of implementation of the recommendations contained in the Commission's findings. As far as communications are concerned, the Commission should collaborate with NGOs in obtaining information about implementation.

These data should not be the exclusive source on which the Commission relies, though.

(g) Support to state reporting

Genuine introspection on the part of states would see the participation of civil society, including NGOs, in the process of preparing and drafting the state report. This ideal has been reiterated by the Commission, at least in posing questions to those states that have reported. However, this ideal course is followed only exceptionally. Extensive 'shadow' or 'parallel' reports, as NGOs present in the UN system, are very uncommon in the African system. More regularly, though, NGOs have provided pertinent information to legal officers at the Secretariat, and to Commissioners, enabling the Commission to direct pertinent questions to government delegates.

NGOs with observer status and national human rights institutions (NHRI) are often not even aware that a particular state (even the one in which the NGO functions) has submitted its state report. They are not informed about forthcoming examination of reports either. NGOs and NHRIs may only learn that a report will be examined at a forthcoming session when they receive the agenda for that session (maybe a month before the session). The Secretariat should at the earliest opportunity inform NGOs enjoying observer status with the Commission (or at the very least those in the particular country) of the fact that a particular state party's report is scheduled for examination at a particular session. Copies of reports by a country that have been submitted electronically should be sent to NGOs with observer status and NHRIs in that particular country, to enable them to prepare 'shadow' or alternate reports (If only hard copies are available, these may be copied at the expense of the NGO or NHRI). All other NGOs with observer status and affiliated NHRIs should be furnished with reports at their request.

One of the problems is that NGOs are not given access to state reports, even when they request them. Under the Rules of Procedure these reports are 'documents for general distribution'.[51] The Commission (through its Secretariat) should be proactive, and should send copies of submitted reports to all the NGOs with observer status in the country that is reporting as soon as the report has been received. Other NGOs should be informed that a particular state has submitted its report and that its report has been scheduled for examination, thus enabling them to request a copy of the report. If the process of electronic submission of reports, suggested above, is strictly adhered to, there seems little reason no to send a copy of the report to all NGOs enjoying observer status with the Commission.

Once concluding observations are issued, they should be communicated to all NGOs with observer status (or, again, at least to those within the particular country).

(h) Special Rapporteurs, Working Groups and Focal Points

NGO lobbying was an important factor in the establishment of all the Special Rapporteurs under the Commission. The most successful of these, the SR on Prisons, initially relied quite heavily on Penal Reform International (PRI), not only for financial assistance but also for technical support, such as organising visits, as well as drafting and publishing of reports.

National Human Rights Institutions

A number of national human rights institutions have been established in African states. There is some cause for concern about the adherence of some of these bodies to the 'Paris Principles', requiring their independence from government. As early as 1989, the Commission adopted a resolution calling on states that have not yet done so to establish national human rights institutions.[52] The Commission subsequently formalised its relationship with these institutions, when it adopted a resolution to grant affiliate status to them. One of the requirements is that these bodies have to meet the 'Paris Principles'.[53] At the 34th session, there were twelve such affiliated institutions, from Algeria, Cameroon, Malawi, Mauritius, Niger, Nigeria, Rwanda, Senegal, Sierra Leone, South Africa, Tchad and Togo. These institutions have the right to attend and participate in sessions.

Suggestions:

- The Commission should strengthen its collaboration with these institutions, and should take proactive steps to ensure the involvement of some of the highly-regarded institutions, such as those from Ghana and Uganda, to apply for affiliate status.

- There should be greater clarity about the role of these institutions in strengthening the Commission. Obvious possibilities are the translation of the Charter into local languages, dissemination of the Charter, ensuring that the topic of human rights and the Charter is included in school and tertiary curricula, especially for lawyers, interacting with and lobbying the state to comply with its reporting obligations under the Charter, the provision of technical assistance with reporting, and collecting information about follow-up of Commission decisions and recommendations. The Commission should engage with national human rights institutions about their role in part of the session, or at a designated workshop or other event.

Other Institutions

There are many more partners with which the Commission interacts. These include AU institutions, in particular the Committee of Experts on the Rights of the Child and the Peace and Security Council, UN institutions and bodies and other regional human rights bodies. Over the years a number of Commissioners have paid visits to the Inter-American Commission on Human Rights, and benefited from being exposed to its activities. Such an exchange should continue. One recent development, the conclusion of a memorandum of Understanding between the African Commission and the UNHCR, should be highlighted.

Suggestion:

- The Commission's working group on the relationship with the AU should be revived and should urgently consider the Commission's co-existence with the AU institutions. Consultations should continuously be held with the Committee of Experts on the Rights of the Child on ways of avoiding duplication and of ensuring collaboration.

Implementation (Follow-up)

Three of the procedures and mechanisms are embodied in recommendations to state parties: complaints, state reports and visits by Special Rapporteurs. (To these may be added the increasing practice of recommendations to states as part of promotional visits.)

Communications

No systematic follow-up exists to establish if states that had been ordered to remedy violations are in fact doing so. There is no person assigned to monitor this aspect either at the level of the Secretariat or the Commission. No consequences arise from a state' (even blatant) disregard for a decision taken and remedy recommended by the Commission. Neither the African Charter nor the Commission' Rules of Procedure explicitly require follow-up.

To a very limited extent, some follow-up to decisions has been initiated. The most notable example is the questions posed about implementation of decisions on individual communications during examination of state reports.[54] Another example is the inclusion, as part of a remedy ordered by the Commission, of the recommendation that the state party advises in its periodic report about the implementation of a decision.[55] Some of the remedies ordered also imply a system of follow-up, such as the remedy in Communication 155/96, SERAC v Nigeria. In that case, the Commission urged the government of Nigeria to keep the Commission informed of the outcome of the work of the Ministry of the Environment addressing environmental issues particularly in Ogoniland, and about the outcome of the Judicial Commission of Inquiry investigating human rights violations. These requests imply a continuous monitoring role on the part of the Commission, a role that the Commission was—paradoxically—not geared towards playing.

Arguments about follow-up are embedded in the bigger debate about the status of the Commission's findings, which, in turn, is closely linked to differences about the nature and role of the Commission. From the outset, there has been a tension between the view of the Commission as a diplomatic body with a limited capacity to make recommendations to governments, and the view that the Commission is a quasi-judicial body. The first view found support in the provisions of article 58 of the Charter, which stipulates that the Commission should report to the Assembly on massive human rights violations and then await an instruction to undertake studies. In the absence of any such instruction from the Assembly, the Commission adopted an approach allowing it to deal with such cases itself, leading to a finding of violation. It also extended its competence to deal, not only with massive violations, but also with individual communications. Based on a holistic reading of the African Charter, the second view holds that findings are binding decisions. This approach is reflected in the Commission's Rules of Procedure, which allow the Commission to deal with all communications, and not only massive or serious allegations.

A holistic reading of the Charter lends support to the Commission's approach. The state parties undertake to promote and protect the rights in the Charter, and to give effect to the rights in the Charter in their legal systems. The oversight body is the Commission, which does this by way of findings on the merits of communications before it. If states were allowed to disregard these findings, it would make a mockery of the endeavour to protect the rights, an endeavour entrusted to the Commission. A duty to respect the findings also derives from the general principle of pacta sunt servanda, which is enshrined in the Vienna Convention on the Law of Treaties.[56] It therefore follows that states have to give effect to the recommendations contained in the findings of the Commission. What the finding of the Commission amounts to, is a pronouncement about the failure of states to give effect to the rights. Not remedying such shortfalls would thus undermine the essential obligation in Article 1. This is exactly what the Commission has found in a communication against Nigeria, when the Commission declared that by ignoring a previous decision, Nigeria had violated Article 1 of the Charter.[57] This finding may be interpreted as departing from the premise that the findings are binding, as non-compliance with them leads to a violation in itself.

Even if the findings of the Commission as such are not legally binding, it is argued here that the subsequent adoption by the AU Assembly of the Commission's Annual Activity Report, in which these findings are contained, provides the findings with a binding status. The AU Constitutive Act, read with its Rules of Procedure, distinguishes between decisions (regulations and directives) and recommendations made by the AU Assembly. Decisions are binding, while recommendations are not.[58] After considering the Commission's Annual Reports, the AU Assembly takes a decision to adopt the report. While the situation was less clear under the OAU Charter, the AU legal framework clarified the issue, clearly establishing a legal obligation on states to abide by the Commission's findings.

Against this background, follow-up of recommendations in findings become pertinent. So far, follow-up has been ad hoc and haphazard. The most visible form of follow-up has been during the examination of state reports, when some Commissioners posed questions to state delegates presenting country reports about compliance with findings against that state. Although such attempts should be applauded, they suffer from some of the shortcomings of the state reporting procedure. By way of illustration: At the last session, questions were posed to the Sudanese delegation about compliance with a number of findings against Sudan. None of these questions were answered, and it remains very unclear to what extent the state reporting follow-up will address these concerns.

Any useful system of follow-up requires information about steps that states have indeed taken to implement recommendations contained in findings. The Secretariat should have a dedicated legal officer assigned to follow-up, who should collect data from states and complainants and legal counsel. This information should be contained in the annual activity reports, and should be disseminated at sessions of the Commission.

Factual disputes are likely to arise about the extent of compliance. To some extent, this may result from the nature of the recommendations themselves. Initially, the Commission adopted recommendations of a very terse, general and non-specific nature. Remedies (or recommendations) phrased in such a way invite uncertainty and dispute about steps to implement and comply with findings. In its later practice, the Commission has fortunately, on some occasions, given very specific and detailed recommendations. For example: In Communication 155/96, SERAC v Nigeria, the Commission detailed the steps the Nigerian government should take to protect the rights of the Ogoni people, by 'stopping the attacks on the Ogoni communities...', 'conducting an investigation into the human rights violations...', 'undertaking a comprehensive cleanup of lands and rivers damaged by oil operations', 'ensuring that appropriate environmental and soil impact assessments are prepared for any future oil development', and urged the government to keep the Commission informed of the outcome of the work of the Federal Ministry of the Environment, and a Judicial Commission of Inquiry. However, the practice of the Commission is still, by no means, uniform, and is seemingly dependent on the legal officer preparing the draft finding and the Commissioner acting as rapporteur in the matter. But not all states report, or are regularly visited. It thus becomes necessary to seriously consider the establishment of a Special Rapporteur (or Focal Point) on Follow-up, in terms of which one Commissioner will be assigned the responsibility to co-ordinate activities, work with the legal officer, establish facts if required, and to intervene with governments in respect of non-compliance.

Ultimately, the matter has to be referred to the political body responsible, the AU, to thus invoke the naming and shaming at the political level.

Suggestions:

- The legal basis of follow-up has to be clarified.[59] The Commission should adopt a resolution reiterating the importance of implementation by states, and the obligation to cooperate to ensure compliance.

- A bilingual legal officer (or two legal officers) at the Secretariat should be made responsible for following up decisions. The duty of the legal officer will be to collect information about follow-up by states. An electronic Register on Follow-up should be kept, in which cases finalised on the merits should be noted, with remedies ordered by the Commission. The Register must be kept up to date with regard to steps taken by state parties that have been found in violation of the Charter to give effect to these decisions. The legal officer will have to engage in vigorous correspondence with both the state party and the complainant, to establish the facts about implementation of the decision, and to be informed of problems encountered in this regard.

- The Rules of Procedure may have to be amended to reflect these proposals. However, this is not imperative, as the Rules do not explicitly exclude these developments in the practices and procedures of the Commission, as they flow logically from the framework of the present Rules.

- One of the Commissioners may be appointed as Special Rapporteur on Follow-up. This Special Rapporteur would remain in contact with the Secretariat, and would report to each session of the Commission about follow-up of decisions. If the need arises, the Special Rapporteur may have to visit the states in question. If a Special Rapporteur on Follow-up is not appointed, the Commissioner who acted as rapporteur in respect of a particular decision, should be required to play the role indicated above. The main problem with the latter possibility is that the follow-up of decisions may and certainly will remain on the agenda longer than the term of many Commissioners.

- The issue of implementation should be integrated into all the relevant activities of the Commission: State reporting, promotional visits and the activities of Special Rapporteurs. The Guidelines for State Reporting should be amended to make explicit the obligation of states to report about the implementation of decisions of the Commission. Questions must be posed whenever relevant during the examination of a state's report, using the information in the Register on Follow-up. Promotional visits should consistently have this issue as part of their agenda for discussion with government officials and NGOs. Where decisions overlap with activities of any Special Rapporteur, that Rapporteur should take up the issue and report to the Secretariat and the Commission. Effectively integrating follow-up into the existing activities will go some way to resolving and addressing concerns about a lack of follow-up implementation. Implementation of findings should feature prominently in all examination of state reports. The practice of the Commission of calling on states to 'report back to the African Commission when it submits its next periodic report in terms of article 62 of the African Charter on measures taken to comply with the recommendations and directions of the African Commission in its decision' should become a standard part of each decision.

- When a decision is adopted, the remedy should be made clear and implementable. The decision should declare that the state should report to the Commission, through its Secretariat, within 90 days after the decision have been taken, about steps the state had taken to give effect to the remedy recommended.

- The implementation of decisions should become a permanent point on the agenda of the Commission, to be discussed during public sessions.

- The Commission should at each session adopt a report on the status of follow-up by states, in schematic form, as is the case with the submission of state reports. Government representatives should be required to respond to the state of implementation of recommendations in their states during the Commission's public sessions, on a new regular agenda point on this issue. These reports should be made public as widely as possible, and should also be contained in the Commission's Annual Activity Reports to the AU Assembly.

Concluding Observations Emanating from Examination of State Reports

Follow-up to state reporting is lacking at two levels. There is no consistent follow-up to ensure that governments provide additional information promised during the examination of their state reports. Governments frequently do not answer questions, promising instead to provide the Commission's Secretariat with the required information once they have returned to their countries. There is also no practice or procedure in place to ensure the implementation of recommendations contained in the 'Concluding observations' addressed to state parties.

A system of follow-up of state reports depends on concluding observations. Initially, the Commission examined reports without adopting any concluding observations at the end of the examination. The practice has now evolved, and it seems to be adopted consistently. However, the problem with concluding observations is the lack of specificity in the recommendations, and the lack of awareness and dissemination of these observations.

The concluding observations are not disseminated widely, and they enjoy minimal visibility at all levels, including at the Commission level. They are not included in any of the communiqués or in the Annual Activity report. The consequence is that implementation is hidden, and that recommendations are not effectively followed up.

Suggestions:

- A legal officer should be dedicated to keeping a systematic record of questions and responses during the process of examination. Such information serves as the minimum requirement for a continuing dialogue between the Commission and the reporting state. Too often states do not answer all the questions posed, promising instead to send their replies upon return to their countries. This information should be systematically followed up.

- The Commission should adopt specific and detailed concluding observations at the end of the examination of state reports, and should disseminate them as widely as possible. Concluding observations should serve as the starting point of subsequent examination of state reports by that particular state.

Special Rapporteurs' Recommendations

The two functioning Special Rapporteurs, the one on Prisons (SRP) and on the Rights of Women in Africa (SRW), issue recommendations at the conclusion of visits. Implementation of the SRW is difficult to assess, as the reports of visits are not easily accessible and because the SRW has a not yet conducted follow-up visits to countries.

The SRP has undertaken a number of follow-up visits. As part of these visits, the SRP assessed the implementation of recommendations made previously. However, it remains inherently difficult to establish the impact of the work of the SRP. To a large extent the question is whether the recommendations have been implemented. The problems in establishing implementation are numerous. The information used to assess implementation is often based on hearsay, or the mere say-so of an official. It is not always possible to verify the assertions. The causal link between reforms of changes and the visit by SRP is also sometimes a matter for conjecture.

In Mali, seriousness about penal matters and reform was noted in the SRP's second report, and was confirmed by my visit. There is openness to criticism and reform. This is reflected in the two visits of the SRP. Further evidence is found in the ease with which Commissioner Dankwa was allowed to see ex-President Traoré and the ease with which the evaluator was allowed free access to prisons and NGOs. Greater openness is also illustrated in the inclusion of penal issues in the national dialogue. NGOs and legal professionals have taken an active interest in the rights of detainees. A project was launched in terms of which advocates took on cases in order to limit the overpopulation of prisons.

Legal reform has also taken place to ensure that periods of detention are shortened. In terms of Loi No 01–080 of 20 August 2001, dealing with the 'Code de Procedure Penal', a person accused of a crime for which the maximum penalty is two years or less, the maximum permissible period of detention, once he had appeared before a 'juge d'instruction', is limited to a month.[60] In the case of a possible penalty exceeding two years, the maximum period of detention is six moths.[61] These terms limit those previously in operation, which allowed for detention up to one year.

Commissioner Dankwa noted two prisons where physical facilities have markedly improved—Banguineda prison farm, and Mopti prison. The evaluator was informed that a great number of prisons had been built recently: The Women's Prison at Bollé as well as Markala, Kimparana, Fana, Kignou, Ouelissebougou, Youfolia, Gao and Bankass Prisons. A further approximately 15 prisons have undergone renovations or repairs. During a visit to Bamako Central Prison, the newly constructed mosque, church and library were pointed out. The relationship between prison staff and prisoners also improved, the SRP noted in the report of the follow-up visit. The Director of the prison at Mopti had been changed, as he recommended, but apparently only very shortly before his second visit. One of the underlying problems, that of the duplication of authority over staff responsible for detention, was addressed in that all staff now fall under the Ministry of Justice.

But some problems persist all the clearer for having been recommended and not complied with: A first clear example relates to the imprisonment of two women in Mopti, despite assurances to the contrary. At the Commission's 24th session, the SRP reported that the Minister of Justice had indicated that two women at Mopti prison had been granted a presidential pardon. When the SRP arrived for the follow-up visit, the same women were still being detained, and he was informed that they were being considered for presidential pardon. Deep-seated problems, in particular lack of medications and overcrowding, persist. As in other countries, overcrowding is a major problem in the Malian prisons. One of the main reasons for the overcrowding is the high percentage of non-sentenced detainees—those under provisional detention and awaiting trial pending the finalisation of their trials. A small decrease in the percentage of non-sentenced prisoners has been observed sine the first visit of SRP.

According to Commissioner Chirwa, who undertook the second visit to Mozambique, some aspects of the situation of detainees in Mozambique have deteriorated. The overcrowding has become worse, and prisons in Tete were in a terrible state. Given the limited resources, few material conditions have changed. The length of detention still remains unacceptable. The November 2000 incident at Montepuez[62] has not been finally resolved. In some respects, conditions have, however, improved. The separation of juveniles and adult prisoners is more strictly adhered to. Efforts have been made to ensure that male and female detainees are separated. A new, modern prison has been built in the rural area. Some prisons (Xai-Xai) have been rebuilt, while others are under reconstruction (Beira). In other cases, reconstruction has been planned (Maputo, Gaza). NGOs agree that there is much greater openness about penal matters, and that NGOs are encouraged to participate in improving living conditions. After the first visit, NGOs report that they were able to discuss penal matters and reform freely with the Minister. NGOs have been allowed, and even requested, to undertake human rights training of prison staff. There are also reports of greater freedom of speech of detainees. A process of review of the penal system is underway, in terms of which the duality in the penal system (involving two different departments) is addressed and the 'Commission to strengthen legality' has been instituted.

The Special Rapporteur visited Uganda from 11 to 22 March 2002. In a very encouraging development, the Ugandan government provided an eleven-page report on the 'implementation of the recommendations' of the SRP. In this report, the government points to steps it has taken so far to address the recommendations (such as ensuring that defilement cases are heard at the level of Chief Magistrates Courts, rather than the High Court, and the proposed Prisons Bill 2002) and to constraints (mainly budgetary).

Suggestions:

- The mandates of each of the Special Rapporteurs should make explicit reference to follow-up of recommendations.

- The follow-up visits of the SRP should be continued. Such visits should use the recommendations of previous visits as point of departure. Follow-up should, however, not be restricted to visits, but should also be effected by way of continuous correspondence with visited states. Accurate information is essential to good follow-up. Many of the steps mentioned by the Ugandan government are of an ongoing nature (such as the Prisons Bill 2002 and the amendments before the Constitutional Review Commission), and need to be followed up through correspondence. In short, visits should not be regarded as one-off events, but should lead to sustained interest and exchange of information.

- It is essential that reports of visits be adopted and published as soon as possible after a visit. These reports should be disseminated widely, and should reach at least all the individuals and institutions that have been involved in the visit. Reports should be accessible through the Commission's web site and should be included in the Annual Activity Reports.

- Follow-up of recommendations should not be viewed as the responsibility of the Special Rapporteurs alone, but should be integrated systematically in the promotional visits of Commissioners to countries that have been visited by these Rapporteurs.

- The lack of demonstrable impact of the work of the SRP in The Gambia is particularly disappointing. Given that the Secretariat is based in Banjul, ease of access to prisons and government officials, enabling a continuous dialogue with the government and sustained follow-up and implementation, would have been assumed.

Conclusion

The suggestions made here are not drastic, derive from common sense, and do not require significant resources. Some of them are indeed already hinted at in the Commission's own Strategy Plan (2003–2006). Attention should now shift to their serious consideration and possible implementation, to ensure the continued strengthening and growth of the Commission. As the African Court on Human and Peoples' Rights becomes a reality, as a supplement to the Commission's protective mandate, there is even more at stake to ensure the effective functioning of the Commission.

Notes

1. This paper is based partly on research about and a report on the procedures of the African Commission, conducted with Professor Salif Younaba, Burkina Faso, as consultants to Interights, and on research and a report on the African Commission's Special Rapporteur on Prisons, conducted as a consultant to Penal Reform International.
2. These states are Algeria, Burkina Faso, Burundi, Comoros, Côte d'Ivoire, The Gambia, Lesotho, Libya, Mali, Mauritius, Niger, Rwanda, Senegal, South Africa, Togo and Uganda. (Three more states have reportedly ratified since then.)
3. Communications against non-state parties are not included.
4. Communications 108/93-126/93, all submitted at the same time by the Centre for the Independence of Judges and Lawyers, against 16 state parties and two non-state parties, are included as one case, as to do otherwise would give a skewed picture.
5. Communications 164/97 to 196/97 are taken as one, as they were submitted simultaneously against the same state. The same applies to Communications 205/97-207/97, against The Gambia.
6. The first inter-state communication was submitted in 1999, Communication DRC v Burundi, Rwanda, Uganda. As this is not an individual communication, it is not included in the number for that year.
7. As of mid-September 2002.
8. Communication 231/99, Avocats Sans Frontières v Burundi, Fourteenth Annual Activity Report, para 14.
9. S ee Rule 102(1) of the Rules of Procedure.
10. Rule 104(1).
11. Communication 25/89, 47/90, 56/91, 100/93, World Organisation Against Torture and three others v Zaire, Ninth Annual Activity Report.
12. As indeed the Rules of Procedure allow the Commission to do if it 'deems it good' (Rule 114(2)).

13. Communication 27/89, 46/91, 49/91, 99/93, Organisation Mondiale Contre La Torture and three others v Rwanda, Tenth Annual Activity Report.
14. See for example Communication 102/93, Constitutional Rights Project and another v Nigeria, Twelfth Annual Activity Report, para 35.
15. Rule 117(4).
16. Rule 119(2).
17. See for example paras 32 and 33 of Communication 220/98, *The Law Offices of Ghazi Suleiman v Sudan*, Fifteenth Annual Activity Report.
18. Para. 12 of the decision.
19. Para. 33 of the decided case.
20. Para. 16 of the decided case.
21. Paras. 18, 19 of the decided case.
22. This happened from the 24th to the 29th sessions—see paras. 21 to 32 of the decided case.
23. Rule 117(4).
24. When the Secretariat published the Thirteenth Annual Activity Report of the Commission, with (financial) assistance from the European Union and the Danish Centre for Human Rights, the Report contained everything except arguably the most important part—the Commission's decisions on communications.
25. Communication 137/94, 139/94, 154/96, 161/97, International PEN and three others v Nigeria, Twelfth Annual Activity Report.
26. See for example the SERAC case referred to, and Communication 241/2001, Purohit and Moore v The Gambia, Sixteenth Annual Activity Report.
27. Rule 62(3).
28. Rule 61.
29. Rule 64.
30. The two reports were examined together, but were dated 1989 and 1992 respectively.
31. This was presented as a single report, combining the second and third reports.
32. A former Commissioner.
33. Commissioner from Ghana.
34. Committee on the Elimination of Racial Discrimination.
35. See, for example, A. Bayefsky The UN human rights treaty system: Universality at the crossroads (2001) at 13.
36. Published in the name of the African Commission, by the Danish Centre for Human Rights. Edited by A.Danielsen and J.Harrington.
37. By way of illustration: In 2000: Sierra Leone (14–19 February 2000), Commissioner Chirwa and Dankwa; Ethiopia (27 February–4 March 2000), Commissioner Dankwa; Uganda (18-21 March 2000), Commissioner Butegwa; Rwanda (22–26 March 2000), Commissioner Ondziel; Burundi (14–22 March 2000), Commissioner Ondziel; Tanzania (15–23 June 2000), Commissioner Chirwa;

Mozambique (7–9 August 2000), Commissioner Pityana; Benin (7–11 August 2000), Commissioner Johm. In 2001: Saharawi Arab Democratic Republic (9–16 February 2001), Commissioner Rezzag-Bara; Niger (10–23 March 2001), Commissioner Sawadogo; Djibouti (14–22 March 2001), Commissioner Rezzag-Bara; Botswana (2–6 April 2001), Commissioner Pityana; Côte d'Ivoire (1–5 April 2001), Commissioners Dankwa, Rezzag-Bara, Johm; Namibia (1–7 July 2001), Commissioner Chigovera; Seychelles (2–6 July 2001), Commissioner Dankwa; Burkina Faso (22 September–2 October 2001), Commissioner Nguema; South Africa (25–29 September 2001), Commissioner Chigovera. In 2002: Gambia (22 December–5 January 2002), Commissioner Johm; Sudan and Libya (26 March–2 April 2002), Commissioner El Hassan; Senegal (August 2002), Commissioner Johm.

38. Especially given that a comprehensive, but unofficial, draft report is available in the Documentation Centre.

39. The resolution called on the OAU to set up an international Commission of Enquiry in which the African Commission should be involved to 'investigate all human rights abuses' that occurred in October 2000.

40. See for example Tenth Annual Activity Report, para 29.

41. The International Centre for the Legal Protection of Human Rights, based in the U.K (www.interights.org).

42. Human Rights Information and Documentation Systems International—a global network (www.huridocs.org).

43. See Annex IV to the Tenth Annual Activity Report.

44. Penal Reform International (www.penalreform.org).

45. Formerly the Canadian International Centre for Human Rights and Development.

46. According to Commissioner Ondziel-Gnelenga, at a private part of the Commission's 30th session (Report of the 30th session of the Commission). The report could not be found at the Secretariat, though.

47. Rule 24 places a duty on the Secretary to provide information about the financial implications of a proposal 'entailing expenses'.

48. See also 7.4 below.

49. Art 45(1)(a).

50. Human Rights Institute of South Africa (http://wn.apc.org/hr/hurisa/hurisa.htm).

51. Rule 78.

52. Resolution on the establishment of committees of human rights or other similar organs at national, regional or sub-regional level, adopted at its 5th session.

53. Resolution adopted at the Commission's 23rd session in 1998.

54. As was done by Commissioner Johm in respect of the state reports of Mauritania, examined during the Commission's 31st session.

55. See Communication 211/98, *Legal Resources Foundation Centre v Zambia*, Fourteenth Annual Activity Report, remedy ordered.

56. Art. 3(1).

57. Communications 137/94, 139/94, 154/96, 161/97 (joined), International Pen and Others v Nigeria, concluding para.

58. Rules 33 and 34 of the AU Assembly's Rules of Procedure.

59. The African Charter does not provide explicitly for follow-up of decisions to be undertaken by the Commission. This lacuna has prompted some Commissioners to argue that the Commission would overstep its competence if it undertakes follow-up of decisions. Given that the Charter provides rights to individuals, and that states through ratification of the Charter undertake to give effect to the rights therein, it would be perverse for the Charter's implementation mechanism to remain unconcerned about the reality of 'giving effect' to its decisions.

60. Art 125 of Loi 01–080.

61. Art 127 of Loi 01–080.

62. Violence erupted after RENAMO supporters attacked the district administrative headquarters, the prison, the local market, the police headquarters, the house of the District Administrator of Montepuez, the Municipality Office Telecom Office, the secondary school, the hostel and local shops. In the fighting that followed 35 people, of whom eight were police officers, died and more than 150 people were wounded.

Chapter 8

The African Commission on Human and Peoples' Rights and the New Organs of the African Union[1]

Ibrahima Kane

In this chapter I will introduce the subject of the relationship between the African Commission on Human and Peoples' Rights (hereafter referred to as the African Commission) and the new organs of the African Union. As you undoubtedly know, since the Constitutive Act of the African Union came into force on 26 May 2001, the African continent has experienced a minor institutional 'revolution'. The Organisation of African Unity (hereafter, the OAU), which was created in 1963 in order to eradicate all forms of colonialism from Africa and defend the sovereignty, territorial integrity and independence of the newly-formed African States,[2] has been succeeded by an 'African Union' whose stated aim is to build 'a united and integrated Africa; an Africa imbued with the ideals of justice and peace; an inter-dependent and virile Africa determined to map for itself an ambitious strategy; an Africa underpinned by political, economic, social and cultural integration which would restore to Pan-Africanism its full meaning',[3] solely comprising 'democratic States respectful of human rights and keen to forge equitable societies'.[4]

This initiative, in which Libya took the lead, aimed to make Africans 'both the actors in and beneficiaries of the structural changes engendered by development; and development should enable humans to accept their identities and conditions, rather than fall victim to them'.[5] The Union calls upon each of its members 'to promote and protect human and peoples' rights, consolidate democratic institutions and culture, and to ensure good governance and the rule of law',[6] to 'promote peace, security, and stability on the continent'[7] and to always base their actions on fundamental principles such as 'respect for the sanctity of human life',[8] 'respect for democratic principles, human rights, the rule of law and good governance',[9] the 'promotion of gender equality',[10] the 'condemnation and rejection of impunity and political assassination, acts of terrorism and subversive activities'[11] as well as the 'condemnation and rejection of unconstitutional changes of government'.[12] The famous principle of non-interference in the internal affairs of African states is replaced by one of non-indifference to the problems experienced by African countries, and the Union, as an institution, has an obligation to supervise the application of these norms by the States Parties and, whenever necessary, grants itself the right to 'intervene in a Member State pursuant to a decision of the Assembly in respect of grave circumstances, namely war crimes, genocide and crimes against humanity'[13] and to impose sanctions[14] on those States which do not act in conformity with its decisions and policies up to and including their suspension,[15] in particular when governments come to power through unconstitutional means.

This normative change has been reflected in the institutional structure through the creation of new organs,[16] some of which have been vested with very specific mandates regarding the promotion and protection of human rights. This is likely to pose problems of 'cohabitation' or coexistence with the institutions created for the promotion and protection of human rights on the continent by the now defunct OAU[17] and which have been recognised as such by the Union itself.[18]

I shall attempt to describe the African mechanism for the protection of human rights originating in this transformation of the OAU. I intend to identify the legal obstacles to harmonious relations between the African Commission and the political organs of the African Union, by means of a comparative analysis of the mandates of the new structures. I also aim to identify the new opportunities that would enable the African Commission to effectively fulfil the role set out for it by the African Charter and lay the foundations 'for dynamic interaction and coordination'[19] with these new structures. With this in mind, I shall successively review the relations of the African Commission with the organs whose theoretical role is to assist it in carrying out the mission of promoting and protecting human and peoples' rights, as laid down by the African Charter, and which could further its participation in the ambitious integration programme currently being explored by the African continent.

Cooperation with the Bodies of the African Union Whose Role Is to Contribute to Fulfilling the Mandate of Promoting and Protecting Human Rights

The African Commission was established by the OAU in 1981, under the African Charter on Human and Peoples' Rights (hereafter referred to as the African Charter). It was vested with the mission of undertaking research, organising seminars, giving opinions and making recommendations to the states parties, formulating principles and rules relating to the enjoyment and exercise of fundamental rights, and working with the principal institutions responsible for human rights.[20] Its role also included reviewing complaints made by states,[21] individuals or non-governmental organisations;[22] interpreting the African Charter at the request of states parties, OAU institutions or other African organisations recognised by the OAU,[23] and performing any other tasks which may be entrusted to it by the African states.[24]

In carrying out this mandate, the African Commission received support from the bodies of the OAU;[25] they were responsible for electing its members, reviewing and adopting the annual reports on the activities of the African Commission and assisting it in its day-to-day mission of protecting human rights on the continent,[26] in particular by providing adequate staff and financial means.[27] And, since its establishment in Banjul, The Gambia, in 1987, the African Commission has, not without some difficulty, developed close working relationships with these bodies, particularly with the Assembly of Heads of State and Government and the General Secretariat. This has allowed it to refine the content of specific Charter clauses, to promote the African Charter within Africa and to dialogue with the states parties regarding practical methods of implementing the African Charter within their respective legal systems. Overall, it has been able to make a notable contribution to the reinforcement of the region's system for the protection of human rights from both the normative[28] and the institutional[29] standpoint.

When the Constitutive Act came into force, some of the roles within the deliberative and executive bodies of the African Union were redistributed in terms of their relationship with the African Commission.[30] I will now explore the changes that have been made and their impact on the operations of the African Commission today.

Principal Changes in the Supervision of the Activities of the African Commission

Under the terms of the African Charter, the Assembly of Heads of State and Government and the General Secretariat of the OAU are the principal partners of the African Commission. The former is responsible for all the major decisions involving the operations of the African Commission, the latter, for its day-to-day administrative and financial management.

In 2002,[31] these mandates were distributed amongst the Assembly of the Union, the Executive Council, the Peace and Security Council (hereafter referred to as the PSC) and the Commission of the Union. However, while this new division of labour was implemented quite judiciously where the deliberative and executive bodies of the Union are concerned, the fact remains that the decision was taken, as we shall see, in violation of the relevant clauses of the African Charter. Despite this fact, these changes have consolidated the relationship between the African Commission and the Commission of the Union.

(i) A division of roles in the supervision of the African Commission amongst the deliberative bodies of the Union which is pragmatic but which stands in violation of the letter of the African Charter

In the interest of efficiency, transparency, good management and, doubtless, the respect of the basic rules of democracy within the African Union, the African States have laid down new rules to enable the deliberative bodies to carry out their missions more efficiently. Although it remains 'the supreme body'[32] of the regional organisation, the Assembly now shares its decision-making powers with the Executive Council,[33] the PSC, the Court of Justice and, to a lesser extent, with the Pan-African Parliament (hereafter referred to as the PAP) and the Economic and Social Council (hereafter referred to as ECOSOC). Its role has been restricted to determining the common policies of the Union,[34] taking decisions on reports and recommendations from other Union bodies,[35] monitoring the implementation of policies and decisions and ensuring Member State compliance,[36] and giving directives on the management of emergency situations (conflicts and wars) and the restoration of peace on the continent.[37] It may delegate any of its powers and functions to any organ of the Union38 as needed.

The Assembly of the Union also works closely with the Executive Council, which is 'responsible'[39] to the Assembly and co-ordinates and takes decisions on policies in areas of common interest to the Member States.[40] In so doing, the Executive Council prepares the meetings of Heads of State and Government, determines the issues to be submitted for decision and implements the decisions that are taken, coordinates and harmonises policies, activities and other initiatives of the Union in areas of common interest, takes decisions on the questions submitted to it by the Heads of State and Government and, above all, reviews the programmes and budget of the Union.[41]

In more direct relation to human rights issues, since July 2002,[42] the Executive Council has been responsible for electing the members of the African Commission and the African Committee of Experts on the Rights and Welfare of the Child[43] and for examining the African Commission's[44] annual activity reports. These two major prerogatives make it the foremost partner of the African Commission on the continent.

The PSC 45 has extensive powers in matters of prevention,46 management[47] and resolution48 of conflict in Africa as well as in the protection of human rights,[49] which is undoubtedly the reason why it has been given an obligation to seek 'close cooperation with the African Commission on Human and Peoples' Rights in all matters relevant to its objectives and mandate',[50] especially those involving emergency situations.[51]

Yet, while the involvement of these specialised structures in the management of the activities of the African Commission is to be welcomed, the same cannot be said for the means used to achieve this end, which can be described as a covert revision of the African Charter. To transfer the power to elect the members of the African Commission from the Assembly of Heads of State, as provided by the African Charter, to the Executive Council by means of a mere clause in the internal Rules of Procedure of the latter, amounts to a violation of the letter of the African Charter. Where possible, it is indeed preferable to avoid the complex procedure of revising the African Charter, but this should only be done without transgressing the provisions of the founding instrument of the African Commission. It is our belief that, while a revision of the African Charter has become inevitable, it must be carried out with due respect for legal formalism, and that the interests of the African Union would be best served by avoiding the development of practices which, in the long run, may run the risk of rendering the substance of the African Charter null and void.

(ii) Towards an intelligent restructuring of the executive authority of the Union so as to better meet the needs of the African Commission

Whereas the executive body of the OAU, the General Secretariat, was made up of one General Secretary and four deputy general secretaries with restricted powers,[52] the executive body of the African Union, the Commission of the Union, is composed of ten individuals[53] and has specific political powers. It is responsible for implementing, coordinating and controlling the execution of decisions taken by the deliberative bodies of the Union as well as representing and defending its interests, preparing its budget and programme, managing its budgetary and financial resources, developing the Union's strategic plans and conducting its studies and taking action in specific areas of responsibility as may be delegated by the Assembly and the Executive Council.[54]

The present structure of the Commission[55] includes a Chairperson, a Vice Chairperson and eight Commissioners elected by the Executive Council for a term of four years, once renewable.[56] Apart from the Chairperson and Vice Chairperson, who have their own specific powers,[57] each Commissioner is responsible for the implementation of the programmes, policies and decisions of the Union concerning the portfolio58 for which he or she has been elected.

Because it inherited the mandate of the General Secretariat of the OAU and because the Constitutive Act of the African Union has vested it with specific

powers in the sphere of human rights,[59] the Commission maintains close relations with the African Commission. Given that the Commission is a collegial
body, these functions are theoretically shared between the Chairperson[60] of the
Commission of the Union and the Political Affairs Commissioner, who is
responsible for human rights.[61] Given the close links between human rights and
the problems of peace, security and development referred to in the African Charter[62] and the Grand Bay[63] and Kigali[64] Ministerial Declarations of the OAU and
the AU, there can be little doubt that the Peace and Security and Social Affairs
Commissioners who are respectively responsible for Conflict Prevention, Management and Resolution and Combating Terrorism, and Health, Children, Population, Migration, Labour and Employment as well as Sports and Culture, will
also be involved in the management of human rights issues. Indeed, the Social
Affairs Commissioner supervises the activities of the African Committee of
Experts on the Rights and Welfare of the Child while the Peace and Security
Commissioner acts as Secretary of the PSC, which is, as we have seen, an important partner of the African Commission. This type of 'duplication' of mandates
within the same team is unfortunately not of a nature to promote the adoption
of coherent programmes and policies on human rights issues within the Commission and therefore to enhance the clarity of its actions in that sphere.

In the months to come, pending a serious review of this issue by the Commission, the Commissioner in charge of Political Affairs will continue to be the
principal partner of the African Commission. It is his responsibility to represent
the Chairperson of the Commission of the Union at the ordinary sessions of the
African Commission,[65] to manage its administrative and financial affairs and to
assist its Bureau during the review of the annual activity report before the Executive
Council. Should there be a difference of opinion between the Political Affairs
Commissioner and the African Commission over the management of the affairs
of the latter, both bodies may seek remedy through the arbitration of the
Chairperson of the Commission of the Union. This is undoubtedly one of the
major innovations of the new system.

These institutional changes open up new perspectives for the African Commission in its interaction with regional institutions. It is therefore incumbent
upon the African Commission and these bodies to seize the opportunity they are
being given to meet the challenge of the changes desired by the African Union in
the sphere of human rights, in particular by adapting its working methods to
these new standards of excellence.

Challenges the African Commission must Overcome to Properly Fulfil its Mandate

Amongst the numerous challenges which the African Commission must overcome in order to cooperate more efficiently with the organs of the Union, we

shall focus on the revision of its working methods and the reinforcement of its independence and its operational capacities.

(i) Revision of its working methods

In our opinion, this is an important priority for the African Commission. Apart from the need to adapt its rules of procedure to its new institutional environment, the Commission, in the light of the powers conferred on the organs with which it is called upon to cooperate, will have to set up systems and procedures which will enable it to maximise the advantages of this relationship instead of being reprimanded, as it was in July 2004, by one of the organs of the Union. At that time, during the first session of the review of the annual report of the African Commission by the Executive Council, a delegate from a state party who had been 'severely criticised' by the Commission protested vehemently that he had not had the opportunity of officially commenting on the report made on the human rights situation in his country. The Executive Council was forced to suspend the publication of the report in question, after requesting that the African Commission 'in future, ensure that the reports are submitted along with the comments of the States Parties concerned and the steps taken in this respect are indicated during the presentation of the annual activity reports'.[66]

In truth, the African Commission has been afforded with an ideal opportunity to review the very format and content of the report which it submits for review by the African Ministers. By improving the structure of the report and including a section devoted to the decisions which it would like to see the Executive Council take concerning the promotion and protection of human rights, it could, in our opinion, facilitate the work of the Council.

Furthermore, increased contact with the members of the Executive Council may provide an opportunity to plead the Commission's cause to the Union. For example, the review of the annual activity report could become a prime opportunity for dialogue on the conjunctural and structural problems of the African Commission, not only with the state parties, but also with the decision-making body.

The revision of the working methods should also focus on the relationships between the new organs of the Union and the other mechanisms such as the special rapporteurs, the working groups and the focal points. Once these relationships have been clarified, the African Commission and the bodies in question should integrate these changes into their respective rules of procedure to ensure that their users have a clear idea of their roles, responsibilities and powers concerning the promotion and protection of human rights.

(ii) Reinforcement of independence and operational capacities

If they are to have an impact, these actions should be implemented by an African Commission which has adequate human and material resources. For the time being, this is not the case. It is clear after some fifteen years' experience that the present size and non-permanent status of the bureau are amongst the most serious problems of the African Commission. And these issues can only be resolved by an increase in its annual budget. Currently, the Commission has a budget of approximately US$760,000, or roughly 2.5 percent of the budget of the African Union[67] to hold its two statutory annual sessions, undertake missions of promotion and protection and carry out the core activities required by its mandate. In reality, this restricted budget only enables it to operate with an administration of about twenty people, only six of whom are legal experts. Recently, consultants admitted that 'The office equipment of the Secretariat of the Commission is woefully inadequate... The urgent need for computers as well as for printers is obvious'.[68] This explains why, when the PCS requested they undertake a mission of inquiry in Darfur, it was only able to mobilise four of its members and one legal councillor for a stay of some ten days in this region of Sudan in the grip of a civil war, in order to verify whether or not serious violations of international human rights and international humanitarian law had taken place in the country. In comparison, over the same period, the Office of the United Nations High Commissioner for Human Rights, which has a budget of US$2 million, sent a mission of about twenty human rights experts to Sudan, led by skilled specialists recognised for their expertise on the issues being examined, for a stay of three months.[69] The result was that the African Commission produced a report in which it explained that the 'mediocre' quality of the work carried out was due, amongst other things, to the lack of time to adequately examine the human rights situation in the country as the PSC had requested. Worse still, financial reasons almost prevented the report from being adopted before the deadline established by the PSC. It was only through the support of a group of NGOs that the extraordinary meeting was finally held in Pretoria, South Africa, in September 2004, three months after the mission to the country.

Raising the awareness of the Commission of the Union, which prepares the budget of the Union, and of the Executive Council, which grants the credits, would help in substantially increasing its budget. The African Commission could, in this respect, remind them of the Kigali Declaration of May 2003, in which the African Ministers of Justice called upon 'the AU policy bodies to provide the African Commission with suitable Headquarters, an appropriate structure and adequate human and financial resources for its proper functioning'.[70]

These budgetary issues cannot fail to have an impact on the independence of the African organisation[71] which is already compromised by the blatant incompatibility between the important executive positions which several of its members occupy in their country of origin[72] and their status as Commissioners. In order to fulfil its responsibilities where cooperation with political bodies is concerned, the African Commission should definitely apply the rule which states that members of the personnel of the Commission of the Union '(...) in the performance of their duties (...) shall not seek or receive instructions from any government or from any other authority external to the Union'.[73]

Relations Between the African Commission and Organs that may Further Its Effective Participation in the Process of Regional Integration being Implemented by the African Union

Europe, which is viewed today as a universal model for successful regional integration, teaches us that there is a dialectical relationship between integration policies and human rights, namely that adequate protection of human rights can only be ensured in an environment where economic integration is developing and that regional integration is only possible if the rights of the individual are fully respected throughout the geographical space involved. This, moreover, is why, in the context of the strengthening of regional integration, the European Union has provided itself with a European Charter of Fundamental Rights, which, if the new European constitution is adopted by its member countries, will replace the European Convention on Human Rights.

Being at the beginning of its process of integration and therefore not in a position to imitate this model, the African Union—which has also, as we have recalled, made respect for human rights a cornerstone of regional integration— has made do with giving the various bodies it has created a mandate in matters of human rights; at the same time, it has requested that the African Commission establish 'interaction and dynamic coordination [with them] with a view to reinforcing the African instruments for the promotion and protection of human and peoples' rights'.[74]

But, after having been so haughtily ostracised when the Union was created, how can the African Commission coordinate its actions with structures which, to date, have practically not allowed it to take part in their activities?[75] After a brief presentation of the facts of the matter, we shall attempt to examine the conditions under which this could become possible.

The Facts of the Problem

To understand the difficulties of the African Commission in participating in the process of integration currently underway in Africa, one must know that, since the entry into force of the Constitutive Act of the Union and the establishment of its organs, the promotion of human rights is no longer the exclusive domain of the African Commission. With the establishment in the near future of the African Court on Human and Peoples' Rights, the African Commission will undoubtedly also lose its monopoly on the protection of those same rights, which it was granted by the African Charter. Moreover, despite the rectification of the 'oversight' to which it fell victim during the drawing up of the Constitutive Act of the Union, the African Commission continues to be excluded from all major discussions initiated by the majority of the organs of the African Union[76] in the sphere of human rights. For example, since the inception of the Commission of the African Union, it has almost never been involved in any of the activities organised by the African Union in the areas of promotion or protection of human rights. This includes the writing of major documents such as the 'Draft Protocol to the OAU Convention on the Prevention and Combating of Terrorism,'[77] the 'Maputo Declaration on Malaria, HIV/Aids, Tuberculosis, and other related infectious diseases'[78] the 'Solemn Declaration on Gender Equality in Africa'[79] and the 'Draft Plan of Action on the Family in Africa'[80] or 'The African Union Extraordinary Summit on Employment and Poverty Alleviation in Africa',[81] not to mention the first two high-level intergovernmental meetings on the Prevention and Combating of Terrorism in Africa in Algiers.[82]

In this climate of almost systematic marginalisation of the regional organ for the protection of human rights, only the PSC seems to have called upon its services. This is assuredly due to its obligation to establish 'close cooperation with the African Commission (...) in all matters relevant to its objectives and mandate'.[83] In its search for solutions to the crisis in the Darfur region of Sudan and to the situation in the Ivory Coast, it did not hesitate to call upon the African Commission to send two commissions of inquiry to look into the allegations of human rights violations in these countries.[84]

Now, as sole interpreter of the African Charter, which is the basis for all actions by the Union in the sphere of human rights,[85] the African Commission is the only African institution capable of advising and even guiding the actions of the organs of the Union in the exercise of their respective jurisdictions. The experience it has garnered in the course of some sixteen years is an asset which cannot be ignored. To ignore that fact would amount to compromising the implementation of the integration which is the aim of this new union of African States. In other words, the best way to successfully implement the integration process would be to recognise the expertise of the African Commission and enlist it in the construction of African integration.

Possible Solutions

Interacting and or cooperating with organs whose powers, duties and functions are so different is not an easy task for the African Commission, especially in the light of the fact that, from an organisational point of view, it is not yet well equipped to assume responsibilities of this nature. For the requirements of our present considerations, we can examine here some of the conditions that must be met by the African Commission and the organs of the Union in order to accomplish this mission whose success could constitute the foundation for genuine economic, social and political development on the continent.

Indeed, if we confine ourselves to the relevant clauses of the African Charter,[86] the African Commission is theoretically the ideal partner for all organs of the Union which have a mandate to coordinate, control and facilitate the implementation of the policies and aims of the African Union, or even to write drafts of joint positions, strategic plans and studies.[87] Their work would be facilitated because the African Commission, using the experience of the United Nations system for the protection of human rights, has endeavoured to adapt its means of intervention to the realities of the continent by adopting new instruments for the promotion and protection of human rights such as special rapporteurs, thematic working groups and focus groups. But to ensure efficient cooperation of this kind, it would be necessary to:

(i)   Review the frequency of meetings of the African Commission and make it a structure with permanent activities. Failing that, some thought should be given to the possibility of making the positions of certain members of its bureau, such as the Chairperson and Vice Chairperson, full-time positions. One cannot expect to develop bonds of close cooperation between an African Commission which only meets twice a year and organs provided with permanent structures and ready at any time to request its help. Given that it is difficult to conceive of a rapid revision of the African Charter in the near future, a decision by the Assembly of the Union with a view to making the positions of Chairperson and Vice Chairperson the African Commission full-time positions could be envisaged. In any event, the internal rules of procedure of the African Commission and its relevant bodies should be revised so as to integrate these new relationships.

(ii) Once that vital decision has been made, the African Commission should systematically participate in the activities of the relevant organs of the African Union. In the event of this being impossible to implement immediately, regular meetings between the organs of the Union concerned and the African Commission should be envisaged. This would enhance synergies between them and contribute to the development of special bonds in the management of human rights issues. For example, the African Commission could help the PSC to determine the grave circumstances under which the Union would be compelled to take action and, as a last resort, to envisage the use of force against one of its members.[88]

(iii) Provide the African Commission and its Secretariat with adequate human and financial resources for its proper functioning and initiate consideration of the establishment of a Fund to be financed through voluntary contributions as provided for in the Kigali Declaration.[89]

(iv) Envisage an in-depth reform of the African Charter with a view to adapting it to the new African reality. This could lead to a complete redefinition of the mandate of the African Commission which would be restricted to activities for the promotion of human rights on the continent, given the existence of an operational African Court on Human and Peoples' Rights.

In sum, the African Commission should give serious thought to the numerous requests by the Union to review its relationships with the organs of the African Union and endeavour to introduce into this important process questions which could lead to a substantial reform of the present mechanisms for promoting and protecting human rights. Since the entry into force of the Constitutive Act, the protection of human rights has become an issue which is both individual and collective; for this reason the involvement of African civil society in this process should not be overlooked—indeed, its contribution to the legitimisation the system has been decisive. In fact, an efficient system for the protection of human rights is one which combines both the legal and the political mechanisms for the protection of human rights and which is oriented towards the satisfaction of fundamental needs.

Notes

1. Paper presented at the conference organised by the Nordic Africa Institute (NAI) and CODESRIA on 'The African Commission on Human and Peoples' Rights: New Challenges and Opportunities for Human Rights Promotion and Protection', Uppsala, Sweden, 9 & 10 June 2004.
2. Article 2 of the OAU Charter.
3. See 2004–2007 *Strategic Framework of the Commission of the African Union*, Volume 2, May 2004, page 6.
4. See *Vision and Mission of the African Union,* May 2004, page 24.
5. See *Vision and Mission of the African Union,* op. cit. page 24.
6. See the ninth whereas clause in the Preamble to the Constitutive Act of the African Union.
7. See Article 3 (f) of the *Constitutive Act of the African Union.*
8. Article 4 (o) of the *Constitutive Act of the African Union.*
9. Article 4 (m) of the *Constitutive Act of the African Union.*
10. Article 4 (l) of the *Constitutive Act of the African Union.*
11. Article 4 (o) of the *Constitutive Act of the African Union.*
12. Article 4 (p) of the *Constitutive Act of the African Union.*
13. Article 4 (h) of the *Constitutive Act of the African Union.* On the legal problems raised by this clause, see 'The normative and institutional framework of the African Union relating to the protection of human rights and the maintenance of international peace and security: A critical appraisal', *African Human Rights Law Journal,* 2003 (3) pages 105-110.
14. See paragraph 2 of Article 23 of the *Constitutive Act of the African Union.*
15. See Article 30 of the *Constitutive Act of the African Union.*
16. According to Article 5 of the Revised *Constitutive Act of the African Union*, the organs of the Union are: The Assembly of the Union, the Executive Council, the Pan-African Parliament, the Court of Justice, the Commission, the Peace and Security Council, the Permanent Representatives Committee; the Specialised

Technical Committees, the Economic, Social and Cultural Council; and the financial institutions which include the African Central Bank, the African Monetary Fund and the African Investment Bank. In comparison, the Organisation of African Unity (OAU) comprised only four: the Assembly of Heads of State and Government, the Council of Ministers, the General Secretariat, and the Mediation, Conciliation and Arbitration Commission.

17. These are: the African Commission, the African Court on Human and Peoples' Rights, the African Committee on the Rights and Welfare of the Child, and the Commission on Refugees.

18. Contrary to the assertions of Rachel Murray in Human Rights in Africa: from OAU to the African Union, Cambridge University Press, 2004, page 71 and following, the Assembly of Heads of State and Government formally recognised the African Commission for Human and Peoples' Rights and the African Committee on the Rights and Welfare of the Child as being institutions of the African Union. See Assembly/AU/Dec.1 (I) XI.

19. Cf. Decision on the 16th Annual Activities Report of the ACHPR Doc. Assembly/AU/7(II)

20. Article 45 (1)(a)(b) of the *African Charter*.

21. Articles 45(2), 47 and 49 of the *African Charter*.

22. Article 55 of the *African Charter*.

23. Article 45(3) of the *African Charter*.

24. Article 45(4) of the *African Charter*.

25. We are referring to the Assembly of Heads of State and Government, the Council of Ministers and the General Secretariat of the OAU (Article 7 of the OAU Charter).

26. Namely, the Assembly of Heads of State and Government (Articles 33, 52, 54, 58 and 59 of the *African Charter*).

27. Namely, the General Secretary of the OAU (Article 41 of the *African Charter*).

28. The African Commission has in particular contributed to the formulation of the Protocols regarding the African Court on Human and Peoples' Rights and the Rights of Women in Africa. It has dealt with almost 300 complaints, giving it the opportunity to provide insightful interpretations of the *African Charter*.

29. It also set up internal working groups to deal with specific themes, focus groups and special rapporteur positions.

30. In its first regular meeting, the Assembly of the Union (formerly the Assembly of Heads of State and Government) delegated certain of the prerogatives granted to it by the *African Charter* to the Executive Council, on condition that the Council refer back to it any questions it is unable to resolve.

31. With the official creation of the Peace and Security Council by the African Union in Durban, South Africa, in July 2002. See Assembly/AU/Dec. 2(I).

32. Article 6 of the *Constitutive Act of the African Union*.

33. Made up of the Ministers of Foreign Affairs of the States Parties.
34. Article 9 (1)(a) of the *Constitutive Act of the African Union*.
35. Article 9 (1)(b) of the *Constitutive Act of the African Union*.
36. Article 9 (1)(e) of the *Constitutive Act of the African Union*.
37. Article 9 (1)(g) of the *Constitutive Act of the African Union*.
38. Article 9(2) of the *Constitutive Act of the African Union*.
39. Article 13(2) of the *Constitutive Act of the African Union*.
40. Article 13 (1) of the *Constitutive Act of the African Union*.
41. See Rule 5 of the internal Rules of Procedure of the Executive Council [Assembly/ AU/2(I) b].
42. The date of entry into force of its Rules of Procedure.
43. Article 5(f) of the internal Rules of Procedure.
44. See Assembly/AU/Dec.11 (II): Decision on the 16th annual report of activities of the ACHPR Doc. Assembly/AU/7 (II) taken during the second ordinary session of the Assembly of the African Union, 10-12 July 2003, in Maputo, Mozambique.
45. The PSC is made up of fifteen elected members, ten of whom are elected for a 2-year term and five, for a 3-year term (Article 5 of the Protocol on the creation of the Peace and Security Council of the African Union).
46. See in particular Article 7(a)(I)(j)(k)(m) of the Protocol on the creation of the Peace and Security Council of the African Union.
47. See Article 7(b)(c)(d)(o) of the Protocol on the creation of the Peace and Security Council of the African Union.
48. See Article 7(e)(g)(p) of the Protocol on the creation of the Peace and Security Council of the African Union.
49. Its aim is to 'promote and encourage democratic practices, good governance and the rule of law, protect human rights and fundamental freedoms, respect for the sanctity of human life and international humanitarian law, as part of efforts for preventing conflicts' [Article 3(f)] and it is guided in its actions by the principles of 'respect for the rule of law, fundamental human rights and freedoms, the sanctity of human life and international humanitarian law' [Article 4(c)].
50. See Article 19 of the Protocol on the creation of the Peace and Security Council of the African Union.
51. See Article 58 of the *African Charter*.
52. Articles 16 and 17 of the *Charter of the OAU*.
53. Article 2 of the *Statutes of the Commission of the African Union*.
54. Article 3 of the *Statutes of the Commission of the African Union*.
55. According to the Statutes of the Commission [article 2 (2)], the Heads of State and of government, may, when they deem it necessary, review the number of commissioners.
56. Article 10 of the Statutes of the Commission of the African Union.

57 See Articles 8 and 9 of the Statutes of the Commission of the African Union for the respective attributions of the President and Vice-President.

58. The eight portfolios of the Union are the following (Article 11 of the Statutes of the Commission of the African Union): Peace and Security, Political Affairs, Infrastructures and Energy, Social Affairs, Human Resources, Science and Technology, Trade and Industry, Rural Economy and Agriculture, Economic Affairs.

59. Its aims include the promotion of peace, democracy, security and stability, and ensuring the mainstreaming of gender issues in all the programmes and activities of the Union. It is competent to take action in the areas of: control of pandemics, disaster management, prevention of international crime and terrorism, environmental management, population, migration, refugees and displaced persons, and food security.

60. Amongst other things, the Chairperson is responsible for appointing the staff of the Commission, liaising closely with the organs of the Union to guide, support and closely monitor the performance of the Union in the various areas to ensure conformity and harmony with agreed policies, strategies, programmes and projects [Article 8 of the Statutes of the Commission of the African Union].

61. See Article 12(1)(b) of the *Statutes of the Commission of the African Union.*

62. See Articles 22 and 23 of the *African Charter.*

63. 'Observance of human rights is a key tool for promoting collective security, durable peace and sustainable development' (3rd Preamble of the Declaration Cf. CONF/ HRA/DECL. (I) page 1).

64. 'Respect for human rights is indispensable for the maintenance of national, regional and international peace and security and constitutes the fundamental bedrock for sustainable development' [3rd Preamble of the Declaration Cf. MIN/CONF/ HRADecl.1(I) page 1].

65. We note with satisfaction that the Commission of the Union participates regularly in the ordinary sessions of the African Commission through the person of the Political Affairs Commissioner, in contrast with the Secretary General of the OAU.

66. Cf. Decision EX/CL/Doc.155 (V), paragraph 4.

67. See the Review of the Procedures in force before the African Commission on Human and Peoples' Rights: Report of the mission carried out for the Secretariat of the Commission, 9 to 14 September 2002, Banjul, by Salif Yonaba and Frans Viljoen, page 8 and following.

68. Cf. 'The Review of the Procedures'. Op cit., page 9.

69. See Report of the International Commission of Inquiry on Darfur to the United Nations Secretary General pursuant to Security Council Resolution 1564 of 18 September 2004, Geneva, 25 January 2005, pages 11-13.

70. Paragraph 23 of the Declaration of the first Ministerial Conference of the African Commission on Human and Peoples' Rights, Kigali, 8 May 2003.

71. See also paragraph 24 of the *Declaration of the first Ministerial Conference of the African Commission on Human and Peoples' Rights*, Kigali, 8 May 2003, in which the bodies are called upon 'to review the operation and composition of the African Commission on Peoples' Rights with a view to strengthening its independence and operational integrity'.

72. At the time of writing, one member of the African Commission is a minister in his own country, while the Chairperson exercises the functions of Ambassador in an African country.

73. Article 4(1) of the Statutes of the Commission of the African Union.

74. Cf. Decision on the 16th annual report of the activities of the ACHPR Assembly/AU/Dec.11 (II).

75. With the notable exception of the Pan-African Parliament and the Economic, Social and Cultural Council which have not yet begun their activities. Moreover, that is why their relation with the African Commission will not be examined here.

76. With the notable exception of the PSC. See infra.

77. Cf. Assembly/AU/Dec.36(III).

78. Cf. Assembly/AU/Decl.6(II).

79. Cf. Assembly/AU/Decl.12(III).

80. Cf. EX.CL/115(V).

81. Cf. EXT/Assembly/AU/3(III).

82. Cf. Doc. EX.CL/146(VI).

83. Cf. Article 19 of the Protocol relating to the establishment of the Peace and Security Council of the African Union.

84. Cf. PSC/AHG/Comm.(X) pages 2 and 4.

85. According to Article 3(h) of the Constitutive Act, one of the aims of the Union is to 'promote and protect human and peoples' rights in accordance with the African Charter on Human and Peoples' Rights'.

86. Cf. Article 45 of the *African Charter* which states that its functions are to '(...) undertake studies and research on African problems in the field of human and peoples' rights, organise seminars (...) and should the case arise, give its views or make recommendations to (African) Governments (...) to formulate and lay down, principles and rules aimed at solving legal problems relating to human and peoples' rights (...) to co-operate with other African and international institutions concerned with the promotion and protection of human and peoples' rights (...) and (...) to interpret all the provisions of the present Charter at the request of a State party'.

87. For instance, the PSC, the Commission of the African Union, the Pan African Parliament and the Economic, Social and Cultural Council.

88. Cf. Article 7(e) of the Protocol relating to the establishment of the Peace and Security Council of the African Union.

89. Cf. Paragraph 23 of the Declaration. According to the African Ministers for Justice, this fund would be financed by contributions from Member States and international and regional institutions.

Chapter 9

Strengthening the African Commission: Procedures, Mechanisms, Partnerships and Implementation/Follow-up

Hannah Forster

Introduction

Let me say at the outset that the contributions of NGOs to the promotion and protection of human rights around the world and in Africa, particularly, mostly on shoestring budgets, have been remarkable. NGOs have been in the frontline of the human rights struggle, fighting to promote human rights within the international arena while leading similar efforts at the regional, national and local levels.

Through their work, they have, among other functions, to

(a) frame policies and influence the decision-making process in a good number of countries at most levels;

(b) give voice to causes that have been ignored, forgotten and or marginalised;

(c) raise legal awareness within targeted communities, often providing basic legal representation in high-risk or neglected human rights cases;

(d) generate expert analysis on the ground and are integral to both the field and headquarters operations of virtually every human right mission, often working around the African Commission;

(e)   send early warning or urgent appeals when no one seems to be paying attention to an emerging crisis;

(f)   promote legal accountability to address past abuses;

(g)   play a leading role in any transition or post-conflict reconstruction process; and

(h)   create standards and engage existing systems to bring about constructive change.

During this brief presentation, I will attempt to define the concept of 'civil society' to create a common understanding before looking at the mandate of the African Commission vis-à-vis the role of NGOs in the promotion and protection of human rights in Africa. It would be appropriate to review the opportunities that exist for civil society participation in the work of the African Commission followed by a close appraisal of the challenges presented. Before concluding, ways in which the African Commission could facilitate the contributions of NGOs will be explored.

Definition of 'Civil Society'

To focus on this task one has to take a closer look at the definition of 'civil society'. Depending on perspectives, the definition of 'civil society' is sometimes vague and often confusing and as such remains a subject of ongoing debate. Various models have been suggested around the concept of 'civil society', aimed at helping us to distinguish that sphere of society outside of the state. It is generally believed that civil society organisations manifestly provide a countervailing force to the overbearing power of the state and their functions are tied to a basic theory of socioeconomic transformation. Whereas some radical scholars claim that 'civil society' gives democratisation the proper bearing in terms of the role the people can play to ensure that democracy serves their interests, liberals highlight the advantages of civil society as laying the foundation for a shared political culture from which pluralist, rather than class, politics emerges. In short, civil society is seen at best as a framework that has the immanent possibility of becoming more democratic and whose norms call for democratisation.[1] [2]

The concept also refers to those associations and institutions that enhance the prospects for individual liberties and personal freedom by operating outside of the state's control and that possess the capacity to confront the state when these liberties are threatened.[3]

For the purpose of this brief presentation, civil society organisations refer to those human rights and development organisations who are actual and potential partners of the African human rights movement and therefore by extension, of the African Commission. These groups include unions, professional associations, religious and cultural organisations, gender organisations, political parties and other non-governmental organisations.

Mandate of the African Commission on Human and Peoples' Rights and the Role of NGOs in the Promotion and Protection of Human Rights

We are all aware that the main mission of the Commission as stipulated in Article 45 of the African Charter[4] is as follows:

(i)   the promotion of human and peoples' rights;

(ii) ensuring the protection of human and peoples' rights in accordance with the provisions of the African Charter;

(iii) the interpretation of the provisions of the Charter at the request of States Parties, OAU (now AU) institutions or African organisations recognised by the OAU;

(iv) the carrying out of other tasks which may be entrusted to it by the Assembly of Heads of State and Government.

Consequently, it can be said generally that the African Commission and civil society organisations on the continent share the same objective, which is to promote common policies to guarantee social justice and the well-being of humanity. The importance of their independent yet complementary roles in the promotion and protection of human rights cannot be overemphasised. This responsibility has already been recognised by the African Commission and taken seriously by the NGOs and civil society organisations working in this area both at the national and regional level.

Over a period, the roles of civil society organisations have included

(i)   Influencing the development of national and regional law and promoting the use of the African Human Rights mechanisms for human rights;

(ii) Monitoring state compliance under various treaties and if necessary criticising policies not compatible with obligations;

(iii) Advocacy regarding issues of public policy and sensitisation on the provisions of national and international instruments.

Opportunities for Civil Society Empowerment and Participation in the Work of the African Commission

Strengthening relationship between civil society and the African Commission and its other partners is laudable considering that the African Commission offers a unique and neutral opportunity for all groups working on the ground to bring their human rights concerns and those of their constituencies.[5] To date, about 314 NGOs and civil society organisations have been granted observer status with the African Commission. This status gives NGOs the possibility of attending and participating in its public sessions as well the responsibility to present reports of their activities and the status of human rights in their various constituencies at regular intervals.

In general terms, it is of interest to note that civil society organisations also have the opportunity, at the level of the African Union, as provided for in its Constitutive Act,6 to:

- access and be represented at ECOSOCC;

- access the Peace and Security Council; and

- be represented in the African Parliament.

These organs offer a multi-pronged approach to the debate and can be capitalised on to integrate human rights issues on the agenda of the AU.

The granting of observer status to NGOs engaged in the promotion and protection of human rights,[7] is subject to certain criteria which entail the provision of the following information regarding the NGO to the Secretary of the African Commission well in advance of its next session:

- Its constitution;

- Structure;

- Leadership;

- Membership, if applicable;

- Activities, including publications, reports, and so on.

Consequently, if the application is accepted, observers will be informed and will then have a right to:

- participate in the public sessions of the African Commission;

- send and or present reports of their activities at regular intervals;

- send and or present 'other communications' under the Commission's protection mandate;

- send and or present reports on the situation of human rights in their constituencies, particularly when state reports are being considered;

- give support and collaborate with Commission and its Members as the case may be;

- put pressure and advocate directly to a body that is open to NGO contributions;

- receive documents and publications of the African Commission; and

- propose draft resolutions to be considered by the African Commission.

The organisation of an NGO Forum8 preceding each African Commission session by the African Centre for Democracy and Human Rights Studies in collaboration with the African Commission over the years also provides a unique opportunity for representatives from civil society organisations working in or on the African Human Rights System to

- meet, discuss and review together the agenda of the Commission;

- speak out with one voice on human rights issues of common concern;

- share experiences and advocacy strategies, particularly best practices and indeed challenges;

- develop and maintain partnerships on thematic issues;

- display and share their publications and other material prepared by different human rights organisations;

- make contact between representatives of NGOs and Commissioners; and

- provide support and on the spot information to Commissioners, as may be necessary.

The Forum also offers the Commission a platform to engage these organisations and to harness their various contributions towards the strengthening of its work. Considering that all Commissioners work part-time, the NGO Forum provides Commissioners with the possibility to meet with a large number of civil society representatives and to get a bird's eye view of the state of the art on the continent as well as specific countries.

Challenges

The main challenge for the African Commission and interested civil society organisations and even governments is to encourage the building of the institutions required to enforce human rights and erection of protective mechanisms while concurrently disseminating information to the grassroots level of society—a delicate yet essential balance indeed!

However, even after having achieved so much at the international and regional levels where human rights standards, courts and complaints mechanisms grow stronger every year, there is the need to ask ourselves: Why has so little changed in the lives of ordinary human beings, Africans, to say the least? Why the stubborn persistence of human rights abuses within repressed, neglected and often inaccessible communities in every corner or African country? How can NGOs make a difference to the lives of ordinary people while contributing towards strengthening the work of the African Commission?

For NGOs to be more effective, they would need to be more outward looking and to reach beyond the traditional NGOs focus on civil and political rights to address economic, social and cultural rights with equal respect and intensity. This could contribute towards making human rights more meaningful and the struggle for human rights more balanced. NGOs must connect their mission to the struggles and dreams of the average African to have more impact. They must be independent of governments. As a result of civil society becoming stronger and more organised, Governments are creating NGOs to pursue their objectives and policies. There is sometimes difficulty in maintaining their independence when so much funding and support comes from Government sources. While it is important for NGOs to actively participate at the national and regional systems, their independence should be maintained, which is a guarantee for freedom of action and speech.

NGOs must foster a better understanding of and greater participation at the national and regional levels by promoting collaboration among themselves as well as with international NGOs, the African Commission and the public at large. While cooperation between NGOs is important, there is a need to maintain separate identities rather than merging. These bodies must also develop organisational transparency and accountability to maintain their credibility as trusted partners in co-operative relations.

In addition, they should encourage more organisations to apply for observer status and thereby be in a position to attend and participate in as many of the public sessions of the Commission as possible; and to submit communications, shadow reports and other materials on human rights violations particularly, to the Commission and individual Commissioners, Special Rapporteurs and Focal Points as may be necessary.

How to Enable NGOs to Strengthen the Work of the African Commission

As we explore ways of enhancing the work of the African Commission through the participation and contribution of NGOs, it would be prudent for that august body to consider activities which would promote awareness of the reporting requirement under the African Charter in collaboration with these partners. The Commission should provide NGOs with copies of the state reports and sufficient advance notice of the date that reports will be reviewed so that NGO input can be prepared and circulated to individual Commissioners prior to the review session. This is a best practice of the UN System which has been utilised to provide and enable an inclusive report of the situation in a particular country or on a specific theme. The African Commission could encourage the involvement and greater participation of independent NGOs in the preparation of these state reports in order to gain a balanced account of the situation in a given state.

It would be desirable for the Commission to publish the list of promotional visits to be carried out well in advance, indicating the dates so that NGOs could also make themselves available to the mission if needed. Further improvement of the information flow is necessary by providing reports of missions, concluding comments and other reports of the Commission to NGOs at the shortest possible time. The Commission could build on and maximise the opportunities provided by the NGO Forum which precedes each African Commission Session for the Commissioners, its Special Mechanisms and Secretariat to meet NGOs at regular intervals and to discuss difficult human rights matters of common concern. Collaboration with NGOs might enable the Commission to explore ways to generate grassroots education based on training materials and sessions organised in conjunction with organisations already engaged, active and respected on the ground. The development of simplified texts and creative methods of bringing the Charter to the people would facilitate such educational work. Finally, it would be very helpful if the Commission were to intervene on behalf of NGOs which are prevented from registering their organisations despite the fact that they have observer status with the African Commission, so that their activities can be carried out legally.

All these possibilities should be explored, bearing in mind that they are not exhaustive of the opportunities for fruitful interaction between the Commission and NGOs.

However, closer collaboration between the African Commission and civil society organisations is essential and should be reinforced by the organisation of any activity geared towards the enhancement of this relationship. The organisation of regular meetings with these partners would be valuable and should be encouraged. NGOs should draw lessons from their individual and collective experiences as development agencies and share them with the African Commission to improve its effectiveness; while the improvement of information flow between the African Commission and the NGOs as well as with other stakeholders, particularly National Human Rights Institutions, should be encouraged. Moreover, the African Commission should recognise the diversity, creativity and contribution to innovation by civil society organisations and needs to capitalise on the NGO Forum. By doing so it could engage civil society representatives with local and professional expertise and by building in a day for public hearings; establish mechanisms for liaison, networking and strategic alliances; and share good practices and other relevant information.

Another challenge concerns the lack of long-term financial security facing many NGOs. It is imperative, therefore, that funding and donor groups recognise the difference between and roles of grassroots, national, sub-regional and regional structures and to establish direct relationships, particularly in the strengthening of the work of the African Commission. This support which would include capacity building of these organisations can be more effective through regional and national co-ordination and directly to groups after relevant evaluation. It could be counterproductive to provide support to these groups through governments or through the African Commission.

Conclusion

It has become more evident that standard setting by itself is not enough and that the importance of bringing human rights standards closer to home cannot be overemphasised. The task of making paper rights real by formulating appropriate implementation strategies and mechanisms is of the utmost significance to the process, as is the obligation of working together to strengthen ourselves and our continent's human rights system. The development of a strategy for making the Commission accessible to the vast numbers of people who are illiterate, live in remote areas or experience other sorts of obstacles in utilising the Commission is therefore crucial to the process.

As the Commission moves forward into the future, it would be useful to explore the possibility of using local committees or NGOs as conduits in this process rather than to reinvent the wheel. Now is the era of ensuring that the paper rights signed and ratified by our governments are implemented and it is imperative that these policies and processes are known and accessible to the ordinary person. Who best to entrust these tasks than the ordinary person? Once empowered these persons could collectively make a difference in ensuring that the African Human Rights System is strengthened.

Notes

1. Blaney, David L. and Pasha, Mustapha Kamal, 1993, 'CivilSociety and Democracy in the Third World: Ambiguitiesand Historical Possibilities', in *Studies in ComparativeInternational Development,* 28(1) (Spring): 3-24

2. Hutchful, E., 'The Civil Society debate in Africa', *International Journal,* vol. 15(1), p. 60.

3. Ekeh, P., 1992, 'The constitution of civil society in African History and Politics', in Caron, Gboyega and Osaghae, eds., *Democratic Transition in Africa,* Ibadan, CREDU, p. 207.

4. *African Charter on Human and Peoples' Rights,* adopted 20 June 1981. OAU Document CAB/LEG/67/3, rev. 5, 21 I.L.M. 58 (1982), entered into force 21 October 1986.

5. Resolution on the co-operation between the African Commission on Human and Peoples' Rights and NGOs having observer status with the Commission, adopted in Banjul, *The Gambia,* 31 October, 1998.

6. Constitutive Act of the African Union, adopted in Lome, Togo 12 June 2000. OAU Document CAB/LEG/23.15, entered into force 26 May 2001.

7. Resolution on the criteria for granting and enjoying observer status to non-governmental organisations working in the field of human rights with the African

Commission on Human and Peoples' Rights, adopted in Bujumbura, Burundi, 5 May 1999.

8. The Forum on the Participation of NGOs in the Sessions of the African Commission on Human and Peoples' Rights and African Human Rights Book Fair is organised by The African Centre for Democracy and Human Rights Studies twice a year, since 2001, preceding the Sessions of the African Commission. The Forum dates back to the early 1990s. Copies of reports, including resolutions and recommendations, are available at the ACDHRS Headquarters in Banjul.

Index

11 September 2001 attacks, 68, 70

Abacha, Sani, 63

Abu Ghraib prison, 71

accountability, 59

Afghanistan, war in, 70, 71

Africa: causes of conflict in, 44; poor human rights record of, 19; post-colonial, 42

African Centre for Democracy and Human Rights Studies, 30, 137, 175

African Charter on Human and People's Rights, 3, 4, 5-6, 12, 27, 32, 34, 36, 38, 41, 42, 43, 48, 49, 50, 62, 63, 75, 78, 80, 112, 123, 128, 137, 138, 143, 155, 156, 163, 173; lack of public awareness of, 114; promotion of, 37, 138-9; revision of, 158; translation into local languages, 141; weaknesses of, 5, 29

African Charter on the Rights and Welfare of the Child, 21, 47-8, 98, 123, 129, 138

African Commission on Human and Peoples' Rights (ACHPR), 4, 5-14, 15, 16, 17, 33, 41, 42, 43, 63, 98; Annual Activity Reports, 126, 128, 131, 134, 137, 143, 146; budget of, 136; challenges to be overcome, 159-62; Commissioners, 25 (election of, 24); Declaration on Freedom of Expression, 123; electronic submission of reports to, 140; establishment of, 19; expression of minority views proposed, 121; functioning of, 6, 29-30; funding of, 22, 32, 46, 131, 133, 134, 161, 164; Guidelines for State Reporting, 122-3, 145; impartiality and independence of, 46; implementation of findings see implementation and follow-up; inability to finalise Nigeria mission report, 116-17; inadequate publicity of decisions, 119; institutional consolidation of, 23-39; lack of clarity of procedures of, 120; lack of credibility of, 125-6; lack of precision and dissemination of conclusions of, 126; mandate and functions of, 24-5, 36-8, 127-30, 173; missions of see missions of ACHPR; non-attendance by state representatives, 124-5; oral hearings in, 139; relation with the new organs of the AU, 154-70; reports of, 121-2; Rules of Procedure, 28-9, 136, 140, 143, 145; Secretariat see Secretariat of African Commission; Special Rapporteurs see Special Rapporteurs of ACHPR; state reports of (non-submission of, 123-4; not translated, 122; inaccessibility of, 127); Strategy Plan, 35-8, 150; strengthening of, 112-53, 171-9; structure of, 8-9; website and newsletter of, 26, 114; working languages of, 30; Working Group on Communications, 118

www.ingramcontent.com/pod-product-compliance
Lightning Source LLC
Chambersburg PA
CBHW021906020426
42334CB00013B/498